POLITICS AND STRUCTURE

Essentials of American National Government

Sixth Edition

POLITICS AND STRUCTURE

Essentials of American National Government

Sixth Edition

THOMAS G. INGERSOLL

ICF Incorporated

ROBERT E. O'CONNOR

Pennsylvania State University

ROBERT F. PECORELLA

St. John's University

Wadsworth Publishing Company
Belmont, California
A Division of Wadsworth, Inc.

Wadsworth Publishing Commpany
A Division of Wadsworth, Inc.

Printed in the United States of America.
10 9 8 7 6 5 4 3 2 1—96 95 94 93

Library of Congress Cataloging-in-Publication Data

Ingersoll, Thomas G.
    Politics and structure : essentials of American national
Government / Thomas G. Ingersoll, Robert E. O'Connor, Robert F.
Pecorella. — 6th ed.
        p. cm.
    O'Connor's name appears first on the previous edition.
    Includes bibliographical references and index.
    ISBN 0-534-18840-0
    1. United States—Politics and government.   I. O'Connor, Robert
E., [date].   II. Pecorella, Robert F., [date].   III. Title.
    JK274.I43 1993   92-29523
    320.973—dc20   CIP

Sponsoring Editor: Peggy Adams
Editorial Associate: Cathleen S. Collins
Production Editor: Penelope Sky
Interior and Cover Design: Jeanne Calabrese
Cover Photo: Oi Jakrarat Veerasarn
Interior Illustration: Susan Haberkorn
Typesetting: Bookends Typesetting
Printing and Binding: Malloy Lithographing, Inc.

To Charley and Betty O'Connor, Ed and Jane Ingersoll, and Joseph and Charlotte Pecorella. They taught us a long time ago the value of understanding, which we hope is reflected in this treatment of the politics and structure of American national government.

PREFACE

Politics and Structure provides

- a description of how politics and government combine to produce public policy.
- an in-depth examination of the four essential institutions: the presidency, Congress, the federal courts, and the federal bureaucracy.
- a demonstration of how the four institutions interact, using as a single case study (cross-referenced to the text) the multibillion-dollar "Superfund" hazardous waste cleanup program.
- an Introduction and Addendum that highlight the contexts of American national government: constitutional, socioeconomic, and political.
- margin notes that help students follow the main arguments and review the material.
- authoritative references and a detailed index.

We developed this book more than a decade ago because we (and our students) were dissatisfied with large, expensive hardbound texts. For pedagogical reasons, each of us preferred to use one of the popular point-of-view texts or a series of topical paperbacks. New texts appear every year, and we liked having access to fresh insights and challenging and unorthodox perspectives. But the point-of-view texts cannot cover the essential operating functions of government adequately and remain relatively concise. We discovered that others shared our conviction that a true "essentials" text was needed.

Because the policy decisions made in Washington affect the lives of all Americans, all of us should understand how these decisions are made. This requires learning about both politics and structure, the two interrelated aspects of American national government, neither of which can be understood in isolation from the other. Students will learn that similar influences operate at different levels of government, and that each level influences the others. In the Introduction, we consider the influence on policy of Federalism, of separating the institutions that share power, and of the two-party system. In the Addendum, we analyze the relationship between politics and economics. These sections complement the four main chapters, and the focused coverage that has been standard from one edition to another remains undisturbed.

The single case study that recurs throughout the four main chapters demonstrates the interrelatedness of political reality. We use the Comprehensive Environmental Response, Compensation, and Liability Act of 1980 and 1986 ("Superfund") to illustrate the pervasive nature of politics and to delineate the separate structures within which politics operates. Page numbers in the margins of the case study indicate where the relevant powers or interactions are discussed in the text. This book is organized flexibly enough to suit many different teaching styles. The chapters can be assigned in the order the instructor prefers.

Acknowledgments

This book is truly a common endeavor in every sense. We have in fact changed the order of our names on the cover with each edition to emphasize the shared nature of our responsibilities.

We remain deeply indebted to many people who assisted us in this and earlier editions. Particularly helpful were the reviews of John Buckley, Orange Coast College; Kennith Hunter, The University of South Dakota; Alan Siegel, Franklin Institute of Boston; John Soule, San Diego State University; Marc Triebwasser, Central Connecticut State University; Christopher Warren, Florida International University; and Paul Winston, Oakland Community College.

Bob O'Connor appreciates the warm support of Mon Petit Baby, Molly Maguire, and Janice Hensyl O'Connor. Tom Ingersoll continues to be grateful for all that Barbara has done. Bob Pecorella is ever grateful to his three Ms: Melody, Moshannon, and 'Mica. Yet, with all the assistance, all errors and weaknesses that remain are solely our own.

Thomas G. Ingersoll
Robert E. O'Connor
Robert F. Pecorella

CONTENTS

INTRODUCTION   **THE CONTEXT OF POLICYMAKING: THE RULES OF THE POLITICAL GAME**   1

Constitutional Prerogatives and Limitations   2
Liberals, Conservatives, and Political Consensus   8
Managing Conflict through the Two-Party System   11
Summary   14

CHAPTER ONE   **THE PRESIDENCY**   17

Constitutional Prerogatives   17
Presidential Leadership   31
Electoral Procedures   38
Term of Office and Succession   42
The Institutionalized Presidency   47
Conclusion   56
Case History: Superfund   59

CHAPTER TWO   **THE CONGRESS**   65

Constitutional Prerogatives   65
Congressional Leadership   71
Electoral Procedures   75
Senators and Representatives   77
The Leaders of Congress   80
Congressional Committees   90

How a Bill Becomes a Law   **96**
The Budgetary Process   **103**
Conclusion   **107**
Case History: Superfund   108

CHAPTER THREE   THE FEDERAL JUDICIARY   117

Constitutional Prerogatives   **117**
Judicial Leadership   **123**
Judicial Activism versus Judicial Restraint   **130**
Judicial Recruitment   **132**
The Judges   **135**
The Operation of the Court System   **140**
Conclusion   **145**
Case History: Superfund   145

CHAPTER FOUR   THE FEDERAL BUREAUCRACY   151

Characterizations on Bureaucratization   **151**
The Organization of the Federal Bureaucracy   **152**
The Bureaucrats   **169**
Bureaucratic Leadership   **174**
Limitations on Bureaucratic Leadership   **178**
Conclusion   **183**
Case History: Superfund   185

ADDENDUM   POLITICS AND ECONOMICS   191

Individualism, Laissez Faire, and the American Ideal   **191**
Government Regulation of the Economy   **193**
The Modern Welfare State   **195**
Summary   **199**

THE CONSTITUTION OF THE UNITED STATES   201

INDEX   215

THE CONTEXT OF POLICYMAKING:

The Rules of the Political Game

Because individuals and groups are in competition for scarce resources, conflict is an inherent part of politics. The intensity of social conflict and the way it is managed are two major components of political life. In some societies, conflict develops over fundamental social goals and purposes; politics then is characterized by bitter disagreements and the threat of social upheaval. In other societies, conflict is more moderate because of a fundamental social consensus, and the political differences arise over which means best secure agreed-upon ends. Political conflicts are then resolved through normal channels.

In relatively stable political systems, governments are the normal channels through which public issues are debated and policies made. However, governments do not operate in a vacuum. They reflect larger social values, including views of human nature, perspectives on the rights and responsibilities of individuals, and ideas about the role of the state. Together, these values are the context of political decision making. They provide opportunities for and place limitations upon governmental policymakers. In codified or legal form, these values are incorporated into national constitutions, which delineate more or less clearly the basic *rules of the political game.* This term is not used to trivialize politics or to imply that the rules are necessarily fair. Rather, it indicates that politics is a competitive struggle among diverse interests for favorable public policies, within a larger framework that organizes, channels, and mitigates political conflict.

In American society, policymaking is constrained by constitutional history, which reflects a fundamental yet dynamic consensus on basic social values. Moreover, an extraconstitutional two-party system emerged early in American history and became the basic mechanism for conflict resolution. Before considering the specific politics and structure of American government, it is useful to explore how each of these elements, alone and in unison, constrains policymakers in the United States. This introduction starts with an analysis of the Constitution (the most fundamental codification of American political values), reviews American political consensus, and concludes by examining the two-party system.

CONSTITUTIONAL PREROGATIVES AND LIMITATIONS

The Constitution of the United States resulted from an inherently political process of debate and compromise. After achieving independence from England, the thirteen original states were bound together loosely by the Articles of Confederation. The Articles established a league of independent states with little central authority to enforce national policies. The rules of the political game were heavily weighted toward state governments at the expense of the national government. Indeed, Congress under the Articles had no independent taxing power, no real authority to regulate interstate commerce, and no capacity to fashion a coherent foreign policy. The Constitutional Convention that met in Philadelphia in the summer of 1787 was charged by the state legislatures with the task of revising the Articles of Confederation. However, the convention went well beyond its mandate when the reformers of the Articles became the framers of the new Constitution.

Meeting secretly, fifty-five delegates produced a document that has been the legal framework of American government for more than 200 years. Because the Constitution's framers had lived first under the British crown and later under the Articles of Confederation, they were well aware of the problems associated with both unaccountable central power and with fragmented, decentralized governance. Nevertheless, despite their shared political experiences, the framers represented diverse interests and philosophies that were very much in evidence during their debates. Some represented the commercial interests of New York and Massachusetts, whereas others were from agricultural areas. Some, like Alexander Hamilton of New York, believed in a strong central government with a powerful president; others, like William Paterson of New Jersey, wanted guarantees of state sovereignty and restricted national power.

By compromising on a number of issues and addressing others in ambiguous terms, the framers fashioned a document that incorporated their diverse viewpoints and managed to hold a variety of interests together. For example, the representatives of small states wanted a legislature based on "one state, one vote," and those from larger states wanted representation based on population. This was resolved by establishing a bicameral (two-house) Congress. In the House of Representatives, state representation would be based on population; in the Senate, each state would have two representatives. Some delegates wanted Congress to choose the president, and others wanted a popular election; this was resolved by creating an electoral college, with each state legislature choosing members who would select the president. The debates between those who wanted a strong president and those who wanted the executive tightly constrained by Congress were glossed over when the president's powers were defined only in general terms.

The Constitution established a political system of shared responsibilities and divided powers, placing limitations on government. The loose confederation of states under the Articles became the federalism of the Constitution, and national power, absent under the Articles, was located in separate institutions. The Constitutional Convention of 1787 dramatically altered the rules under which the United

States would operate. In order to understand politics and structure in the United States today, it is necessary to examine the constitutional notions of limited government, federalism, and the separation of institutions sharing powers, as well as the evolution of these concepts since 1787.

Limiting Government's Powers

To many Americans, the idea of limited government is synonymous with the Bill of Rights, the first ten amendments to the Constitution. These amendments begin with the powerful five-word prohibition, "Congress shall make no law." They place restrictions on the national government by securing certain rights for individuals, including freedom of religion, speech, and the press (Amendment I); the right to be secure from unreasonable searches and seizures (Amendment IV); the right to avoid self-incrimination (Amendment V); the right to a speedy trial (Amendment VI); the right to a trial by jury (Amendment VII); and the right to be protected from cruel and unusual punishment (Amendment VII). Over the years, the judicial system has interpreted these rights, defining and redefining them in light of changing circumstances not foreseen by the framers. For example, the development of electronic surveillance techniques required updating the Fourth Amendment's protection from unreasonable searches. The development of the radio and television industries meant updating First Amendment press protections. When the Fourteenth Amendment passed in 1869, the slow process of extending the protections of the Bill of Rights to citizens interacting with state governments began.

However, the Bill of Rights is not the only component of the Constitution that limits government powers. The seven Articles that comprise the main body of the document also contain restrictions. Foremost are the sections involving federalism and the separation of powers, which limit the power of the national government. The Constitution also constrains government by formalizing accountability through elections. Aside from these general limitations, the Constitution contains other, more specific prohibitions. Article I, Section 9, prohibits Congress from suspending the requirement for a writ of habeas corpus (the right to be brought before a judge and charged upon arrest); from passing bills of attainder (laws declaring an individual or group guilty of a crime without benefit of a trial) or *ex post facto* laws (laws that make past acts a crime); and from conferring titles of nobility.

The net effect of these constitutional codifications is an institutionalization of libertarian philosophy in American government. Libertarian thought supports minimal government involvement in the private sector. It should come as no surprise that this philosophy has effects on political decision makers and their policies. Among all industrialized nations, the United States is the most reliant on private-sector production; state-run enterprises are anathema. The United States was one of the last industrialized nations to adopt social programs for the underprivileged and did so only because of the upheavals during the Great Depression of the 1930s. Basic welfare grants in the United States are less generous and public housing less available than in other Western countries. The United States is also the world's only industrialized nation, except for South Africa, that lacks national health insurance.

The emphasis on individual rights and limited government touches almost all segments of American society. The commonly used expression, "I know my rights," reflects just how embedded a general notion of civil liberties is. Ideologically, most Americans support individual rights against government actions that might violate constitutional rights. More concretely, however, many are troubled by the emphasis on civil liberties in criminal prosecutions. Further increases in the social problems associated with drug abuse, for example, may result in future demands for more intrusive police actions, fewer protections from invasions of privacy, and less emphasis on the rights of the accused. However, the current level of resistance to widespread drug testing proposals is one more affirmation of the principle of individual rights and limited government.

From Federalism to Intergovernmental Relations

Federalism and the Constitution   At the heart of many debates at the Constitutional Convention was the issue of state versus national responsibility. To be accepted by state conventions, the Constitution had to ensure the states a formally guaranteed role in the new government. To be an effective blueprint for nationhood, it had to establish a strong, responsible national government providing "for the common defense" and ensuring "domestic Tranquility."

Federalism guarantees the jurisdiction of two governments over the same territory and population. The Constitution provides both a strong central government and a permanent political role for the states using this system. The framers found three benefits in federalism. First, it allowed both states rights proponents and national power advocates to support the Constitution. Second, dividing responsibility between the national and state governments helped limit the power of government generally. Finally, federalism permitted the diversity of American society representation in state capitals and, through state representatives, in the national government.

The Constitution established a viable central government. Article I, Section 8, gives Congress many powers not granted the legislature in the Articles of Confederation. These include the powers to levy taxes, to borrow money, to regulate interstate commerce, to coin money, to declare war, to raise armies, and "to make all Laws . . . necessary and proper" to accomplish its functions. Article II vests executive power in a president, an office neglected in the Articles of Confederation. Article VI states the Constitution and all its national laws and treaties "shall be the supreme Law of the Land." This means that when state laws conflict with national legislation, the latter must be obeyed. Furthermore, Article I, Section 10, prohibits the states from engaging in numerous activities, including entering into treaties, coining money, passing bills of attainder or *ex post facto* laws, impairing the obligation of contracts, and levying taxes on imports or exports.

While creating a strong central government, the Constitution provides a number of protections to the states. Article IV guarantees each state its territorial integrity, "a Republican Form of Government," protection from foreign invasion and, upon a state's request, national assistance in dealing with internal violence. Article V guarantees that "no State, without its Consent, shall be deprived of its equal Suffrage in the Senate." Article V also provides a role for the states in the amendment process: Upon petition of two-thirds of state legislatures, the Congress "shall call a Convention for proposing Amendments." Furthermore, all constitutional amendments need ratification by three-quarters of either state legislatures or special state conventions.

In the early years of the American Republic, the general and sometimes vague precepts of the Constitution needed definition. Many issues were resolved by Supreme Court decisions, which established a relatively broad sweep of national powers. For example, in *Martin* v. *Hunter's Lessee* (1 Wheaton 304 [1816]), the Court assumed for its own authority to review state court decisions involving national laws. In *McCulloch* v. *Maryland* (4 Wheaton 316 [1819]), the Court provided Congress and the national government wide legislative discretion by interpreting the "necessary and proper clause" quite broadly. In *Gibbons* v. *Ogden* (9 Wheaton 1 [1824]), the Court struck down a state law because it infringed on the national government's power to regulate interstate commerce. Nevertheless, it took the Civil War to decide the most fundamental issue of federalism. Following the Union's victory, it was clear that the United States was a sovereign nation composed of states, rather than a collection of sovereign states comprising a nation.

Modern intergovernmental relations   Since the Civil War, the United States has redefined federalism. All governmental levels have grown in size and importance, and the relationships among levels of government have changed. The phrase *intergovernmental relations* characterizes national-state interactions in recent years. More than a semantic choice, the term implies extensive interaction and numerous cooperative undertakings between the national and state governments, suggesting the evolution of federalism from a demarcated to a more interactive system.

In the early years of the Republic, sporadic federal grants to the states were for education and for maintaining local militias, with no larger policy of direct federal aid. The Federal Highway Act in 1916, however, formalized the process of allocating federal grants to the states. Before the passage of the Highway Act, nationalstate relations were characterized by *dual federalism,* with each level of government maintaining its own unique responsibilities. With this new ongoing system of grants-in-aid, the federal government changed national-state relationships dramatically. In place of dual federalism, federal grant programs provided for policy cooperation between the national and state governments and ushered in an era of *cooperative federalism.* In subsequent years, first with Franklin Roosevelt's attempts (known as the New Deal) to cope with the Great Depression in the 1930s and then with Lyndon Johnson's efforts (known as the Great Society) to eliminate poverty in the 1960s, cooperative federalism grew in importance.

Funds allocated by Democratic administrations were generally in the form of categorical grants-in-aid. Categorical grants are given to state governments with requirements of how the money can be spent and constitute an indirect method of implementing national policy priorities. The Nixon and Reagan administrations attempted to reestablish more distinct spheres of policy responsibilities (a modern dual federalism) by substituting block grants for categorical grants-in-aid. Block grants give local governments wider discretion over the use of federal funds than the latter. Targeted programs of aid, reflecting national policies, were also modified by the growth of formula grants, which allocate funds more broadly, again resulting in increased local policy control. Despite these Republican efforts to broaden grant programs and reinstitute a form of dual federalism, cooperative federalism remains a mainstay of intergovernmental relations in the 1990s and probably for the foreseeable future.

Federalism and intergovernmental relations have marked effects on the politics and structures of American government. Federalism reinforces American pluralism by giving the diverse groups in the United States a variety of access points at which to make policy demands. For example, education, police protection, and land-use planning are considered primarily state and local responsibilities, while Aid to Families with Dependent Children (AFDC) unites federal, state, and county jurisdictions in the nation's primary welfare program. Federalism also encourages pluralism because states and regions develop their own political subcultures. In the early part of this century, some states opted for progressive legislation limiting child labor and improving work conditions for their citizens, often in the face of Supreme Court resistance. These state laws became the models for subsequent federal social legislation. Of course, the development and protection of subcultures can also be socially destructive, exemplified by the Southern states' attempts to maintain their systems of racial segregation in the 1950s and 1960s.

Cooperative federalism has resulted in extensive lobbying efforts in Washington on the part of states and localities. As these levels of government began to rely on federal aid money, they organized like any other interest group to defend programs beneficial to them. Some maintain individual offices in Washington, while others joined organizations like the National League of Cities, the National Association of Counties, and the National Association of State Legislatures. Members of Congress now have the dual role of appropriating federal funds and of representing constituencies and local governments that demand federal money. Such local pressures often result in the practice of *logrolling,* whereby members of Congress trade votes on programs for their local constituents. This keeps constituents happy but may result in substantial budgetary pressures.

The Separation of Institutions Sharing Powers

In Federalist 51, James Madison wrote:

> In framing a government which is to be administered by men over men, the great difficulty lies in this: you must first enable the government to control the governed; and in the next place oblige it to control itself. A dependence on the people is no doubt, the primary control on government; but experience has taught mankind the necessity of auxiliary precautions.[1]

[1]James Madison, "Federalist 51," *The Federalist Papers* (New York: Mentor Books, 1961), pp. 320–325.

With these words, Madison summarized a basic tenet of American government in general and of the separation of institutions sharing powers in particular. National government must be strong enough to rule while remaining accountable enough to be controlled. The framers chose to do this by separating institutional powers within the national government, producing a system of checks and balances. At its most basic level, the separation of institutions provides for three branches of government: a Congress primarily responsible for legislating, a president primarily responsible for executing the law, and a court system responsible for adjudicating any disputes that arise. Checks and balances provide each branch with powers that can constrain the actions of the other branches. For example, only Congress may legislate, but the president has the power to veto legislation, which Congress can then override with a two-thirds vote. The president can be impeached by the House and tried by the Senate, with the Chief Justice of the Supreme Court presiding.

With separate institutions sharing powers, each actor in national government can, and often does, strive for an increased role but one actor's ambition runs headlong into another's and the overall thrust for government power is controlled. Obviously, such a system generates conflict within government. Over the years, such friction has resulted in swings in the balance of influence among the three branches, particularly between the president and Congress. The twentieth century saw increases in presidential prerogatives, particularly during and following Franklin Roosevelt's years in office. However, a succession of "failed presidencies"—Johnson and the Vietnam war, Nixon and Watergate, Carter and the hostages in Iran—increased congressional influence. Although Reagan's eight years reestablished presidential stature in part, his second term was marked by an activist Congress that challenged many of his initiatives. Early in his own administration, George Bush reestablished some of the momentum toward increased presidential stature begun in the first Reagan administration. Although Bush, unlike Reagan, was not identified with any particular domestic policy agenda, his presidential approval ratings rose to all-time record levels following the Persian Gulf War. However, Bush's popularity dropped rapidly in the wake of the economic downturn of the early 1990s.

The constitutional division between the president and Congress has been reinforced in recent years by divided party control. From 1988 through 1992, President Bush was forced to deal with a Congress in which both houses were controlled by Democrats. Such a situation, faced by many recent Republican presidents, adds a distinctly political component to the doctrine of separate institutions sharing powers. Bush reached out to the Democratic majority for votes to pass his programs and, at the same time, continued to nurture his natural political base among the Republican minority. This division, also faced by Presidents Eisenhower, Nixon, Ford, and Reagan, presents a difficult but not insurmountable problem, evidenced by the relative success these Republican presidents enjoyed with Democratic Congresses early in their administrations. Conversely, Jimmy Carter, with a Congress controlled by his own party, was generally no more successful in his relations with the legislative branch than were recent Republican presidents.

The federal courts are not immune from controversy in the realm of separation of powers. The lifetime tenure of federal judges is balanced by the fact that they are nominated for their positions by the president and confirmed by the Senate. Historically, this constraint on court actions has been as effective as (though less direct than) other checks. Periodically, the courts have been accused of legislating, in other words, making policy rather than adjudicating policy disputes. In the 1930s, for example, an activist, conservative Supreme Court was initially checked by Roosevelt's unsuccessful attempt to use his nomination power to pack the Court. Although the president's court-packing threat was blocked by Congress (another example of separation of powers), it did succeed in changing the Court's rulings ("the switch in time that saved nine").[2] Subsequently, FDR's eight Supreme Court appointments moved the Court in a more liberal direction. In the 1960s, complaints about Earl Warren's activist liberal court were a focal point of Nixon's 1968 campaign. Subsequently, Nixon's, Ford's, Reagan's, and Bush's appointments to the Court made it a more conservative body.

In a parliamentary system like Great Britain's, one party or coalition of parties controls both the legislative and executive branches, and policy is more readily formulated with accountability more easily determined. The American system of separate institutions makes it more difficult for the federal government to produce a coherent national policy. Citizens also have difficulty calling political leaders to account for failed policies, particularly during an era of divided party control. Between 1981 and 1992, for example, the United States amassed huge budget deficits and nearly quadrupled its national debt. However, the Republicans in the White House blamed the Democrats in the Congress, and vice versa. This separation of institutions also makes it more likely that local district issues, by definition parochial or limited in scope, will have substantial influence on national policy. Such local influence, as in the case of congressional logrolling mentioned earlier, can have negative effects on national budgetary policy.

In summary, the Constitution is the primary codified constraint on policymakers. It structures the American political game, outlining the responsibilities of the national and state governments and of the three institutions that share power within the national government, and limiting the powers of national political leaders in their exercise of those responsibilities. Since 1787, great social and political change has occurred within the Constitution's general framework. Nevertheless, it remains a fundamentally sound document, which continues to control the exercise of power more than 200 years after its adoption.

LIBERALS, CONSERVATIVES, AND POLITICAL CONSENSUS

With the exception of the Civil War, American politics has generally been a contest over appropriate means to an end rather than a battle over basic philosophies. On a day-to-day basis, political conflict is characterized by a fundamental

---

[2]Justice Owen Roberts changed his votes following the confrontation and helped establish a five-to-four majority in favor of New Deal legislation.

consensus, around which liberal and conservative ideological interpretations have developed. The conservative-liberal split is basically managed through the two-party system. Because the range of American ideological differences is relatively narrow, it adds a degree of overall coherence to an essentially fragmented political order.

Over the course of American history, national consensus evolved in light of changing political and economic values. Therefore, it is useful to consider how the current range of ideological differences around that consensus constrains the public policy options available to political leaders. In the United States today, four basic precepts define the American political consensus. First, there remains basic agreement that government in the United States should be limited, thereby protecting individual rights. Second, the competitive free market, properly regulated by government, is considered the most effective mechanism for economic growth and development. Third, over the past fifty years, the social consensus has incorporated the notion of governmental responsibility to the disadvantaged. Fourth, there is a fundamental recognition that the United States needs an effective military defense against a dangerous world.

Consider these consensus views in light of conservative and liberal interpretations. Compared to the diversity of ideologies and parties in Western Europe, the American ideological continuum is relatively narrow. Generally, conservatives subscribe to the notions of limited government involvement in economic matters, more extensive government involvement enforcing basic moral values, and a forceful American military presence around the world. Liberals generally believe in extensive government involvement in the market, less government involvement in social issues such as abortion and school prayer, and an emphasis on diplomacy in international relations. A caution is in order here: These are not the classic characterizations of conservative and liberal thought in political theory. However, they are reasonable characterizations of these terms as currently employed in the United States.

Before proceeding, it should also be noted that *conventional* politics is the subject of this discussion. Many individuals and groups speak, sometimes eloquently, to a different world view. On the ballot in the last presidential election were candidates offering a variety of nonconsensus political views, ranging from communism to extreme libertarianism. This analysis excludes them because they do not demonstrate anything approaching broad-based support among the American people. Nevertheless, if history is a guide, some of their policy suggestions in less radical form may become part of a future consensus. For example, social security was once considered a radical idea until economic circumstances prompted the Democratic party to adopt it in the 1930s. Now this formerly radical proposal is part of the fabric of conventional American politics.

Although concepts of individual rights and limited government cross ideological lines, there are different interpretations of what these values mean. Generally, liberals emphasize the notion of limited government by interpreting literally the rights conferred directly by the Constitution and by extending the notion of basic rights to include such concepts as a right to privacy. In the balance between the individual and society, they tend to weigh individual rights more heavily than society's prerogatives. Because of their focus on individual rights, liberals are sometimes thought incapable of exercising governmental authority. Conservatives, while supportive of individualism, are more inclined to tilt the balance between individual rights and society in favor of the society. Many conservatives believe that government is obligated to enforce moral norms with measures like banning abortion and making school prayer mandatory. Because of this focus on social obligations and stability, conservatives are sometimes accused of being authoritarian.

Conservatives are usually enthusiastic supporters of the free market. They distrust government regulation and government attempts to macromanage the economy. Because of their strong promarket position, conservatives sometimes favor business interests over the general interests of society. Liberals, while supportive of competitive markets, are more inclined to regulate and macromanage the economy. They often view corporate America with suspicion and favor policies to constrain its activities. Because of their economic activism, liberals are occasionally charged with promoting inefficiency in the free market.

Liberals are supporters of the welfare state and the notion that the social environment directly affects individual behavior. They see a societal responsibility to the poor and favor extended social programs financed through the redistribution of wealth. Liberals also evidence a strong commitment to civil rights through support of affirmative action programs for minorities and women. Because of their social-welfare commitments, liberals are often tagged "bleeding hearts" and social engineers who disrupt society's economic base in favor of helping the poor. Conservatives acknowledge the welfare state but seek to limit its size and scope, viewing social programs a drain on both the larger economy and the individual initiative of recipients. They believe that economic growth will solve many of the problems faced by the poor. Because of their position, conservatives are sometimes accused of being hard-hearted and short-sighted in their approach to the disadvantaged.

Conservatives view the international arena with great suspicion, wary, for instance, of the calls for defense budget cuts in the wake of the Soviet Union's collapse. Indeed, in the period before its collapse, conservatives were particularly distrustful of the Soviet Union and saw that nation as the root cause of many international problems, particularly in the Third World (the undeveloped nations in Africa, Latin America, and Asia). Because of their distrust of negotiations and their support for the use of American military power, conservatives are sometimes termed reckless in their foreign policy positions. Liberals acknowledge the world's dangers, but argue that the breakup of the Soviet Union represents an opportunity to decrease military expenditures and increase domestic social program spending. Even before the breakup of the Soviet Union, liberals saw many of the Third World's problems as indigenous to those nations, not as the result of Soviet expansionism. Because of their distrust of the defense establishment and military power, liberals are often labeled idealists and appeasers.

Obviously, these positions are generalizations. Americans are not usually rigidly ideological; indeed, they are likely to cross ideological lines, depending on the broad policy concern being considered. For example, conservatives such as former Arizona Senator Barry Goldwater do not support attempts to enforce moral norms on society, and liberals such as Senator Edward Kennedy (D.-Mass.) have supported strong anticrime legislation despite the opposition of many civil liberties groups. Nevertheless, these generalized conservative and liberal positions constitute the viable alternative approaches in the United States today. American political leaders take them into account when they approach problems, and American voters give expression to them when they exercise their franchise.

MANAGING CONFLICT THROUGH THE TWO-PARTY SYSTEM

The primary tool of conflict management in the United States is the two-party system. The American two-party system is the world's oldest; indeed, the Democratic party is the world's oldest political party. Such longevity is particularly impressive in light of party history. Parties are not mentioned in the Constitution, were opposed at their inception by powerful political leaders (including many of the Constitution's framers), and have been the subject of a hundred years of reform efforts often directed at hindering their operations. Nevertheless, American political conflict since 1860 has been managed primarily through the Republican and Democratic parties. Indeed, in 1992 all but one of the 535 members of the 102nd Congress (Bernie Sanders, an Independent from Vermont), all but two of the state governors (Lowell Weicker of Connecticut and Walter Hickel of Alaska), and nearly all of the 7,248 state legislators were either Republicans or Democrats.

Why has the two-party system survived for so long? One explanation lies in election procedures. A number of Western democracies have *proportional representation,* with the proportion of seats a political party receives in the nation's legislature reflecting the proportion of votes it received in the election. For example, if a party receives 40 percent of the popular vote, it captures 40 percent of the seats in the legislature. In the United States, however, congressional elections are based on single-member districts; there is one winner in each of the 435 congressional district races. This system favors the two major parties because a district's congressional seat is awarded to a party only if its candidate receives a plurality (more votes than any other candidate) of the district vote. A winner-take-all system makes it highly unlikely that minor-party support will be reflected in Congress. Therefore, it discourages voters from wasting their votes on minor-party candidates and encourages them to select the "lesser of two evils"—one of the two major-party candidates.

Minor parties face three other difficulties that help perpetuate the two-party system. First, except for crisis situations, the average American voter is relatively moderate in his or her political views. The major parties, broad-based coalitions of many diverse interests, are well suited to attract this moderate voter with political appeals centered around the American consensus. Minor-party candidates who stray from the moderate center have, by definition, only minority support, and those who court the political center risk losing their original supporters and appearing simply redundant to the majority of voters.

Second, the major parties' control of the political process means that electoral rules are written to favor them. In most states, for example, it is difficult to get on the ballot without major-party endorsement. State rules usually require minor-party candidates to submit petitions containing signatures from a specified number of registered voters in order to appear on state ballots. The highly technical requirements for collecting and submitting such petitions virtually ensure that political opponents will challenge their validity. In New York, for example, the unspoken rule for ballot petitions dictates that two signatures be collected for every one required. Such state rules are particularly onerous to minor-party presidential candidates, who must deal with them on a state-by-state basis. In 1992, before Ross Perot would announce his independent candidacy for the presidency, he insisted that volunteers committed to him get his name on state ballots.

Finally, minor-party candidates frequently receive insufficient media attention. The media cover the major candidates because one of them is expected to win. However, supporters of minor candidates argue that such media decisions are self-fulfilling and assure a major-party victory. On the other hand, the media wish to avoid the charge that granting equal coverage to a minor party creates a candidacy.

Conservatives, Liberals, and the Two-Party System

To some degree, the conservative and liberal variants of the American consensus are reflected in party politics in the United States. However, in contrast to multiparty systems, in which each party represents a relatively coherent ideological perspective, the national Republican and Democratic parties are large umbrella organizations, incorporating widely diverse sets of interests. Generally speaking, the Democratic party tends to be liberal and the Republican party conservative, but this characterization conceals as much as it reveals. For example, the Democratic parties in Texas and Mississippi are more conservative than the Democratic parties in Massachusetts and New York, and the Republican parties of Pennsylvania and New Jersey are less conservative than the Republican parties of Florida and Utah.

In fact, each party's national candidates have to consider the views of several distinct and influential groups within the party's national coalition. Republican candidates have to address the concerns of a supply-side, entrepreneurial wing seeking to diminish the influence of the welfare state, a moralist faction's social agenda wanting to outlaw abortion and reinstate school prayer, and a regular or moderate wing concerned with balanced budgets and social stability. National Democrats must address the interests of a Southern wing relatively conservative on foreign policy issues; a large group of New Deal Democrats concerned with labor issues, social policy, and crime; and a vocal liberal wing emphasizing social issues and redistribution of society's wealth.

Balancing these various interests and priorities, some of which are incompatible, is very difficult. National party leaders commonly avoid specific policy positions and allow regional and ideological factions within the party relatively free rein. This results in a "babble of voices" presenting party positions and in attempts to smooth over these differences with balanced national tickets such as the 1988 match between Governor Michael Dukakis and his more conservative running mate, Senator Lloyd Bentsen. However understandable given the circumstances, such adaptations do not lead to meaningful national coordination of the political process through the party system. Because of the ideological divisions within party coalitions, national candidates avoid specifically defined policy positions during campaigns and, once elected, they cannot always depend on party support in governing.

Political Parties and Political Fragmentation

In theory, the two-party system should help counterbalance the political fragmentation resulting from federalism and the separation of institutions sharing powers. In practice, however, the two-party system not only fails to counterbalance but actually reinforces this fragmentation. The term *two-party system* is in some ways a misnomer. Although there are national Republican and Democratic party committees as well as congressional campaign committees located in the House and the Senate, American political parties are essentially state-based organizations. Consequently, it is not unreasonable to speak of fifty Republican and fifty Democratic parties. Within each state and subject to state law, parties are organized in a hierarchical fashion. At the lowest level is the precinct or election-district organization. Participants in precinct organizations select representatives for the county organization, which remains an important source of party patronage and influence in many states. At the top of the hierarchy sits the state party committee, which has the primary responsibility for party organization, with day-to-day management in the hands of a state chairperson.

Under this decentralized party system, candidates for Congress are not selected by national party leaders, so they do not have to reflect the national party's position on issues (assuming the national party has positions on issues). In fact, congressional candidates may not even be chosen by state party leaders. Because of the variety of elective positions in a federalist system, state party officials concentrate on those offices that affect them most directly. Accordingly, these officials take great pains to influence the selection of candidates for governor, state attorney general, state legislature, and other local offices. Generally, state party officials are less interested in federal offices. A party's candidates for Congress often run relying more on their own resources and assistance from local or state interest groups and political action committees (PACs) than on the party they nominally represent. Because members of Congress frequently develop closer political ties with interest groups than with their own party organizations, they may represent group and not party concerns within Congress.

Another reason that parties are weak national coordinators involves the history of party reform in the United States. In the late nineteenth and early twentieth centuries, the backlash against the corruption associated with party politics in general (and the urban political machine in particular) instilled a series of reforms intended to curtail party power. The substitution of primary campaigns for party conventions as methods of selecting candidates made it more difficult for party leaders to control their own internal operations, thereby securing political loyalty among elected officials. Also, the rise of civil service (as opposed to party patronage) as the means of recruiting public-sector employees greatly lessened party influence over government workers.

In recent years, additional reforms have served to weaken the power of party leaders, particularly among Democrats. After their 1968 electoral defeat, the Democrats attempted to open up the party's presidential nomination procedure. Several commissions revised the rules to increase the influence of party reformers by deemphasizing the input of party regulars. Party rules were rewritten to include quotas specifying the percentages of minorities, women, and young people to be represented in the party's national conventions. Such reforms, coupled with the emphasis on the presidential primary system for selecting national candidates, resulted in an increasingly volatile nomination process. Since 1982, attempts to recentralize the party included requiring that more Democratic officeholders be included among national convention delegates and instituting regional primaries in the South, ostensibly to generate more moderate (read less liberal) candidates. However, because each such attempt represents political advantage for one faction and disadvantage for another, Democrats will probably find these procedural battles highly injurious to party unity in the coming years.

SUMMARY

The United States Constitution, the world's oldest, acts as a fundamental constraint on political leaders. It established the basic rules of the political game in 1787. The original document, together with its twenty-six amendments, still serves today as the "supreme Law of the Land." Because of the constraints of limited government, federalism, and separate institutions sharing powers, governance in the United States is more difficult and less efficient than in many other societies, but that is precisely the point! Government was designed to be difficult from the beginning. Minority rights were protected; the states were guaranteed a role in the nation's political life; and leaders who sought to extend their powers beyond the pale of constitutional acceptance found themselves in political trouble.

Because conflict is an inherent part of politics, the political context of a society cannot be understood without some knowledge of conflict intensity and conflict management. American politics operates around a fundamental consensus, including notions of individual rights, limited government, a capitalist economy, the welfare state, and the need for a viable military defense. Liberal and conservative ideologies interpret that consensus, weighing social values differently but not departing very far from these core agreements (compared to politics in other industrialized nations). Generally, conservatives desire relatively free markets, social enforcement of moral norms of conduct, and a strong American military presence around the world. Liberals, on the other hand, support government regulation and management of the economy, extensive civil liberties protections, and a reduced American military presence around the world. At times, the consensus undergoes revision, as during the Civil War or the development of the welfare state in the 1930s, and American politics may then take on a hard ideological edge. However, such periods are exceptions to the general rule.

Conflict management in the United States is a function of the two-party system. This system is supported by the congressional election process, which provides for winner-take-all elections conducted in single-member districts. Unlike proportional representation, the system of single-member districts does not provide for minor-party representation in the national legislature. Such an electoral system encourages voters to avoid minor-party candidates for fear they will waste their votes. The two-party system is further reinforced by the political, procedural, and public-relations problems minor-party candidates face in seeking elective office.

The two-party system has the potential to provide effective coordination of American politics, but for structural, ideological, and procedural reasons, that potential remains largely unfulfilled. Structurally, party control is not concentrated in national party commissions or in the Congress but instead is found in each of the fifty states. Ideologically, both parties include widely divergent viewpoints and orientations making political coordination very difficult. Also in terms of procedures, the influence of national party leaders has been dramatically reduced over the years by reforms intended to open the political process.

In terms of day-to-day policy, such a constrained and fragmented system is inevitably conservative—not in ideological terms, but in the sense of favoring the status quo. The fragmented American political system, provided for in the Constitution and further decentralized by the local orientation of American political parties, makes it very difficult for national public policy to change by great leaps and bounds. Instead, political changes are best characterized as a series of incremental adjustments (that is, small changes in existing policy), which may or may not proceed in any particular direction. Only in crisis periods (such as war) does American government produce dramatic policy changes guided by an overall design. Even in the Great Depression of the 1930s, the Roosevelt administration did not apparently operate with any great policy design. Roosevelt's approach to the crisis was essentially one of trial and error, so even the development of the American welfare state was the result of a series of incremental adjustments in the existing situation.

Although political conflict is constrained and policy change generally incremental, policy is not wholly determined by context. Political leaders have options and are relatively free to select from among a variety of policy alternatives. Following this review of the context in which policy decisions are made, succeeding chapters will examine the policymakers themselves: the president, Congress, the judiciary, and the bureaucracy.

THE PRESIDENCY

The political institutions created by the Constitutional Convention of 1787 evolved so dramatically that today's institutions bear little resemblance to those of the 1790s. For example, the early presidents scheduled a weekly open house in the White House; today, citizens touring the White House rarely even glimpse a government official. The early Congresses met for only a couple of months per year; today, Congress is almost constantly in session. In 1787, Alexander Hamilton wrote that the judiciary is the "weakest of the three departments of government"; today, federal judges are involved in nearly every aspect of American life, and the Supreme Court has declared more than 100 laws passed by Congress and signed by the president unconstitutional. In 1802, the federal bureaucracy numbered only 2,875 nonmilitary employees; at last count, just under three million nonmilitary employees received paychecks from the national government. However, the four institutions of the presidency, Congress, federal courts, and the bureaucracy have evolved within a framework of stability provided by the Constitution.

CONSTITUTIONAL PREROGATIVES

The president's constitutional prerogatives group conveniently under six presidential roles: commander in chief of the armed forces, chief diplomat and director of foreign relations, chief executor of the nation's laws, chief administrator of the executive branch, chief policy initiator, and chief of state. (See Table 1-1.)

The President as Commander in Chief

The president's power as head of the armed forces Article II, Section 2, of the Constitution declares that the president "shall be Commander in Chief of the Army and Navy of the United States, and of the Militia of the several States, when called into the actual service of the United States." The Constitution makes no attempt to define the duties of the commander in chief or to establish any sort of

TABLE 1-1   The President: Constitutional Prerogatives and Powers

1. Commander in Chief	Power as head of armed forces (Art. II, Sec. 2)
2. Chief Diplomat	Power to negotiate treaties and executive agreements (Art. II, Sec. 2)
	Power to nominate ambassadors (Art. II, Sec. 2)
	Power to receive ambassadors (Art. II, Sec. 3)
3. Chief Executor	Power to execute the nation's laws (Art. II, Sec. 3)
4. Chief Administrator	Power to command the executive branch (Art. II, Sec. 2)
	Power to appoint top administrators (Art. II, Sec. 2)
5. Policy Initiator	Power to convene/adjourn Congress (Art. II, Sec. 3)
	Power to address Congress on the state of the union (Art. II, Sec. 3)
	Power to veto legislation (Art. II, Sec. 7)
	Power to nominate judges (Art. II, Sec. 2)
6. Chief of State	Power to grant reprieves and pardons (Art. II, Sec. 2)
	Power to commission officers (Art. II, Sec. 3)

guidelines. Ordinarily, presidents have delegated their authority in this area to career military officials while retaining the ultimate responsibility for all military actions to ensure civilian control over the military. There are no constitutional provisions, however, requiring a president to delegate this or any other executive authority. For example, George Washington personally commanded the forces that crushed the Whiskey Rebellion in 1794.

> The president is not required to delegate any of his powers.

Succeeding presidents, some with little or no previous military experience, have assumed the role of ultimate military strategist in addition to performing their function of assuring civilian control over the military. During the Civil War, for example, Lincoln, with no previous military experience at all, often visited the Army of the Potomac and instructed the generals on military strategy. Similarly, Jimmy Carter, formerly in the U.S. Navy, took personal command of the ill-fated rescue attempt of the American hostages in Iran in 1980.

As this power has evolved, the president can never forget the enormity of this responsibility. He* is constantly shadowed by a military aide who carries the "black box" containing the cryptographic orders the president needs to initiate a nuclear attack. Although U.S. nuclear-strike capability has been used only once (during World War II), the threat to use it was made by Dwight D. Eisenhower in 1953 and by John F. Kennedy in 1962.

*Regrettably, the male pronoun is used when referring to the president, to avoid awkwardness and because no woman has yet been elected to the office, although it is only a matter of time before this is no longer true.

Presidential authority in
military affairs is broader
than congressional
powers.

The undefined constitutional provision for presidential authority in the area of military affairs places few limitations on presidents. In contrast, the constitutional provision for congressional authority in this area is quite specific. Congress has constitutional authority to tax for the common defense, declare war, make rules concerning capture on land and water, raise and support armies, provide and maintain a navy, make rules governing the armed forces, and call out the state militia and provide for its training and discipline. However, Congress cannot send an army anywhere, and its decision *not to* declare war has not inhibited presidents from engaging U.S. troops in armed conflicts.

Extensions and limitations of commander-in-chief powers The president's power as commander in chief authorizes him to mobilize and use United States forces anywhere in the world. Although only Congress can declare war (and has done so five times in the War of 1812 against Britain, the Mexican War, the Spanish-American War, and the two world wars), the president has always requested such declarations. Without such a request, presidents have initiated military conflicts on more occasions than those authorized by Congress. For instance, no declaration of war accompanied United States involvement in the naval war with France (1798–1800), the first and second Barbary wars (1801–1805 and 1815), the Mexican-American disputes (1914–1917), the Korean War (1949–1953), or the Indochina War (1960–1973).

Caution must be exercised
in "interpreting" the
meaning of constitutionally
granted powers, because
their scope has changed
considerably over time.

The Founders did not intend that the power to wage war should reside with the president, but the evolution of the meaning of *commander in chief* has resulted in this acquired constitutional power. This is a particularly good example of the need for caution when interpreting phrases of the Constitution. The title *commander in chief* initially conferred upon the president the authority of military commander in the event of an internal insurrection or a congressionally declared war with a foreign power. Over the past 200 years, however, *commander in chief* changed, now meaning the president can order troops into combat in any area of the world. This is far from the original intent of the Constitutional Convention. Titles of public officials change their meaning over the years and this serves to illuminate how a political system operates. The British monarch, for example, is also the commander in chief of the United Kingdom's armed forces, but the queen holds that title for ceremonial reasons only and has no actual military power. Clearly, a uniform meaning of the term *commander in chief* is not possible. The title may be employed in both British and American political systems, but the powers it confers are dramatically different.

The president's power as commander in chief is not unlimited. Although he can commit troops to combat anywhere in the world, his actions are more likely to go unchallenged if the conflict is over quickly. For example, in January of 1991, a 52 to 47 Senate vote supported George Bush's deadline for Iraqi withdrawal following that country's invasion of Kuwait. Although the Senate vote indicated substantial opposition to the policy, the Persian Gulf conflict's limited duration helped maintain congressional support for the president's policy. However, if the

The War Powers Act was an attempt to limit the president's powers.

conflict to which troops are committed is likely to be prolonged, the political tenor of the times influences the extent to which Congress tolerates the use of military power. After the unpopular Indochina War, Congress passed the 1973 War Powers Act forbidding the president to commit troops for an extended period without congressional consent. This accounted for Reagan's close consultation with Congress when he committed troops in Lebanon in 1983; he acted only after Congress passed a joint resolution permitting commitment of troops for no longer than eighteen months.

Congress scrutinizes presidential military actions in varied degrees, even within a single presidential term of office. In 1981, for example, Congress offered little resistance to President Reagan's plans for massive increases in military spending. The takeover of the U.S. embassy in Iran, combined with Soviet interference in Afghanistan and Poland, produced popular and congressional support for an enormous military buildup. By 1985, the pendulum had swung back; Congress treated Reagan's requests for additional military spending with skepticism and, in some cases, outright rejection. Indeed, in 1987, a joint congressional committee investigated the Reagan administration's violations of the 1986 Boland amendment limiting U.S. military aid to the Nicaraguan contras.

The President as Chief Diplomat

The president speaks for the nation in foreign affairs.

A second crucial area of presidential authority relates to foreign policy. The Constitution gives the president three specific powers in this area: (1) "He shall have Power, by and with the Advice and Consent of the Senate, to make Treaties, provided two-thirds of the Senators present concur"; (2) "he shall nominate, and by and with the Advice and Consent of the Senate, shall appoint Ambassadors, other public Ministers and Consuls"; and (3) "he shall receive Ambassadors and other public Ministers." As with his power as commander in chief, this area of presidential authority is important not because of the specificity of the original grant but rather because of its evolution. The president is now the nation's principal spokesman in foreign affairs. George Washington set the tone for this evolution as early as 1793, when, despite heated congressional and popular criticism, he declared American neutrality during a war between France and England.

Power to negotiate treaties and executive agreements Although the Constitution requires senatorial consent to treaties, treaty making initiative rests with the president. The law empowers only the president or his representatives to negotiate with other nations. The president thus decides the kinds of treaties he wants to negotiate.

Treaties have the force of law, even overriding previously passed legislation.

Once approved by the Senate and ratified by the president, treaties have the force of law. If a treaty conflicts with a state law, the latter is null and void; if the conflict is with a federal law, whichever was enacted or ratified last prevails.

The Senate usually defers to presidential initiative in foreign affairs. The Senate has rejected only about 1 percent of all treaties proposed; another 15 percent were conditioned or passed with specific reservations, and the rest were consented to without alteration. The most notable exception was the Senate's 1920 rejection of the Treaty of Versailles and U.S. participation in the League of Nations, a rejection of Woodrow Wilson's lead. With this in mind, Franklin D. Roosevelt was careful to include key members of the Senate Foreign Relations Committee in crucial negotiations during World War II. The inclusion of senators in those negotiations was motivated not by constitutional or legal necessity but by political wisdom. Although Presidents Nixon, Ford, and Carter did not directly involve senators in the negotiations concerning the Panama Canal, all three kept key senators well informed and sought their advice to ensure future Senate approval. When Reagan resumed arms control talks with the Soviet Union in March 1985, an official delegation from both houses of Congress accompanied negotiators to Geneva. Including Congress early in the process usually means a warmer reception to subsequent negotiation outcomes.

Congressional-executive international agreements require the approval of Congress as well as the president.

Congressional-executive international agreements   In addition to formal treaties, the United States enters into numerous compacts with foreign governments that are never presented to the Senate for ratification. Known popularly as *executive agreements,* and to the State Department as *international agreements other than treaties,* they are of two distinct types. The first, known as a *congressional-executive international agreement,* concerns matters over which Congress has specific powers granted by the Constitution. An example of such powers (which will be discussed in Chapter 2) is Congress's constitutional responsibility "to regulate Commerce with foreign Nations" (Article I, Section 8). This point stipulates that any matter concerning foreign trade regulation falls under the power of Congress, not the president. However, the power to *negotiate* with foreign nations lies with the president alone. Therefore, in matters of foreign trade, both the president and Congress have constitutional powers, and agreements concerning such matters constitute congressional-executive international agreements.

Furthermore, such agreements are ratified by a simple majority vote of *both* houses of Congress, even though this ratification may sometimes precede the actual negotiation. In 1934, for example, Congress gave advance ratification when it passed the Reciprocal Trade Agreements Act, which *authorized* the president to conclude certain types of trade agreements with foreign nations. Under this act, presidents have negotiated many such agreements, which have the same force of law as treaties. Inverting the procedure is also possible, so that the president negotiates first and then presents the agreement to Congress for ratification. Such was the case with the congressional-executive international agreements annexing Texas (in 1845) and Hawaii (in 1889) to the Union. The case of the annexation of Texas is interesting because it illustrates that a president may use the congressional-executive international agreement to avoid the two-thirds Senate vote necessary for treaty ratification. During John Tyler's presidency, the United States negotiated a treaty with Texas for its annexation as a state, but on January 8, 1844, the Senate refused ratification by the necessary two-thirds vote. Barely one year later, when President James Polk presented the Texas' annexation to both houses as a congressional-executive international agreement (requiring only a simple majority vote in each house), the Senate approved by a vote of twenty-seven to twenty-five.

Congressional-executive international agreements are "easier" to move through Congress because they do not require a two-thirds majority in the Senate.

By presenting the proposal in this way, Polk accomplished what Tyler had been unable to do. The decision to present a proposed agreement as a treaty (thereby requiring two-thirds consent of the Senate) or as a congressional-executive international agreement (necessitating only majority concurrence in each house) is, with one exception, merely a matter of political receptivity and is determined by the number of votes the president expects to have in the Senate.

The one exception to this general rule is that certain matters can be dealt with *only* by treaty. The Tenth Amendment stipulates that powers not constitutionally granted to the federal government are "reserved to the States respectively or to the people." Under this amendment, certain matters (although none is specifically mentioned) are not within the jurisdiction of the federal government. If a proposed compact with a foreign government includes such matters, ratifying the compact as a congressional-executive international agreement would be unconstitutional, because neither the president nor Congress has constitutional authority in those matters. However, the same proposed compact could be ratified as a treaty, because the treaty power is specifically granted, without limitations of any kind, by Article II, Section 2, of the Constitution. For example, the very first treaty the United States negotiated after ratification of the Constitution (the Jay Treaty of 1794 with Great Britain) contained provisions concerning ownership of private property by British subjects in the United States, even though the Constitution does not give either Congress or the president power over matters of private property. This agreement with Great Britain was presented to the Senate and ratified as a treaty with the necessary two-thirds vote. It could not have been presented to both houses for a simple majority vote because, although treaties may deal with matters reserved to the states, congressional-executive international agreements may not (Table 1-2). Thus any matter that might be handled as a congressional-executive international agreement could also be handled as a treaty, but the opposite is not true.

Treaties may cover matters reserved to the states by the Constitution; international agreements other than treaties may not.

Pure executive agreements The second type of international agreements other than treaties is the *pure executive* (or presidential) *agreement*. Whereas the congressional-executive international agreement relies on powers granted to both Congress and the president, the pure executive agreement stems from constitutional powers granted solely to the president. For example, the president is the commander in chief of the armed forces and may negotiate with foreign governments on military matters without submitting the results of these negotiations to Congress for ratification. It was a pure executive agreement that ended both world wars, even though Congress had declared those wars. In those instances, the president was acting as commander in chief, and Congress was powerless to intervene.

Executive agreements rely for their authority on powers granted exclusively to the president.

In recent years, presidents have increasingly relied on these pure, or "true," executive agreements in foreign policy matters (Table 1-3). Although not specifically granted by the Constitution, presidential authority to conclude such agreements was upheld by the Supreme Court as a "modest implied power" deriving from the president's authority to conduct the nation's foreign relations. As a result, hundreds of such agreements are now negotiated each year by executive-branch officials acting in the president's name and under his authority, and none of these

Executive agreements are another example of the evolution of presidential powers, but Congress has acted to eliminate the secrecy that often shrouded these agreements in the past.

TABLE 1-2   Differences between Treaties and International Agreements Other Than Treaties

Treaties	International Agreements Other than Treaties	
	Congressional–Executive International Agreements	"Pure" or True Executive Agreements
Specified in the Constitution (Art. II, Sec. 2).	Not specified in the Constitution but based on congressional and presidential powers.	Not specified in the Constitution but based on presidential powers.
Two-thirds Senate approval required.	Simple majority vote of each house required.	No congressional action required.
Binding on succeeding presidents.	Binding on succeeding presidents.	Not binding on succeeding presidents.
May include matters reserved to the states.	May not include matters reserved to the states.	May not include matters reserved to the states.
May include congressional, presidential, and judicial prerogatives.	May include congressional and presidential prerogatives.	May include only presidential prerogatives.
Used extensively before 1900.	Used extensively since 1900.	Used extensively since 1900.

TABLE 1-3   Number of Treaties and International Agreements Other Than Treaties Negotiated by the United States (1789–1990)

Period	Treaties	International Agreements Other than Treaties
1789–1839	60	27
1840–1889	215	238
1890–1939	524	917
1940–1979	504	9,079
1980–1990	186	3,922

SOURCE: U.S. Department of State

agreements requires approval by Congress. However, Congress has attempted to curb the president's powers in this area. In 1972, it passed legislation requiring the secretary of state's submission to Congress within sixty days the final text of any pure executive agreements negotiated by the administration. The law's purpose is to assure that Congress has knowledge of the content of such agreements.

Power to appoint ambassadors   Congress has disputed even less the president's prerogative to nominate ambassadors. The more popular ambassadorial posts often

The more popular ambassadorial nominations often go to wealthy campaign contributors who have little or no experience in diplomacy.

go to wealthy campaign contributors whose experience in diplomacy is nonexistent, but the Senate usually concurs with the president's wishes. The trend toward using more Foreign Service officers as ambassadors was halted by the Reagan administration. President Jimmy Carter appointed a committee of distinguished leaders to identify for him the best-qualified individual for each position. The committee was to consider "campaign activities" only if two candidates were equally qualified. When Reagan replaced Carter in the White House, wealthy campaign contributors again formed the pool from which ambassadorial nominees were selected. Although half of Reagan's nominees were Foreign Service officers, they were generally excluded from ambassadorial posts in the more significant nations.

Power to receive ambassadors   The president's power to receive ambassadors carries the implied authority to recognize or refuse to recognize foreign governments, with the implied authority to receive ambassadors. Historically, the president received an ambassador if that ambassador's government had *de facto* (actual) control over the territory that it claimed to govern. This criterion was applied to all governments in the late eighteenth century when the Constitution was drafted.

Today, the power to receive ambassadors is a political tool used by presidents to grant or withhold official recognition of other governments.

American presidents have used this authority (as have other heads of state) as a political tool in the conduct of foreign policy. For example, the USSR was not recognized until November 1933, although the Soviet government had been in power for more than sixteen years. From the end of World War II through 1978, the United States withheld recognition of China. The process of normalizing relations with that country included its "partial recognition," beginning with Richard Nixon's 1972 trip to China. From then until January 1, 1979, the United States exchanged cultural programs, diplomatic missions, and even Ping-Pong teams—but not ambassadors. Only with the exchange of ambassadors does one country "officially recognize" the existence of the other. As of 1992, the United States is withholding official recognition of Cuba, Vietnam, and Iran. The decision to recognize any one of these countries by receiving its ambassador has become completely political. It rests with the president alone, and neither Congress nor the courts can legally force or forestall his decision.

"Partial recognition" has been applied during the process of "normalizing relations" with other countries—another evolution of presidential powers.

Of course, as a part of his power to receive ambassadors, the president also has the authority to demand their recall as well as the recall of other diplomatic personnel. In recent years, diplomats have been expelled primarily for suspected espionage activities. When a country expels a diplomat, the "offended" nation often retaliates by expelling one of the first country's diplomats.

The President as Chief Executor

Power to execute the nation's laws   The president's constitutional power and duty to "take Care that the Laws be faithfully executed" provides a convenient link between the president's powers in foreign and domestic affairs. This clause provides the president with authority to carry out congressional legislation—that is, because no constitutional provisions permit Congress to enforce its own legislation,

Congress has no authority to enforce its legislation; it must rely on the president to enforce any law it passes.

Laws may be selectively and sporadically enforced by the president.

Presidents usually impound funds to promote efficient management of programs or in response to congressional directives.

Funds are impounded to penalize programs the president disagrees with.

Congress must rely on presidential action. The president, therefore, has tremendous latitude in deciding how vigorously he will enforce a law.

In reality, however, all presidents emphasize certain laws and almost ignore others. The strong antipollution laws passed by Congress at the turn of the century are a case in point. Dumping industrial waste into the nation's rivers and streams has been illegal for over seventy years, but the law has been enforced only sporadically and selectively.

Presidents generally execute laws involving the expenditure of funds appropriated by Congress. Yet, at least since Thomas Jefferson's time, presidents have withheld, or "impounded," funds from programs or projects authorized by Congress. These impoundments have occurred primarily for two reasons: The president wished to promote efficient management, or he had statutory or constitutional authority to withhold money. In 1803, for example, Jefferson impounded $50,000 appropriated by Congress for the purchase of gunboats to be used on the Mississippi River for protection against the French. After Congress appropriated the money, however, Jefferson completed negotiating the purchase of the Louisiana Territory, removing the French from the river and eliminating the immediate necessity for gunboats. Within a year, however, when gunboats of improved design were available, Jefferson released the funds. He had, therefore, impounded appropriated money in the interest of more efficient management and ultimately expended the money for the purpose that Congress intended. In this case, Jefferson withheld money on his own initiative, but a president might also act with statutory direction. Congress may direct the president to impound funds by passing legislation that imposes spending ceilings or unspecified budget cuts. Thus, in 1950, Congress passed an "omnibus" appropriations bill ordering President Harry Truman to cut the budget by not less than $550 million "without impairing national defense," whereupon Truman impounded $572 million of nonmilitary funds.

Presidents also impound funds to eliminate programs for which Congress has appropriated money but which the president dislikes. This is applied especially to domestic programs, often to those that enjoy considerable congressional support. Countering this type of impoundment, Congress passed the Budget Impoundment and Control Act of 1974, requiring that the president report all impoundments to Congress. However, the act is so ambiguously worded that administrations interpret it as legislative permission to impound, at least to a limited extent. In general, since passage of the act in 1974, presidents have deferred expenditures but have eventually spent whatever Congress has appropriated, with little argument that permanent impoundment is a presidential privilege.

Chief executor, commander in chief, and foreign relations roles combined The president's power to execute laws, his primacy to conduct the nation's foreign relations, and his role as commander in chief of the nation's armed forces have, in concert, contributed to the evolution of presidential power. One stage of this evolution occurred at the outset of the Civil War, when Lincoln relied on the constitutional mandate that the president faithfully execute the nation's laws. Within ten weeks after the firing on Fort Sumter, he had spent $2 million not appropriated by Congress, called out the militia, ordered a naval blockade of the Southern ports, seized rail and telegraph lines leading to the capital, and suspended the writ of habeas corpus (the power of a court to release individuals held by the police). Lincoln later defended his actions, claiming: "I felt that measures otherwise unconstitutional might become lawful by becoming indispensable to the preservation of the Constitution through the preservation of the nation. Right or wrong, I assumed this ground and I now avow it." In most instances, the courts either avoided the constitutional issues or upheld Lincoln's actions. Lincoln had combined and perhaps exceeded his constitutional prerogatives in justifying his unprecedented actions.

> Presidents have combined specific constitutional prerogatives so that the whole of their powers is greater than the sum of the individual powers.

Many other presidents have increased presidential power through the constant expansion and evolution of their constitutional prerogatives as commander in chief, foreign policymaker, and executor of the laws. Ironically, it is often acts of Congress that permit the president to expand his power at the expense of Congress. For example, during World War I, Congress granted President Woodrow Wilson the extraordinary combination of powers to conscript an army, license international trade, censor all communications with foreign countries, control enemy aliens within the country, and seize and operate the nation's water and rail transportation facilities as well as its telephone and telegraph systems.

During World War II, Franklin D. Roosevelt controlled the national economy by a systematic process of price and rent controls, federal rationing, plant and shipyard seizures, and material allocations. (Only some of these powers ever received congressional approval.) The most extreme application of his wartime powers came in Executive Order No. 9066 of February 19, 1942, under which approximately 112,000 Japanese Americans were removed from their homes in the "military areas" of the West Coast (Washington, California, Oregon, and parts of Arizona) and interned in special camps for the duration of the war. A month after the executive order was issued, Congress passed legislation approving Roosevelt's internment decision.

> Although Presidents have substantial power over foreign policy matters, they are still constrained by the Constitution, the Congress, and public opinion.

Such approvals for presidential actions are not always forthcoming. In a general sense, the public's mistrust of foreign "adventurism," occasioned by the U.S. experience in Vietnam, constrained succeeding presidents from expanding constitutional prerogatives in foreign affairs. Some believe that the swift U.S. victory in the Persian Gulf War in 1991 may have set the stage for a renewed period of increased presidential discretion in international affairs. However, even during the more permissive period of "bipartisan foreign policy" in the 1950s, presidents were restricted. During the Korean conflict, for example, Truman overstepped the limits of "constitutional" authority by seizing most of the nation's steel mills, then on the verge of a strike. In *Youngstown Sheet and Tube Company v. Sawyer* (343 U.S. 579 [1952]) the Supreme Court declared the action unconstitutional.

In summary, successive presidents have combined their military, foreign, and executive powers to gain a wider operating range. As the scope of these powers increased, their combined use resulted in new presidential prerogatives far beyond those specifically listed in the Constitution.

The President as Chief Policy Initiator

The constitutional system of checks and balances involves the president directly in legislative matters. In the role of policy initiator, the president acts as the nation's primary agenda setter. Indeed, because so many congressional decisions involve presidential initiatives, some have called the president the nation's chief legislator. Article II, Section 3, directly addresses the president's relations with Congress. These provide that (1) "he shall from time to time give to the Congress Information on the State of the Union"; (2) he shall "recommend to their Consideration such Measures as he shall judge necessary and expedient"; and (3) "he may, on extraordinary Occasions, convene both Houses, or either of them, and in Case of Disagreement between them, with Respect to the Time of Adjournment, he may adjourn them to such Time as he shall think proper."

Power to convene and adjourn Congress   The third of these cases can be covered rather quickly, because the evolution of this power has been away from presidential authority rather than toward it. Since the adoption of the Twentieth Amendment, Congress convenes each year in January and usually remains in session for nine months or longer, thereby providing few opportunities for calling it into session.

As with the presidential powers considered earlier, the first two powers enumerated under chief policy initiator also carry special import as a result of their evolution. Although neither the first provision (that Congress shall be supplied with information) nor the second (necessitating that it listen to the president's judgments) mandates either legislative direction or content, the exercise of these presidential powers now has that effect.

Because Congress is in session almost year-round, the power to convene Congress has meant little.

Power to address Congress on the State of the Union   The president's annual state of the Union address to a joint session of Congress began with Washington but fell into a prolonged period of disuse with Jefferson, who preferred to send written messages to Capitol Hill. The practice of a personal address was revived temporarily by Wilson and then more permanently by Franklin Roosevelt and has been continued by each successive president, with the exception of Nixon during his second term. Delivering the State of the Union address has become a major television opportunity for the president. It not only allows him influence over the legislative agenda for the upcoming session but also a direct appeal for public support of his programs.

Presidents use the annual State of the Union address to prepare Congress and the public for the president's legislative agenda.

Power to recommend legislation   Presidents now supplement the State of the Union address with actual drafts of bills. As part of this practice, begun by Theodore Roosevelt, the State of the Union address as a philosophical statement is followed by specific proposals to Congress. For example, in 1992 President Bush used the State of the Union address to present the broad outlines of his economic revitalization plan to help the economy recover from recession. Later he presented Congress with draft legislation containing the specifics of his economic program.

The evolution of the president's position as chief policy initiator has even been abetted by Congress. In 1921, Congress passed the Budget and Accounting Act, which requires that the president supplement his State of the Union address with a detailed account of his proposals for the funding of both new and ongoing federal programs. The Budget and Impoundment Control Act of 1974 further legitimated the primary role of the president in the budgetary process. The Employment Act of 1946 required presidential analysis of the nation's economy, with particular reference to maintaining full employment and production and proposals for achieving those objectives. Thus the constitutional provision that the president shall "recommend measures" to Congress is now interpreted to include the planning and presentation of an entire program of legislation.

The president proposes the annual federal budget.

Power to veto legislation   The Constitution clearly grants only one "official" authorization to the president in the legislative process. Section 7 of Article I (relating to Congress) limits presidential authority to veto power over legislation. Significantly, this is one of the few presidential constitutional prerogatives that has not substantially changed. He must still sign every congressional bill, or let it lie on his desk for ten days while Congress remains in session, for the act to have the status of a law.

The veto power gives the president the right to pass on every piece of legislation.

In the event the president decides a bill should not become law, even if his disagreement is with a single provision of the bill, he must return the entire bill to Congress in order to veto it. Neither the Constitution nor (quite understandably) Congress has given him veto power of only selected parts of an act (an "item veto"). Presidents Reagan and Bush have repeatedly urged Congress to grant the president "item-veto" authority, arguing that by giving the president the authority to veto individual items that would increase the federal deficit they were challenging him to balance the budget. Congress, viewing this as an unprecedented power grab on the part of the president, refused the "challenge."

Once vetoed, a measure must secure a two-thirds majority in each house of Congress to become law. If Congress has adjourned for the end of its session, however, the president may exercise his "pocket veto" by simply not signing the bill in the requisite ten-day period.

Power to nominate judges   The president's constitutional involvement with the judiciary is limited to nominating federal judges, so his influence through the courts depends on the actions of others. Article II provides that the president nominate: "Judges of the Supreme Court, and all other Officers of the United States, whose Appointments are not herein otherwise provided for, and which shall be established by Law. . . ." As explained at greater length in Chapter 3, the power to staff the judiciary is shared with the Senate because the president's nominees must be confirmed by the Senate. Normally, the president consults with the senators from

The president nominates all federal judges, although his choices must be confirmed by the Senate.

the state where the vacant federal judgeship exists before a nomination is made. Although the president may nominate whomever he pleases, the Senate may refuse confirmation. Despite the evolutionary increase in presidential power, the president remains far from omnipotent.

The President as Chief Administrator

Power to command the executive branch   Article II provides that "executive Power shall be vested" in the president, and that "he may require the Opinion, in writing, of the principal Officer in each of the executive Departments." Except for these two provisions, however, the Constitution is conspicuously silent on the president's relation to the bureaucracy. It assumes the presence of executive departments but makes no effort to define their composition, duties, powers, or responsibilities, and thereby leaves the bureaucracy's development to statute and evolutionary process. Consequently, the president has wide latitude in deciding how he wishes to administer the executive branch of government. Congress has strengthened the president's role as chief administrator simply by increasing the number of executive departments and the tasks they are expected to perform.

The president decides how laws are to be administered.

Power to appoint bureaucrats   This increase in executive departments was accomplished in accord with the provision that the president shall appoint "such inferior officers as [the Congress] may think proper." There was certainly no expectation by the Founders that the central government would experience the growth accompanying this nation's move into the twentieth century. Until the acceptance of a merit-oriented civil service in 1883, presidents distributed literally thousands of patronage positions to loyal party followers. "To the victor belong the spoils" was a practice only partly curbed in 1883 when Congress passed the Civil Service Act (the Pendleton Act) following President James A. Garfield's assassination by a frustrated office seeker.

The percentage of government positions open to presidential appointment has decreased with the extension of the civil service system, to the point that the number of political appointments is now relatively stable. When James Monroe was inaugurated in 1817, the *total* number of federal employees was only 6,500— approximately the number of new appointments an incoming president can make today in a civilian federal bureaucracy numbering almost three million people. The ground rules have changed with the continued expansion of the civil service, but the practice of presidential appointments to positions of importance in government has remained.

Filling these 6,500 job openings involves negotiations between the White House staff wanting to reward long-term loyal supporters of the president, and cabinet members insisting on making some major appointments in their own departments. In 1981, for example, Secretary of State Alexander Haig rejected White House suggestions that certain long-term Reagan supporters receive high-level State Department positions.

The president nominates the highest-level bureaucrats, although his choices must be confirmed by the Senate.

The Senate has traditionally supported the president's choices for executive positions, even if confirmation hearings sometimes become quite heated. This is not to say a president can be unmindful of the Senate's wishes. When President Bush nominated Robert Gates to become director of the Central Intelligence Agency (CIA) in 1991, the Senate Select Comittee on Intelligence heard widely conflicting evaluations of Gate's previous performance with the agency. Gates, whose nomination for the same post had been withdrawn by President Reagan in 1987, following questions concerning the nominee's role in the Iran-Contra scandal, was confirmed by the Senate in November 1991 by a 64–31 vote.

In 1989, the Senate, by a 53–47 vote, rejected President Bush's nomination of former Senator John Tower as secretary of defense. The repudiation of Tower, following a long and rancorous debate, was the first Senate rejection of a cabinet-level nominee since 1959, when Lewis L. Strauss was turned down as secretary of commerce. Although such Senate rejections are rare, presidential nominees have been withdrawn in the face of popular and congressional opposition. As the Tower case demonstrated, neither the Senate nor the president can take the confirmation process for granted.

The President as Head of State

Power to grant reprieves and pardons and to commission officers   There are two remaining presidential powers enumerated in Article II which correspond to the fifth constitutional role of the president: (1) he has the "Power to grant Reprieves and Pardons for Offences against the United States, except in Cases of Impeachment"; and (2) he "shall Commission all the Officers of the United States." These powers were obviously intended as, and have largely remained, the ceremonial duties of any officer of government in whom the powers of head of state are vested. Occasionally there has been controversy over a "political" pardoning, such as President Gerald Ford's decision to grant a "full, free, and absolute pardon" to Nixon for all offenses he "committed or may have committed" while serving as president—a most exceptional case. Much less exceptional (indeed, more in accord with the tradition of presidential pardons) was Carter's first executive order, which he issued less than twenty-four hours after he assumed office. By "proclamation and executive order," Carter granted a "full, complete, and unconditional pardon" to those Americans who, without violence, had violated the Selective Service Act between August 4, 1964, and March 28, 1973. By this action, which applied to most Vietnam-era draft registers (but not military deserters), Carter may have sought to start his presidency with an effort at putting Vietnam-era controversies to rest. Perhaps acting on similar impulses, early in his administration Reagan pardoned two former FBI officials who had been found guilty of authorizing illegal searches of the residences of antiwar activists. As both these cases show, presidents may use pardons to send political messages to the American people.

The president's power to grant pardons has been used only in exceptional cases.

Thus far, analysis of the president's constitutional powers and their evolution has identified at least the seeds that produced the current presidential roles of head of state, chief executor, commander in chief, chief policy initiator, chief administrator, and chief diplomat. However, the contemporary president's powers are even more extensive. Even careful reference to the Constitution cannot explain the development of the president's position of leadership in the American political scene or the constant blending, overlapping, and even conflicting nature of the roles he fills considered in the next section.

PRESIDENTIAL LEADERSHIP

No combination of constitutional, implied, or evolved presidential powers operates separate from the occupant of the Oval Office. The power of the president has increased over the years, in short, because of the men who have held the office. The judgment of history, by which presidents are labeled strong or weak, capable or inept, even good or bad, can often be reduced to a judgment of their leadership. Because of the unique nature of the office of president, the incumbent has the opportunity to lead the government, his own political party, and the American people. The ability with which various incumbents have handled this leadership role has not only determined their own places in history (subject, of course, to the vagaries of history itself) but has also profoundly affected the possibilities open to their successors.

Leadership as Persuasion

The presidency provides an opportunity for leadership, but no guarantee of success.

Presidential leadership involves the art of persuasion. As Richard Neustadt pointed out the president can rarely compel people to act, but his position offers him advantages that, if he is skillful, he can use to persuade people to do what he wants them to do.[1]

Many individuals the president needs to influence are not under his authority. Members of Congress, for example, are under no obligation to follow the president's suggestions. He cannot compel Congress to act; he must persuade it to do so. He can keep Congress from acting by using his veto power, but, ironically, the use of this power indicates that the president has failed to persuade Congress to pass a bill he prefers. If the president's leadership was more successful, he would not have needed to use the veto.

The president cannot depend on his authority to accomplish a great deal.

The president cannot compel action on the part of individuals not under his authority; he even finds it difficult to compel action on the part of executive-branch officials who are. The president is at the top of a bureaucracy with millions of people, each responsible to his or her immediate supervisor. Presidential commands may be misunderstood or simply disobeyed, and the president may not have knowledge of the noncompliance. Senior members of his staff may initiate programs without his knowledge or consent. If the president exercises his authority to fire cabinet officers, as Jimmy Carter did in 1979 with Transportation Secretary Brock Adams, Treasury Secretary W. Michael Blumenthal, and Health, Education and Welfare Secretary Joseph Califano, the incident may engender unfavorable

[1]Richard E. Neustadt, *Presidential Power* (New York: Wiley, 1960).

publicity. If these persons were not the best possible candidates for their positions, why were they appointed in the first place? Removing a cabinet officer is not indicative of strong leadership but of a failed leadership. It may suggest that the president has little influence on a cabinet officer.

Presidential Persuasion and Congress

In attempting persuasion, the president has advantages in the constitutional prerogatives already outlined. Additionally, there are many bargaining advantages that help him persuade members of Congress to act favorably on his program. A president controls a variety of material resources with political value; he has access to the public through the media; he has a wealth of information at his command; and he enjoys the prestige inherent in the office.

Material resources with political value These include presidential appointments, invitations to important White House functions, presidential appearances during congressional campaigns for reelection, federal projects scheduled for construction or operation in congressional districts, the "pet projects" of members of Congress on which presidential assistance would be helpful, budgets for both new and existing programs—the list goes on.

Conversely, the president can provide or withhold something a member of Congress needs or wants. In this area, the presidents recognized as great leaders were most adroit at communicating their decision to provide or withhold resources. A presidential intervention providing a member of Congress with a federal project in his or her district does not need to be accompanied by the representative's promise of support—but that support had better be forthcoming. John F. Kennedy, for example, excluded members of Congress of his own party from the speaking platform when he was touring constituencies because of their lack of support for his program.

At times this congressional-presidential practice of *quid pro quo* (something in exchange for something else) is so blatant it verges on outright trading. During the 1981 debates over Reagan's budget proposals that sharply modified Carter's fiscal year 1982 plan, several members of Congress from sugar-growing districts visited the White House. Reagan had earlier announced his desire for sugar price supports reductions because he believed such supports were inflationary. After these meetings, the president altered his position, and the representatives emerged supportive of the Reagan budget. When asked whether his vote could be bought, Congressman John Breaux (D.-La.) replied, "No, it can be rented."[2]

Ready access to the public The president's national constituency is a bargaining advantage that can directly influence his relations with other elected officials, because their constituencies must necessarily be included in his own. At least since

An effective president is likely to be persuasive; an unpopular president will have difficulty getting Congress to follow his leadership.

[2]*Congressional Quarterly Weekly Report*, July 4, 1981, p. 1169.

Andrew Jackson, every president has understood and acted on this overlapping constituency to convince congressional recalcitrants that the administration's policies are the ones preferred by "the folks back home." Bush often repeated his contention that his 1988 election be interpreted as a "mandate" for the policies he favored and that members of Congress who opposed his policies were out of step with their constituents.

Appealing for national support is one of the most important elements in the president's arsenal of leadership tactics. In his war against renewing the charter of the Second Bank of the United States, Jackson used the veto to gain popular support. He sent Congress the most strongly worded presidential veto message ever received, but it was actually aimed to incite pressure from congressional constituents on their representatives to vote against the measure the second time around. Wilson's "swing around the circle," a city-to-city tour to inspire popular support for the League of Nations, was a familiar tool of every president in the late nineteenth and early twentieth centuries.

By effectively using the mass media, a president can enhance his popularity and thereby increase his ability to realize his objectives in Washington.

As technological advances permitted increased (and eventually more direct) contact with progressively larger audiences, the power of the presidential office kept pace. First, newspapers, with their fiery editorials and selective perception of the news, assured the president an audience wherever the telegraph could reach a printing press. At least with Wilson, and possibly even Theodore Roosevelt, the presidential press conference became an established means of informing, pleading with, and "educating" the national constituency. The advent of radio provided first Calvin Coolidge and then, in full measure, Franklin D. Roosevelt with one of the most effective communication methods possible—a direct link between the citizen at home and the man in the White House. Roosevelt's "fireside chats" eliminated the journalistic middleman and brought the president into the living rooms of millions of Americans at once. Since the 1950s, presidents have been seen and heard on television at times of their own choosing, on topics they consider important, and under circumstances they deem most appropriate.

Most recent presidents extensively used press conferences to get their messages across to the people. Reagan was an exception, averaging fewer than seven press conferences per year, and after 1981 the federal government actually stopped reporting presidential news conferences in its weekly compilations. To be sure, Reagan still used the media more effectively than any other president in modern history, but at times of his own choosing and in forums of his own selection. The traditional press conference, with reporters freely asking far-ranging questions on national and international policy, was not the forum of Reagan's choice. President Bush reintroduced the practice of holding frequent formal and informal meetings with the press.

These successive technological advances have not eliminated, but rather supplemented, the "swing around the circle." The president still travels throughout the country, aided by a host of helicopters, jets, and limousines, presenting his views to his constituents, hoping to convince them his program is in their best interests and so inform their senators and representatives in Washington.

The president's chances of reelection affect his ability to lead effectively.

Yet persuading Congress and the American people to follow his lead is far from the president's only concern. No president in his first term can dare neglect his reelection prospects. If his electoral victory was relatively close in the last campaign, he will be eager to increase his popular support and enhance his image as the "representative" of all the people. This concern has become even more important as the electoral majority becomes less a reflection of the nation's numerical majority. In 1988, George Bush enjoyed a comfortable victory over Michael Dukakis. However, although 54 percent of all who voted preferred Bush, less than 30 percent of all American adults voted for him. In fact, almost as many Americans cast no vote as voted for Bush and Dukakis combined. The sum of all the votes cast for Bill Clinton and George Bush in 1992 was less than the majority of American citizens, who either cast no vote or voted for Ross Perot. These statistics are hardly likely to lull a president into complacency about his relations with the American people.

Through his access to the mass media, the president can place issues on the national agenda.

Such complacency is most easily avoided by the president's attention to *all* the overlapping roles his leadership includes. As the only federal official with both the responsibility and the facilities to develop a comprehensive legislative program, he has the opportunity to place significant national problems on the political agenda and frame them in a manner to attain legislative majorities. As the chief administrator, he can issue executive orders that can increase his popularity, such as Reagan's early decontrol of domestic oil prices. Issuing such orders is a right either inherent in his administrative responsibilities or stemming from legislation which congressionally provides for presidential discretion over the timing and specificity of policy implementation. The decisions made regarding implementation can affect how the American people view their president.

Availability of information Another presidential advantage is the availability of information in the executive branch, particularly relevant in the area of foreign policy and international affairs. The president receives frequent briefings from foreign policy experts. The executive branch has at its disposal literally thousands of bureaucrats, who form an impressive foreign policy information base. The president is privy to intelligence information that is only sometimes shared with the Congress—and then only with select members. Congress does have expert advice available from in-house staff and witnesses at committee hearings, but such contacts are less numerous and less extensive than those available to the president. Indeed, except for highly visible and controversial foreign policy issues, members of Congress simply do not have the resources to develop independent bases of foreign policy information.

In many cases, members of Congress do not have the resources to develop independent information on foreign policy issues.

For example, in 1965 President Johnson asked Congress to pass the Gulf of Tonkin Resolution, giving the president approval to extend the U.S. effort in Vietnam. Johnson highly exaggerated his report about unprovoked attacks on American destroyers in the Gulf of Tonkin. However, members of Congress had no independent sources of information for evaluating this report, so they gave Johnson increased powers to escalate the war in Southeast Asia.

The prestige of the office of president gives its occupant opportunities to lead.

Prestige of the office   A final advantage the president has over members of Congress is the prestige of the presidency itself. Indeed, presidential popularity is a source of extraconstitutional power, and should be viewed more as a function of prestige of the office than merely a popular judgment of the incumbent. The adroit use of presidential invitations, the friendly phone call to an otherwise obscure public official, the appearance before a citizen's group, even the presidential press conference or television appearance are all persuasive tactics available to any president. The incumbent benefits from the judicious use of such tactics that are his alone to use simply because he occupies the Oval Office. It is *the president,* not a *specific* president, whose intervention often ensures the success of an otherwise doubtful program or policy. His personal prestige and status are automatically assured because of his office.

Some citizens support any program that the president believes is in the national interest.

One result of this prestige is seen in the president's role as a leader of public opinion. In May 1966, just before Lyndon Johnson ordered the bombing of Hanoi and Haiphong harbor, 50 percent of the American people favored such an action; one month later, after the presidential directive was issued, the percentage rose to 85. Two years later, in March 1968, 51 percent of the electorate favored a limitation on the bombing; after this policy was initiated in April, only 26 percent opposed the new policy.[3] Many Americans support or oppose a particular policy simply because they want to agree with the president's position.

Many expect the president to not only be a political leader and a good administrator but also a moral leader providing a model of good behavior.

Elected from a nationwide constituency, the president is the only nationally elected official entitled to speak for all the people. In speaking for them, he is expected to lead not only in terms of politics but in areas of ethics and morality as well. He is therefore understood to be a moral leader, exemplifying those qualities that serve as ideals for most Americans. Thus, FDR characterized the presidency as "preeminently a place of moral leadership."

In addition, the American people look to the president for protection from economic ills, for social justice, for preservation of national security—in short, as the panacea of the political system. In this context, the very existence of the office of the president becomes a source of the incumbent's power with both Congress and the population at large.

Many expect the president to solve all national problems; this is a source of power for the occupant of the office.

However, to say the prestige of the presidency is a source of power is not to imply that unlimited power is in the hands of whoever occupies the office. Richard Nixon, under fire for a series of illegal actions during the Watergate crisis, argued that his critics were weakening the presidency rather than merely attacking the current occupant of the position. Although this argument did garner Nixon some public support, the House Judiciary Committee voted for impeachment and he resigned in disgrace. The prestige of the office is a great resource in the hands of a politically astute president, but his ability to use the resource wisely determines whether he is a powerful or a weak president.

[3]Figures taken from John E. Mueller, "Trends in Popular Support for the Wars in Korea and Vietnam," *American Political Science Review* 65 (1971), pp. 369–370.

The Presidential Political Context

The political milieu of presidential power   The president is the leader of his party. Actually, "party unity" in the United States is largely mythical because, as mentioned in the introduction, the parties are best characterized by decentralization (each "national" party is little more than a confederation of fifty state parties). Given the mythical nature of party unity, the president's position as party leader is generally insignificant. He no longer even controls the thousands of patronage positions once doled out to loyal party followers, since the rise of the civil service system drastically curtailed the "spoils system." The potential consequences of this lack of meaningful party unity and the president's inability to dispense favors as widely as he once could became evident in the summer of 1976. Gerald Ford, a nonelected but nonetheless sitting president, was nearly denied his party's nomination in the face of an extremely strong challenge to his position as party leader by Ronald Reagan.

> American political parties are decentralized, so power in the parties is at the state and local levels.

The president's role as party leader is meaningful today only in conjunction with his role as national leader in the field of public policy. By espousing a given public policy in the name of the party, the president can alter the public's *image* of the party and the party's composition. FDR employed this tactic in the early 1930s rejuvenation of the Democratic party. Appealing directly to an urban-oriented clientele (including labor, blacks, ethnic groups, and intellectuals), he changed the composition of the Democratic party and set the tone of government policy as well.

> The president's position as head of one of the national parties is not a significant source of power.

Those who wielded presidential power most skillfully over the years did so within the context of decidedly political limitations. Working with keen awareness of what is politically possible has usually allowed presidents to expand their range of alternatives; ignoring political possibilities has usually resulted in the loss of presidential power and prestige. Franklin Roosevelt's attempt to "pack" the Supreme Court, by adding justices more favorable to New Deal legislation, is a case in point. The attempt, while perfectly legal constitutionally, was inappropriate in light of the political climate in which Roosevelt had to operate. Because he misjudged that climate, he not only failed to pack the Court but lost presidential prestige as well—even though he had just been reelected by the most substantial electoral majority in United States history.

> Strong presidents understand that politics is the art of the possible.

The task of maintaining presidential power is made especially difficult by issues that the president cannot avoid. After a year or so in office, the president is held accountable for the state of the economy. If the economic situation is perceived as poor, members of Congress increasingly distance themselves from the president, because they are concerned with their own reelection. A president who is perceived as ineffective in dealing with national problems is not a powerful leader.

> Presidents are held accountable for the economic condition of the country.

Aside from the current political scene, a president is also affected by agreements made by his predecessors—most notably in the area of foreign affairs. Disregarding such inherited agreements jeopardizes the continuity of U.S. foreign policy and thereby casts doubt on the president's ability as chief diplomat. Such disregard may in fact damage the entire range of presidential powers, and yet the political climate demands an incumbent not freeze into the policies of his predecessors. A president who fails to recognize the need to alter his inherited foreign policy when domestic dissatisfaction exists weakens presidential leadership.

The president must contend with entrenched interests that develop around public policies. Often, government programs that distribute resources to some segment of the population become almost the private domain of interested political actors from the affected communities, congressional committees, and executive agencies. Such "iron triangles" act to protect programs from budget cuts or unfriendly alterations and can constrain the president. For example, dairy-price subsidies are supported by organized dairy interests, members of Congress from the dairy-producing states, and administrators from the Department of Agriculture. Many other government programs develop similar support networks. Presidents are often constrained by such "iron triangles" when attempting to change government programs.

The president is a *political* actor participating in a process that often demands conflicts be resolved by striking bargains between those wishing certain policies to continue without change and those wishing to implement new policies. Such bargains result in *incrementalism*—the process of gradual policy alteration. However, the president's unique position can enable him to institute dramatic policy changes and, in these instances, override the effects of incrementalism. For a president to lead, he must know when to use the powers of office to force rapid changes and when to settle for incremental changes.

Policy changes generally are incremental, slight movements from the status quo.

The Reagan budget victories of 1981 demonstrate that a strong president can bring about nonincremental changes.

The Reagan administration's 1981 budget battle victories demonstrate the effective use of presidential power to produce nonincremental change. Reagan sought nonincremental shifts in federal spending priorities, with unprecedented peacetime increases in defense spending and drastic reductions in spending for many social programs. He persuaded Congress by shrewdly using his resources in four ways.

First, he reminded Congress of his great popularity at that time—opposing his wishes might lead to defeats at the polls. Reagan acted early in his administration while the traditional "honeymoon" period for new presidents still prevailed. Even the assassination attempt on Reagan in March 1981 increased his ratings in the polls, just after his popularity started a sharp decline. It is difficult for anyone to oppose a president who has recently been shot.

Second, the Reagan administration worked closely with Republican leaders in Congress, developing a strategy so the massive spending changes were accomplished through one vote, rather than many votes on individual programs. This enabled senators and representatives to avoid taking an identifiable stand for or against cuts to popular programs.

Third, employing a tactic mentioned earlier in this chapter, Reagan invited small groups of legislators to the White House for personal chats. He used his charm as well as promises to support their pet projects to garner their votes. It is difficult to sit informally in the White House and say "no" to a popular, charming, wounded president.

Fourth, Reagan twice addressed the nation on television, urging citizens to contact their representatives and demand that they support the president's program.

Using his exceptional speaking skills, developed in his career as a professional actor, Reagan effectively garnered public support for his program. The president used his power to command a national audience most adroitly.

In summary every president has resources that, if used effectively, permit him to persuade others to follow his lead. If the resources are not used effectively, the president will be able to carry out few of his plans. There are no guarantees—only opportunities.

ELECTORAL PROCEDURES

Presidential Eligibility

Constitutional provisions of presidential eligibility   Like presidential power, presidential selection cannot be fully understood by mere reference to the Constitution. The constitutional requirements of presidential eligibility are outlined in Article II, Section 1, and stipulate quite simply that the president be a natural-born citizen, at least thirty-five years of age, and a fourteen-year resident of the United States. The meaning of the first provision was questioned in 1968 when George Romney, born in Mexico of American parents, was considered for the Republican nomination. Constitutional lawyers agreed, however, that any citizen born of American parents probably would be considered "natural born." Similarly, Herbert Hoover had not resided in the United States for the fourteen years immediately prior to his election, but the tenure provision is interpreted as requiring a total of fourteen years in any time sequence.

> The Constitution places few limits on presidential eligibility.

Extraconstitutional considerations of presidential eligibility   Political and personal considerations have taken precedence over the bare constitutional requirements. Of the forty-two U.S. presidents, twenty-six were lawyers, twenty-four served in Congress (four in the Continental Congress), thirty-four could trace their ancestry to prerevolutionary British stock, and of the remaining six, five claimed prerevolutionary Dutch or German heritage. Only John Kennedy, the lone Roman Catholic, could go back no further than a third-generation Irish immigrant. Some presidents were actually born in the proverbial log cabin: Millard Fillmore, James Buchanan, Abraham Lincoln, and James Garfield, and possibly also Andrew Jackson and James Polk. William Harrison, Andrew Johnson, and Ulysses Grant dishonestly claimed during their campaigns that they too were of log-cabin birth. Marriage has not been seen as a requirement of the office; both Buchanan and Grover Cleveland were bachelors. Cleveland subsequently married (and Tyler and Wilson remarried) while occupying the office. Americans have also shown a marked preference for nominating generals after a "successful" war. Most predictably, yet often not mentioned, every major-party nominee for president or vice-president has been a white male, until 1984. Only the nomination of Geraldine Ferraro as Mondale's running mate disrupted this exclusive trend.

> In *practice*, only white males are eligible for the presidency.

Presidential Selection

According to the original prescriptions of the Constitution (Article II, Section 1), each state legislature chose a number of electors equal to its total number of representatives and senators. Each elector voted for two persons (at least one of whom was not to be a citizen of that elector's state) for the office of president. It was to be understood that the electors were free agents who would choose, in the words of Alexander Hamilton, "characters preeminent for ability and virtue." A complete list of all persons voted for and the number of votes each had received was then sent to the president of the Senate. In the presence of Congress, the ballots of all the states were counted, and the person who had the majority of electoral votes was president; the runner-up, vice-president. In the event of a tie or the absence of a candidate with a majority of the electoral votes, the House of Representatives chose the president, and the runner-up was named vice-president.

> The electoral college as a deliberative body ceased to function after the Washington administration.

The advent of political parties   This provision lasted only twelve years, until the crystallization of political parties around the time of Jefferson and John Adams started the practice of electors in the several states pledging their support to one party or the other before their selection by the legislature. The overwhelming majority of electors in 1800 chose the "Democratic-Republican" (or "Anti-Federalist") ticket of Thomas Jefferson and Aaron Burr. The electoral lists received by the president of the Senate showed that the electors who supported this ticket had all cast one vote for Jefferson and one vote for Burr, so that the presidential candidate had the same number of votes as his running mate. The House was forced to select the president even though everyone knew that the electors wanted Jefferson as president and Burr as vice-president. The House quickly chose Jefferson, but the event precipitated passage of the Twelfth Amendment (ratified in 1804), designed to avert similar situations in future years. The new provisions mandated separate ballots for president and vice-president.

Between 1804 and 1828, Jefferson's Democrat-Republican party controlled the White House. The election in 1828 of Andrew Jackson signaled a new era in the candidate-selection process. By 1832, the congressional caucus system of nominating presidential candidates was replaced by the convention system. Each party held a national convention every four years, where party leaders from the states met to choose the party's presidential candidate. The period from 1832 to 1860 witnessed the expansion of the electoral base; with the election of Abraham Lincoln in 1860, the modern two-party system was born.

Current presidential nomination by political parties   The presidential nomination system evolved from the selection of the nominee by state party leaders to the selection of the nominee through a series of state primary and caucus elections. In recent years, the national party conventions have served to confirm the results of these state elections. The candidate was formerly chosen by the national convention; now he or she is simply nominated at the convention.

Each party has its own system for choosing delegates to attend its national convention, at which its presidential candidate is chosen.

Convention delegate selection procedures   Each party has its own rules for selecting delegates to its national convention. The general rules are set by the national party organizations, but the individual states have great latitude in deciding how delegates will be chosen for the national conventions. These rules are modified somewhat every four years, as each party strives for a nominating system fair to potential candidates, accurate in its representation of party supporters, and successful in giving the party's presidential nomination to the strongest candidate. Both parties have witnessed a rise in the number of delegates selected through primary election systems instead of caucus systems. In primary election systems, voters generally choose among delegate candidates pledged to support particular presidential hopefuls at the national conventions. In caucus systems, party members generally hold local precinct meetings to elect representatives to district party meetings, who in turn select representatives to state conventions.

Caucus systems give a greater role to party leaders and others active in party affairs, but in the past few years, caucus systems have evolved toward greater openness in permitting expanded participation by all citizens. The result has been that both caucus and primary election systems encourage potential candidates to appeal directly to the public. Both systems permit potential candidates to attract votes through the media and to garner delegates without consulting party leaders. The rise of primary election systems and the more recent opening of the caucus system have contributed both to the weakness of American parties and to the successful campaigns of the party "outsider," like Jimmy Carter, who had little support among party leaders.

The two parties differ in delegate selection procedures, primarily in the Democratic party's greater concern with the openness and representativeness of its system. Democratic conventions have more blacks, young people, women, Hispanics, and Native Americans than do Republican conventions. In the 1992 Democratic national convention, women accounted for almost half the number of delegates, quite a change from the older convention image of smoky rooms filled with men.

Electoral college operations   Unlike the constantly evolving mechanisms for choosing convention delegates, the means of choosing electors have remained virtually unchanged for more than a hundred years. Each state has electoral votes equal in number to the size of its congressional delegation (members of the House plus two senators). The unit rule, which operates in every state except Maine and Nebraska, means that a candidate who wins a state's popular vote on election day wins all of that state's electoral votes.

The candidate who wins a plurality of the vote in a state wins all of the state's electoral votes.

In mid-December, the electors pledged to the candidate who won their state's popular vote meet in their state capital and cast their votes. Their sealed ballots are then sent to Washington, D.C., where they are counted in early January before a joint session of Congress. A candidate needs 270 of the electoral college's 538 votes (the total number of House and Senate seats plus three votes from the District of Columbia) to become president. In the event that no candidate receives the required 270 electoral votes, the election goes to the House of Representatives where each state casts one vote. A majority of the states, or 26 votes, is required for victory. The Senate chooses the vice president; 51 votes are required for selection.

The electoral college has had its critics. Some people fear that unpledged electors or electors pledged to an independent candidate might run in some states, thereby increasing the uncertainty of the entire process. In addition, most states have no legal provision holding the pledged electors to their announced candidate. This fact, and the possibility that the election might be thrown into the House of Representatives, has attracted regionally based third-party candidates.

A state's importance in the electoral college system rests on its number of votes. Electoral votes range from California's 54 (2 for its senators and 52 for its representatives) to 3 each in Alaska, Delaware, North Dakota, South Dakota, Vermont, and Wyoming, states with a single representative each. Because of the unit rule, winning California by the slightest of margins gives a candidate 54 electoral votes; winning Alaska by a 90-percent margin gives a candidate only 3 electoral votes.

According to the 1990 census, the ten most populous states (California, New York, Texas, Pennsylvania, Illinois, Ohio, Florida, Michigan, New Jersey, and North Carolina) account for 257 electoral votes—only 13 short of the 270 needed for election. It is crucial, then, that any presidential candidate carry these states, the nation's heterogeneous, urbanized, industrialized centers. Accordingly, electoral strategies are influenced by the electoral college system. No candidate can afford to ignore the issues important to the larger states, even if that candidate has a regional base of support such as Carter enjoyed in 1976. Carter managed to carry six of the ten largest states, which, combined with his support from the South and a few scattered states, permitted him to achieve a narrow electoral-vote victory over Ford. With 270 electoral votes needed for victory, Carter gained the White House by accumulating 297—a margin that could have been offset by a single large state. The closeness of the race reinforced the necessity that each candidate know how to appeal to the voters in the large states.

> A presidential candidate must be able to win at least some of the large urbanized states to be successful.

Electoral college reform? Proposals for direct electoral college reform have been of three general types. The first would abolish the electoral college completely and establish a system of direct election. By this method, the candidate with the largest popular vote would be named president, but there is considerable disagreement over whether this should be a majority or whether a plurality would suffice. A second proposal would retain apportionment of the electoral college based on the state's congressional and senatorial seats, but the votes would be cast on a proportional basis, each candidate receiving the fraction of the electoral vote corresponding to his popular vote within the state. The third proposed reform, a district plan, would give the electoral college vote to the plurality vote winner in each congressional district, the two corresponding Senate votes going to the plurality winner in the state as a whole. Under this proposal, a candidate would have to receive a plurality in *each* of California's 52 congressional districts to capture all of that state's 54 electoral votes. This third proposal was actually adopted by Maine: Clinton won all four of Maine's electoral votes in 1992 because he won victories in each of its two congressional districts and, therefore, in the state as a whole.

These kinds of reform ideas have been in the political air for years and are particularly prominent after a close presidential election like that in 1976. Ford would have won that election if as few as 9,245 voters in Hawaii and Ohio had switched their votes to him from Carter, even though the latter had a plurality of 1.7 million votes nationwide. Despite bipartisan support for some kind of change in the system, it is not likely the necessary constitutional amendment (which would affect Article II, Section 1) will be enacted in the near future. Political scientists disagree on the consequences of the proposals, and politicians, no more certain, are not about to exchange a system they have grown comfortable with for one with obscure political implications.

The electoral college is unlikely to be reformed, because no one is sure of the practical consequences of the reform proposals.

TERM OF OFFICE AND SUCCESSION

Term of Office of the Presidency

The Constitution provides that the president and vice-president serve concurrent four-year terms. Until ratification of the Twenty-second Amendment in 1951, there was no limitation on the number of terms an individual could serve in either position. By refusing to serve as president for more than eight years, Washington established a "voluntary" tradition that lasted until Franklin Roosevelt accepted the Democratic nomination in 1940 for an unprecedented third term (a record that stood only until he extended it to four terms four years later). The Twenty-second Amendment, adopted in 1951, provides that no person may be elected to the presidency more than twice (reduced to once if he has served more than half of the term to which another person was elected).

A president can serve no more than two terms.

Eight of forty-one presidents have died in office, and one resigned before completing his term.

Succession to the Presidency

Article II of the Constitution stipulates that the vice-president assumes the presidency in the event of death, resignation, or removal from office of the incumbent, and empowers the Congress to provide for the subsequent line of succession. The problem of succession has produced many proposed solutions, culminating in ratification of the Twenty-Fifth Amendment in 1967 (discussed shortly).

The language of the Constitution did not make clear whether the vice-president, assuming the presidential office in the event of its vacancy, would be invested as president or only as acting president. Tyler settled this question by insisting on full official empowerment after the death of Harrison in 1841. Harrison, the first president to die in office, died of natural causes, as did Zachary Taylor, Warren G. Harding, and Franklin Roosevelt; Lincoln, Garfield, McKinley, and Kennedy were assassinated; and Nixon resigned.

Congressional attempts to stabilize the line of succession Before ratification of the Twenty-Fifth Amendment, Congress attempted three times to settle the question of presidential succession. The Succession Act of 1792 placed the president pro tempore of the Senate and then the Speaker of the House of Representatives immediately after the vice-president in line of succession. This provision stood, unused, until congressional action in 1886 recognized the growth and importance of the executive branch and decided the line of succession should run through the cabinet. The act provided for the secretary of state (followed by the rest of the cabinet in the order of the origin of their department's establishment) to assume office.

With Truman's assumption of the presidency in 1945 upon the death of Franklin Roosevelt, Congress again prepared to change the line of succession. Truman was reluctant to accept the provisions of the 1886 act on the grounds that they were "nondemocratic": He had the power to choose the secretary of state, therefore his own potential successor. The Succession Act of 1947 therefore retained all the provisions of its immediate predecessor but reinserted the Speaker of the House and the president pro tempore of the Senate (reversing the order of 1792) between the vice-president and the secretary of state. This provision was acceptable to Truman because it provided for officials elected to office, not appointed, to succeed to the presidency.

The line of succession now runs from the vice-president, to the Speaker of the House, to the president pro tempore of the Senate, to the secretary of state, followed by other cabinet members (rank-ordered by the date their departments gained cabinet status).

The provisions of 1947 stood until Kennedy's 1963 assassination highlighted the drawbacks of such an arrangement. As Johnson assumed the presidency, John McCormack, the Speaker of the House, was seventy-one years old, and his counterpart in the Senate, Carl Hayden, was almost eighty-seven. The obvious problem of their ages aside, could their selection for the office really be democratic? They held their positions of congressional authority at the behest of their colleagues; congressional leaders are elected to Congress, but not to their leadership positions, by the voters.

The Twenty-Fifth Amendment Inspired by the long-standing custom by which each candidate for president selects his own running mate (originally by agreement and now through his party's nominating convention) and attempting to retain some degree of "democratic procedure," the states ratified the Twenty-fifth Amendment in 1967. According to its provisions, a vacancy in the vice-presidential office empowers the president to nominate a vice-president, who must then be confirmed by a majority of both houses of Congress. This ensures that the Speaker of the House will not succeed to the presidency unless both the president and vice-president die or resign simultaneously—on the presumption that there will always be time to appoint a vice-president. This amendment therefore addresses both presidential and vice-presidential vacancies, the latter having been more numerous than the former, numbering eighteen instances for a cumulative total of forty-five years.

A vacancy in the vice-presidency is filled by a presidential nominee confirmed by majority votes in the House and Senate.

Upon the resignation of Spiro Agnew in October 1973, this newest succession procedure received its first trial. The speed with which the president acted—

House Minority Leader Gerald Ford was chosen as vice-president designate within two days and confirmed by Congress within two months—demonstrated the viability of the amendment.

Less than two months later, the provisions of this same amendment were put into operation again. Ford ascended to the presidency, and the vice-presidential post again fell vacant. In August 1974, Congress received for confirmation the name of Nelson Rockefeller, and for the first time in modern U.S. history a president and a vice-president were chosen by Congress, not elected by the voters.

The office of the vice-president   The first vice-president, John Adams, characterized the office as "the most insignificant . . . that ever invention of man contrived, or his imagination conceived." (Vice-President John Nance Garner, on a somewhat more graphic note, suggested it was not worth a "bucket of warm spit.") The only constitutional provision other than succession delegated to the vice-president is the authority to preside over the Senate, where he votes only in event of a tie— hardly a provision of much importance.

The vice-president has little authority or power.

Each presidential candidate chooses his vice-presidential running mate, generally with the foremost purpose of balancing the ticket to win the election.

Each party's presidential candidate generally chooses his vice-presidential running mate at the party's national convention, which then ratifies the choice. The candidate's choice of the number-two person is often not determined by the latter's qualities of judgment or expertise. Rather, the vice-presidential nominee is chosen for the political expedient of helping the ticket get elected. Dating from the first presidential election, conventional political wisdom dictates there be some attempt to balance the national ticket in terms of age, temperament, ideology, and geographic origin.

The importance of political considerations in selecting vice-presidential candidates has not diminished with the advent of modern media campaigning techniques. Bill Clinton's selection of Al Gore in 1992 was unusual because both men were considered southern moderates. In 1988, however, Michael Dukakis selected Senator Lloyd Bentsen of Texas as his running mate because Bentsen's more conservative positions balanced his own more liberal views. In 1984, running against a president far ahead of him in the opinion polls, Walter Mondale selected Geraldine Ferraro, the first woman vice-presidential candidate put forward by a major political party. Her selection was clearly intended by Mondale to add a shot of adrenaline to his campaign. Ferraro did generate considerable enthusiasm and media attention, but she did not generate sufficient votes for Mondale to defeat Reagan.

In 1968, Nixon's private polls convinced him that he would run best without a vice-presidential candidate because every well-known possibility alienated large groups of voters. Nixon responded to this dilemma by choosing Spiro Agnew, then an unknown figure in national politics. It was as close as Nixon could get to not having a running mate. Five years later, Agnew resigned from the vice-presidency after pleading *nolo contendere* (no contention) to a criminal charge of tax evasion. Nixon's dilemma in 1973 was not the voters but mounting disclosures relating to Watergate. Under these circumstances, Nixon needed a successor to help stem the impeachment tide in Congress. Nixon's logical, albeit futile, choice was Ford, minority leader in the House and a veteran of twenty-three years in Congress.

Traditionally, the presidential nominee announces the choice for vice-presidential nomination during or just before the party's convention. In 1992, Bill Clinton selected Senator Al Gore, a Democrat from Tennessee, as his running mate. Senator Gore was born into a political family; his father had represented Tennessee in the United States Senate in the 1960s. The younger Gore was closely identified with environmental issues in the Senate and had written a book on environmental policy. In 1988, Gore had run unsuccessfully for the Democratic Presidential nomination and there had been some speculation before the primaries that he might seek the presidential nomination again in 1992. The Clinton–Gore ticket was unusual for several reasons. Because both candidates were known as moderate Democrats from Southern states, the ticket was not "balanced" by traditional regional and ideological considerations. The Clinton–Gore ticket also represented a major generational shift in American politics in that, for the first time, the candidates for President and Vice President were both born in the post-World War II period.

The president determines the nature and amount of authority exercised by the vice-president. Until Franklin Roosevelt's presidency, the vice-president did not even attend cabinet meetings, and Truman, although he attended, knew very little about U.S. foreign policy. He was completely ignorant of the substance of most strategy decisions about the conduct of the war, and even about the development of the atomic bomb until after Roosevelt's death.

The current trend is toward greater involvement of vice-presidents in important executive activities; still, vice-presidents spend most of their time representing presidents at state funerals and making speeches.

Recent presidents have elevated the vice-president to a more central role in their administrations, but he continues to function at the discretion of the president rather than by right. In 1977, for example, Carter ordered the vice-president's office moved from the Executive Office Building across the street into the White House itself, intending that Vice-President Mondale would assume a central role in the administration. In 1981, Reagan appointed Bush to chair his administration's crisis management team, over the objections of Secretary of State Haig. Although Mondale and Bush had responsibilities denied to most previous vice-presidents, their responsibilities were given to them (and could be taken away) by the president. In addition, it should be noted that the recent expanded vice-presidential role is primarily in the area of public relations and symbolic responsibilities. The vice-president's influence over the actual development of policy is conspicuously absent, and unlikely to materialize. His nomination on the grounds of political expediency, his lack of an independent power base, and the nature of his duties all prevent him from evolving into a powerful political figure in his own right.

The only constitutional authority added to the vice-president's office came with the ratification of the Twenty-fifth Amendment in 1967. Its passage stemmed from periodic concerns over presidential disability. During Wilson's second term, for example, his wife assumed many presidential duties while her husband was gravely ill. Years later, Eisenhower suffered coronary thrombosis in 1955, followed in quick succession by an ileitis attack and operation in 1956 and a mild stroke the following year, rendering him temporarily incapable of discharging the duties of his office. The military command mode of operation he established from his first years in the White House rose to the occasion, and his "special assistant,"

Sherman Adams, through whom all presidential business had previously been channeled, made all necessary presidential decisions.

In each of these cases, the then vice-presidents, Thomas Marshall and Richard Nixon, respectively, were either unwilling or unable to act according to the provisions of the Constitution. Article II stipulates that in the event of the president's "Inability to discharge the Powers and Duties of the said Office, the Same shall devolve on the Vice President," but it does not indicate how disability is determined or power is transferred.

Passed in 1967, the Twenty-fifth Amendment permits a vice-president to assume the duties of a disabled president.

The Twenty-fifth Amendment therefore provides for two situations. First, it permits either the president himself or the vice-president (in concert with a majority of the cabinet or of anybody designated by Congress) to inform the Speaker of the House and the president pro tempore of the Senate of the president's inability to perform the functions of his office, at which point the vice-president becomes acting president. Second, a formerly disabled president can resume office by transmitting to the same congressional officers a declaration that he is again fit for office. This procedure was first used by Ronald Reagan during his cancer surgery in 1985. If the vice-president and a majority of the executive officers disagree with the president's declaration and advise the Congress within four days, a vote of two-thirds majority in both houses, taken within twenty-one days of the receipt of the vice-president's message, is necessary for his continuation as acting president. If this element of constitutional authority was granted to the vice-president earlier, perhaps history would remember Wilson's vice-president, Thomas Marshall, for more than his hopeful comment, "What this country needs is a good five-cent cigar."

Impeachment and removal from office   The Constitution also provides that "the President, Vice President, and all civil Officers of the United States, shall be removed from Office on Impeachment [by the House of Representatives] for, and Conviction [by the Senate] of Treason, Bribery, or other high Crimes and Misdemeanors" (Article II, Section 4). The only president successfully impeached by the House was Andrew Johnson in 1868. He had requested and then demanded the resignation of Secretary of War Edwin Stanton in defiance of the Tenure of Office Act of 1867. That act, passed by Congress over Johnson's veto, negated presidential authority to remove members of the executive branch without senatorial approval. Johnson (following precedents established as early as Washington's first term) refused to accept this legislation as constitutionally valid.

Andrew Johnson was the only president to be impeached by the House, although he was acquitted by the Senate and remained in office.

In the face of heated partisan debate and intense congressional dissatisfaction with Johnson's "too lenient" reconstruction policies, the Supreme Court declined to rule on the question of constitutionality and set the stage for the trial in the Senate. With the chief justice presiding, in accord with the requirements of the Constitution, the Senate failed by one vote to muster the necessary two-thirds to convict Johnson of the charges brought by the House (one of which included that he used improper language and spoke in a loud voice).

In contrast to the obvious political wranglings of the Johnson impeachment, the events that led to the only presidential resignation in the nation's history were relatively free of partisan overtones. On June 17, 1972 (five months before the

THE INSTITUTIONALIZED PRESIDENCY

presidential election), five men were arrested while planting surveillance equipment in the Democratic National Committee offices located in the Watergate apartment complex in Washington, D.C. An FBI investigation quickly unearthed financial links between the arrested men and the Committee for the Reelection of the President (CREEP), and, through it, to the White House itself. Top Nixon aides, acting on the president's orders, impeded the investigation.

Early in 1973, the web of White House interference with the investigation began to unravel. Federal District Court Judge John Sirica refused to believe that the investigation had uncovered all the relevant facts, and the Senate voted seventy-seven to zero to establish a special select committee to investigate the incident. During the committee's hearings (which documented White House interference), former presidential aide Alexander Butterfield disclosed the existence of a secret taping system in the White House, which recorded presidential conversations. When a special federal prosecutor attempted to gain access to the tapes through court action, he was fired by Nixon—an act that prompted the House of Representatives to empower its Judiciary Committee to begin an investigation into impeaching the president.

The Judiciary Committee launched an extensive ten-month investigation. Even as the committee deliberated, federal prosecutors pressed for new evidence to convict the constantly expanding list of White House personnel who had conspired to obstruct justice by impeding the original investigation. On July 24, 1974, the Supreme Court ruled eight to zero that Nixon would have to surrender more tapes as evidence. Three days later the Judiciary Committee voted twenty-seven to eleven recommending the president himself be impeached on the same obstruction of justice charge.

On August 5, 1974, the tapes that the Supreme Court had ordered released revealed that Nixon had instructed his top White House aide, H. R. Haldeman, to have the CIA block the FBI's investigation into the source of the Watergate funding. In light of this disclosure, congressional leaders informed the president that his impeachment by the House and conviction by the Senate was virtually assured. However, impeachment would not be necessary—the threat of it was sufficient. Richard M. Nixon resigned the presidency on August 9, 1974, and Gerald R. Ford became the thirty-seventh president of the United States.

> After the House Judiciary Committee voted to recommend impeachment to the entire House, Richard Nixon resigned from office.

THE INSTITUTIONALIZED PRESIDENCY

The President as Chief Executive

> Each president sets up mechanisms to decide how his office will process information and make decisions.

Theodore Sorenson, an assistant to President Kennedy, accurately characterized the problems inherent in making a presidential decision as conflictual—that is, involving "conflict between departments, between the views of various advisors, between the administration and the Congress, between the United States and another nation, or between groups within the country: labor versus management, race versus race, or state versus nation."[4] How these conflicts are handled, who decides what to do, and the means used to reach and implement decisions are called the *institutionalization* of a particular presidency.

As the nation's chief executive, the president is in charge of the administrative and executive elements of the federal government. Each president copes with his administrative responsibilities by using his own combination of cabinet officials and personnel from the Executive Office of the President. The cabinet, whose existence is assumed by the Constitution, dates from the time of Washington. The Executive Office of the President (EOP), established in 1937, reached its peak in 1974 during the second Nixon administration, when it had grown to include more than a dozen agencies and 2,568 people with an overall budget of $106,700,000. The well-publicized abuses of presidential power, which could not have occurred without this growth, have induced subsequent presidents to trim these figures somewhat (for example, just under 1,700 people in 1992). However, they have been constrained in their cutbacks by the complex task of overseeing the executive branch.

Every president adopts an institutionalized presidency congenial to his executive style.

Presidential styles   How a president utilizes his personnel and structures his organization are determined primarily by personal style. Franklin Roosevelt, for example, relied on an administrative style characterized by personal involvement in detail and creative tension among his aides. Eisenhower's administration, on the other hand, was marked by a heavy reliance on formally established bodies for advice and even decision making. The creation of the hierarchical structure on the military model was Eisenhower's own brainchild. Nixon and Reagan both developed their organizational styles along the lines of the Eisenhower model. Reagan in particular involved himself only in major policy matters of program direction, not the specifics of bills and policy implementation. In contrast, Kennedy and Carter injected themselves into the decision-making process anytime they had doubts about what might be happening.

There is little agreement among scholars of the presidency on whether the active Roosevelt style or the passive Eisenhower approach is more effective. Although Carter was praised for his extensive knowledge of public policy, he also was criticized for spending too much time on details and not marshaling his efforts to be able to effectively handle major questions. Reagan was praised for a great ability to build political support by focusing his energies carefully, but was also criticized for not learning the actual impact of his policy recommendations.

The degrees to which any president isolates himself from conflicting opinion, relies on formal channels, and attempts to maintain personal authority instead of delegating it are all measures of the tone of his administration. It is this tone that gives life and shape to the institutionalized presidency.

[4]Theodore C. Sorenson, *Decision Making in the White House* (New York: Columbia University Press, 1963), pp. 14–15.

The Cabinet

Franklin Roosevelt once commented: "When I woke up this morning the first thing I saw was a headline in the *New York Times* that our Navy was going to spend two billion dollars on a shipbuilding program. Here I am the Commander-in-Chief of the Navy having to read about that for the first time in the press." His reaction dramatizes the president's lack of communication with the cabinet, the oldest element of the institutionalized presidency.

The president's cabinet includes the secretaries of the federal departments and the UN ambassador.

The cabinet was first formed as a four-member staff under George Washington, and has grown to its current high of fourteen. Its present composition of members, all but one of whom is the administrative head of a sprawling federal bureaucratic structure, includes the United States ambassador to the United Nations, the attorney general, and the secretaries of state, treasury, defense, interior, agriculture, commerce, labor, health and human services, housing and urban development, transportation, energy, and education. Shortly before the 1988 elections, Congress voted to add the Veterans Administration to the cabinet. Members argued that although these changes would not necessarily bring additional staff or money to the Veterans Administration, it would symbolize the government's concern for veterans.

George Reedy, press secretary to Lyndon Johnson, described the cabinet as "one of those institutions in which the whole is less than the sum of its parts."[5] The same factor delineates both the individual strengths and the collective weakness of cabinet members: their relationship to their individual departments. This relationship will be analyzed as the source of their power and influence in the Chapter 4 discussion of the bureaucratic structure itself. However, it is analytically helpful here to clarify that strength in relation to the collective impotence of the cabinet as an element of the institutionalized presidency.

The cabinet member's dilemma   The nearly three million civilian employees who work in cabinet departments wield tremendous power as a result of their acquired expertise, possession of the government's material resources, and a virtual monopoly on the capacity to act. The secretary must cultivate their confidence and respect, which is quickly lost if he or she fails to advance the departmental interests to which many of these men and women have devoted entire lives. Cabinet members change even more frequently than presidents, but their departments remain. Thus a cabinet officer, considered by the president as a "trusted adviser," is viewed by the department as "our man at the White House." This places cabinet members in an extremely tenuous political situation. If they take a parochial, "departmental" stance in cabinet consultations, their worth as presidential advisers on matters of more universal concern may be called into question by White House staff. This was particularly true for the secretaries of domestic policy departments during the Reagan administration; they were appointed to weaken programs in their departments, not to support program-expansion ideas of the civil servants.

[5]George Reedy, *The Twilight of the Presidency* (New York: New American Library, 1970), p. 77.

At cabinet meetings, members have two roles: to represent departmental interests and to provide the president with general advice as part of his "team." These roles are often in conflict.

If, however, a cabinet secretary fails to support departmental positions, especially the views of senior professionals, departmental personnel will believe that their "boss" is costing them influence with the president. They will likely stall implementing the secretary's administrative initiatives, leak damaging information to the press or Congress, and engage in other behavior subversive to the secretary's position. Regardless of how a secretary handles this role of departmental representative to the president, the cabinet as a collective body of presidential advisers does not function well.

Conflicts between cabinet members and the White House staff are frequent as both vie for influence with the president.

The cabinet is often faced with disputes between members, resignations over administration policy (dating from Jefferson's resignation from Washington's cabinet over the economic programs advocated by Alexander Hamilton), the preemptive stature of other presidential officers (particularly the White House staff), and even the sheer uncertainty of individual cabinet members' positions. These problems increase their sense of frustration and often result in retreats into their respective departments, leaving the institutionalized presidency to evolve other means of coping with its difficulties.

Use of the cabinet as an advisory body Eisenhower was probably the last president to try using his cabinet as an advisory body, establishing a special post of cabinet secretary to prepare agenda. Kennedy once referred to meetings of the cabinet as a "waste of time," and his successor never even discussed the conduct of the Vietnam War with the cabinet. Nixon's original pledge to revitalize the cabinet was quickly forgotten, as demonstrated by Interior Secretary Walter Hickel's complaint in 1970 that the president was inaccessible to cabinet members. Ford, Carter, Reagan, and Bush all made similar promises to involve the cabinet in the discussion of crucial matters. In practice, all four relied on other arrangements, generally informal groups with memberships tailored to the subject matter and including people from the Executive Office of the President and one or two other trusted cabinet secretaries.

The Executive Office of the President

Established by President Franklin Roosevelt by executive order under prerogatives granted him by the Reorganization Act of 1939, the Executive Office of the President (EOP) comprises staff agencies that aid the president in carrying out his duties. Table 1-4 lists the major components of the EOP, which has roughly 1,700 employees and a budget well over $100 million.

The White House Office Taking precedence in the EOP is the White House Office (or White House staff), a circle of advisers with the most immediate access to and influence with the president. Its formal duties include advising the president on matters of public concern, briefing him on current activities and problems within the executive branch, acting as liaison with Congress, and providing him with advice on the full range of domestic, foreign, and national security affairs.

TABLE 1-4   Executive Office of the President, January 1989

Office or Council	Year of Establishment	Statutory Head	Senate Approval?	Principal Task
White House	1789		No	Assist the president.
Office of the Vice-President	1789	Chief of Staff	No	Assist the vice-president.
Office of Management and Budget	1970[c]	Director[a]	Yes	Prepare and administer federal budget.
Council of Economic Advisers	1946	Chairperson	Yes	Advise on economy and preparation of annual economic message.
National Security Council	1947	President[b]		Advise on foreign affairs.
Office of U.S. Trade Representative	1963	U.S. Trade Representative	Yes	Coordinate trade agreement programs and administer overall trade policy.
Council of Environmental Quality	1969	Chairperson	Yes	Coordinate national environmental programs.
Office of Science and Technology Policy	1976	Director	Yes	Serve as a source of scientific analysis and advice.
Office of Administration	1977	Director[a]	No	Provide common administrative support services for entire EOP.
Office of Policy Development	1978	Director[a]	No	Advise on and coordinate domestic policies.

[a]Who is also an assistant or special assistant to the president.
[b]Staff operates under an executive director.
[c]The budgetary part of OMB's work had been done by the Bureau of the Budget, which had been in the EOP since 1946.

The White House staff is composed of close, long-term confidants of the president. By controlling access to the president, the White House staff has great influence.

The main characteristic of the White House staff is a strong personal loyalty to the president. Unlike cabinet officers, staff members have no independent base of power or bureaucracy to represent. Their position (like that of the vice-president) is determined by presidential style, but (unlike that of the vice-president) their relationship with the president usually dates from his earlier political career, so he trusts their judgment and advice. This closeness to the president is a source of substantial power for the White House staff. More than anyone else in the government, they are able to get the president's ear. The staff members also set the president's agenda, determining who gets into the Oval Office and which phone calls will be returned. By this role of "gatekeeper," the White House staff can structure the information the president receives.

Some presidents delegate more authority to the White House staff than others. Eisenhower and Reagan gave the staff more leeway to make decisions than did Kennedy, Johnson, Ford, Carter, and Bush. Nixon exhibited strong trust in his staff, which was almost his sole source of advice on matters of national concern. In return, his staff exhibited such loyalty that one member suggested he would go so far as to run over his own grandmother if that would help the president. In addition, the power wielded by the staff was so pervasive that ranking members of the president's own party in Congress, and even cabinet members, complained that they had little access to the Oval Office. The extreme of staff autonomy among recent presidents, however, was Reagan's system. Reagan's "disengaged management style" permitted his staff great discretion to carry out and occasionally form White House policy. Bush reestablished more direct presidential involvement with staff. However, the President's first chief-of-staff, John Sununu, angered a number of Republican members of Congress as well as his fellow administration officials with his reportedly arrogant manner. In December of 1991, Bush replaced Sununu as chief-of-staff with Samuel Skinner, who had been Secretary of Transportation. Skinner himself was replaced in 1992 by James Baker, who was brought in to help with the President's reelection campaign.

This type of system raises serious questions of whether the president gets the necessary information for optimal decision making. In their zeal to serve him, staff members decide what information should be transmitted and what should be repressed. Their intervention may be overly officious, their confidence exceeding their competence. In their desire to remain in his favor (there is no job security for members of the White House staff), they may seek to shield him from all criticism. Consequently, the staff may isolate the president from the information he needs to avoid serious errors in judgment.

Some White House staffs have been criticized for isolating the president.

No treatment of the White House staff would be complete without mention of the president's special assistant for national security affairs. In recent administrations, he has assumed many of the duties of the secretary of state by taking a central role in the formulation of U.S. foreign policy. Thus, McGeorge Bundy under Kennedy, Walter Rostow under Johnson, and Henry Kissinger under Nixon became the "man in the basement" whose rivalry with the respective secretaries of state evolved into the merging of the two positions in Kissinger. This proved to be a short-lived marriage. In November 1975, after considerable intracabinet rivalry, Ford removed Kissinger from his post as assistant to the president, although Kissinger retained his position as secretary of state. Carter maintained the separation of the two positions when he assumed the presidency, appointing Cyrus Vance as secretary of state and Zbigniew Brzezinski as his special assistant for national security affairs. Their public squabbles over policy as well as over who should present the administration's positions embarrassed Carter on several occasions.

Over the years, each national security adviser has had squabbles with the secretary of state.

Conflict between the secretary of state and the national security adviser continued throughout the Reagan administration. In the early months of Reagan's presidency, National Security Adviser Richard Allen publicly bickered with Secretary of State Alexander Haig. The 1981 appointment of William Clark (a novice in foreign policy matters) to replace Allen provided at least temporary relief to this long-standing institutional dispute with the secretary of state. However, nothing was resolved permanently. Other White House staff members leaked material, damaging Haig in the press, and in June 1982 Haig resigned after feuding with Clark. During the Iran-Contra hearings in 1987, the policy differences on a variety of issues between National Security Adviser John Poindexter and Secretary of State George Schultz were dramatically revealed. George Bush's close political and personal relationship with his secretary of state, James Baker, afforded Baker unchallenged access to the president, elevating the secretary of state to a position of acknowledged preeminence in the administration and helping overcome some of the institutional tensions between the secretary of state and the national security adviser. However, as a general rule, the White House staff continues to vie with the secretary of state and other cabinet members for power and influence with the president.

Office of Management and Budget   Another important element in the EOP is the Office of Management and Budget (OMB), which is more powerful than any other single agency in its impact on the development and implementation of federal programs. From its inception, it has coordinated the budget requests of all federal agencies. Without OMB clearance, no executive agency can request funds from Congress, and as of 1970, no appropriated funds can be spent without OMB approval.

Established originally as the Bureau of the Budget under the control of the Department of the Treasury, the agency was transferred to direct presidential control at FDR's request, in accord with the general trend toward presidential leadership in the legislative field. Since its reorganization and renaming by Nixon in 1970, OMB has become even more powerful. Its major responsibility is the supervision and control of budget administration; this responsibility has been constantly expanding in recent years in a White House attempt to control the bureaucracy.

OMB is the locus for executive decisions on expenditures as well as the linchpin in the president's effort at managing the federal bureaucracy.

In preparing the federal budget, OMB gathers requests for expenditures from all departments and agencies of the government eighteen months before the beginning of a given fiscal year. It then coordinates those budget requests in accord with the president's determination of priorities. The director of OMB, nominated by the president with senatorial confirmation, then returns the "trimmed" budgets to each department for further consideration—thereby initiating the process of request, consideration, and return that continues unabated until the presentation of the president's budget to the Congress for approval. At the same time, OMB is also responsible for improving governmental organization, developing information and management systems, and creating programs for the recruitment and training of federal career executives.

The "administrator" or "overseer" role of the OMB is intended to give greater emphasis to the management aspect of the government's operations. It is also an attempt to ensure planning and implementation on a coordinated basis with EOP direction and control. Reagan further strengthened OMB, ordering all federal agencies to clear changes in regulations or administrative procedures with OMB. Under an even more far-ranging 1984 executive order, all federal departments and agencies were required to notify OMB at the beginning of the fiscal year of changes that they would propose during the upcoming year, and to provide OMB with early drafts of policy changes that were being considered. OMB thus emerged at the center of Reagan's effort to gain tight control over the federal bureaucracy. George Bush allowed his OMB director, Richard Darman, to continue the centralizing trend established by Reagan.

Unlike OMB, which has a large staff to gather information, the Council of Economic Advisers works with a small staff to develop an overview of economic conditions to be able to advise the president.

Council of Economic Advisers   Separate from OMB, but also concerned with the federal budget, is the Council of Economic Advisers, established under the EOP by the Employment Act of 1946 and currently operating under that statute and the Reorganization Plan of 1953. Its director and two other members are appointed by the president with senatorial consent and are assisted by a small staff of economists and statisticians. The council relies heavily on the various federal departments and agencies for economic data, as does OMB, but unlike the latter, it cannot dictate appropriations and expenditures. It therefore enjoys a much more cordial relationship with its sources.

In accord with its broad responsibility to analyze the state of the economy, the Council of Economic Advisers issues yearly recommendations to the president on matters of economic growth and stability. It also prepares analyses of economic programs and policies of the federal government and submits advice on economic developments that, although general in nature, form the basis of the president's annual economic report to the Congress.

The National Security Council includes the heads of the essential agencies dealing with foreign affairs and military matters.

National Security Council   The National Security Council (NSC), established in the EOP by the National Security Act of 1947 (amended in 1949), advises the president on the integration of domestic, foreign, and military policies relating to "national security." This phrase is interpreted as including anything that affects the functioning of the United States government as determined by the National Security Council itself. The anomaly here is that the same agency that defines the limits of national security also determines policies delineated by that definition.

The members of the NSC, by statute, include the president, the vice-president, the secretaries of state and defense, and any additional persons by presidential invitation. The NSC considers policies on matters of common interest to the departments and agencies concerned with national security, but its utilization, as with every other element of the EOP, is a function of the personal style of the incumbent president. Eisenhower, for example, used the council extensively, developing an intricate substructure of boards and committees beneath it. Kennedy abolished the substructure, but during the Cuban missile crisis established an Executive Committee of the Council numbering sixteen members (which, when the crisis subsided, was just as quickly abolished). Nixon used the council for advice but frequently sought out non-NSC people like assistants H. R. Haldeman and John Ehrlichman for this purpose. Nixon revitalized the council and gave a central role to Kissinger—a role Kissinger continued to play under Ford even after being removed as special assistant to the president. Carter and Reagan returned to an earlier tradition of extensive use of the NSC, although neither developed the subcommittee structure used by Eisenhower. Again, it is the personal style of the president that dictates how, and how much, he uses specific elements of the executive branch.

The same statute establishing the National Security Council placed the Central Intelligence Agency under NSC control. The CIA, whose director and deputy director hold presidential appointments with senatorial consent, coordinates intelligence activities of the several departments and agencies whose operations are in the interest of national security. It also performs additional services at the request of the NSC. After revelations in the 1970s of illegal and bizarre CIA interference with Americans, Carter issued Executive Order 12036 on January 24, 1978, prohibiting the CIA from spying on any Americans except suspected foreign agents, terrorists, drug traffickers, and current or former intelligence employees suspected of endangering the agency. On December 4, 1981, Reagan rescinded the Carter limits on the CIA by his Executive Order 12333, which permitted the CIA to spy on Americans and to infiltrate domestic organizations, but "only if it is essential to achieving lawful purposes as determined by the agency head or designee." Because neither chamber of Congress objected within sixty days to this executive order, it went into effect. By such executive orders, the president can modify the authorities of any unit in the Executive Office of the President, provided the orders do not violate statutorily granted agency mandates.

Other elements within EOP As summarized in Table 1-4, the White House Office, the Office of Management and Budget (formerly the Bureau of the Budget), the Council of Economic Advisers, and the National Security Council all are elements of the Executive Office of the President with long histories and significant tasks. Each has substantial staffs on the EOP payroll as well as assistants "on loan" from various executive departments and agencies. Other elements are newer and smaller and do not enjoy the relative permanence that the principal agencies experience. Agencies are sometimes established within the EOP to demonstrate special presidential concerns with a problem. The Office of Drug Abuse Policy, for example, established by Nixon and abolished by Carter, falls into this category.

The EOP is subject to administrative reorganization at any time, provided only that the president submits to Congress any reorganization proposals, which automatically become effective if neither house rejects them within sixty days. This arrangement provides each president with the flexibility necessary for managing responsibilities according to his own best judgment. This flexibility can produce drastic changes in the composition of the EOP: Nine of the nineteen organizations in the EOP when Carter took office in 1977 were eliminated within six months. Functions performed by these now-defunct offices were transferred either to cabinet departments or to other offices within the EOP. Reagan generally felt comfortable with Carter's organization of the EOP, although he moved quickly to abolish the Council on Wage and Price Stability (COWPS), an agency he found ideologically distasteful. COWPS employees monitoring wage and price fluctuations lost their jobs, while COWPS employees measuring the impact of governmental regulations were transferred either to OMB or to a new task force on regulatory reform.

The CIA is part of the Executive Office of the President under the National Security Council.

The president can reorganize the EOP or modify the mandate of units within the EOP by executive order, providing neither house of Congress objects within sixty days.

Commissions   Reagan's regulatory reform task force chaired by then Vice-President Bush, is an example of a special ad hoc entity the president may establish at any time. Usually called commissions, they are composed of citizens appointed by the president and supported by paid professional staffs. These presidential commissions operate within the EOP until their reports are completed and presented for presidential consideration. They carry no real authority and are rarely significant in determining presidential policy. They are frequently established not so much to provide a source of information for presidential action as to convey the impression of presidential concern. They may therefore demonstrate attention to public relations more than to public policy, as the fate of recent commission reports demonstrates.

When faced with public pressure to "do something" about a problem, presidents sometimes establish commissions charged with preparing informative reports.

The Kerner Commission blamed white racism for the widespread urban riots of 1966–1967 and called for massive federal programs combating the emergence of what it saw as "two Americas": one white and the other black and poor. The report failed to lavish praise on Lyndon Johnson's civil rights accomplishments resulting in a lukewarm presidential endorsement of the report itself and no subsequent attempt to initiate its proposals. The Commission on Obscenity and Pornography, appointed by Johnson, reported in 1970 that pornography was not causing crime, a conclusion termed "morally bankrupt" by Nixon. Similarly, Nixon announced even before the Commission on Drug Abuse presented its report that he would not abide by its recommendations if they included the legalization of marijuana.

Removal of personnel   The 1867 Tenure of Office Act Andrew Johnson defied to remove a subordinate (precipitating his own impeachment) was declared unconstitutional by the Supreme Court in *Myers* v. *United States* (272 U.S. 52 [1926]). Chief Justice Taft reaffirmed George Washington's position in his first battle with Congress on this point: The president must have the power to dismiss members of the executive branch on his own authority, because he is responsible for the work of the departments involved.

The president can fire high-level administrators he previously appointed.

CONCLUSION

The office of the presidency provides an opportunity for leadership.

In summary, the president's use of political power takes precedence over the exercise of his constitutional authority. Through a series of power evolutions (which reflect the overall development of the American political system) and in response to initiatives not of his choosing, each successive president has been faced with the problem of molding an institution capable of responding to the vagaries of the American political climate. How the incumbent reacts to this challenge is a function of the individual rather than of the office. The means of presidential leadership are available, but their use is dependent on the individual's ability and political expertise.

One cannot attain the presidency without a good deal of political expertise, yet one of the persisting ironies is that many who have reached the presidency have demonstrated a decided *inability* to exercise the kind of leadership one would

To rise to the presidency, the exercise of good political judgment is essential, but the political judgment needed to get elected is not the same as that needed to govern effectively.

expect. The history of Lyndon Johnson's presidency stands as the clearest possible example that shrewd politicians do not necessarily become strong presidents. Johnson's knowledge and mastery of the wily maneuverings on Capitol Hill served him well in his first years in office. He continued to use many of the tactics that had earned him a place among the most illustrious floor leaders in Senate history, but he fared poorly in the end. Johnson's inability to recognize the differences between senatorial and presidential leadership and to read and react to the signs of popular dissatisfaction with an increasingly futile war in Southeast Asia made it impossible for him to continue his early leadership in domestic affairs at a critical period of American history.

In contrast, Richard Nixon enjoyed overwhelming support for his direction of foreign affairs. During his presidency, the United States finally extricated itself from the longest war in its history, established better relations with nations that had once been overtly hostile (including the People's Republic of China), and generally assisted in reducing international tensions. But Nixon's foreign policy successes will not determine his place in history. His misuse of the powers of his office during the Watergate affair and his total disregard of social and political realities combined to produce the only presidential resignation in American history.

The people need not applaud a strong president if they judge his objectives harmful to the nation.

Jimmy Carter brought great intelligence and enormous energy to the presidency, yet his administration produced only a few examples of successful leadership (such as Carter's cajoling the Senate into ratifying the Panama Canal Treaty). His inability to present the people with a clear vision of where he sought to lead them brought about public impressions that Carter was indecisive, weak, and even inept. The more these perceptions took hold, the harder it was for Carter to persuade Congress and his own executive appointees to follow his lead, which thereby reinforced the negative image.

The presidency of Ronald Reagan can be divided into two distinct periods. In the first year, Reagan demonstrated to skeptics that a popular president could overcome opposition to make great changes in national spending priorities as well as bring about a tax cut of unprecedented magnitude. During the early part of the first term, Reagan and his advisers used the opportunities inherent in the presidential office to change national policies. In his second term, however, because of his "lame duck" status and his problems with managing the White House, Reagan lost much of his capacity to influence both Congress and the public. Although he remained personally popular with the public, Reagan's ability to set the national agenda through media appeals was not as impressive in his second term as it had been from 1981 through 1984.

In his second term, President Reagan lost much of his capacity to influence Congress and the public.

George Bush entered the presidency with more national government experience than any of his predecessors. Unlike Carter and Reagan, who had been state governors and who ran against the establishment, Bush was known as a Washington insider. Before becoming the forty-first president, Bush held a number of positions that let him observe Washington politics from a variety of perspectives. As a former member of Congress from Texas, Bush understood the workings of the national legislature; as a former chair of the Republican National Committee, he was directly involved in party politics; as a one-time director of the CIA, he was privy to a large amount of information (much of it classified) on foreign governments and international politics; and as Ronald Reagan's vice-president for eight years, Bush observed the presidency from a particularly close vantage point.

As was the case with Lyndon Johnson, however, Bush's political background did not guarantee him a successful presidency. Like many presidents before him, Bush appeared to prefer the relative autonomy of foreign affairs to the constraints and accomodations of domestic politics. The Bush administration was marked by dramatic events on the international scene, some a result of presidential action, others a consequence of forces beyond U.S. control. The relatively quick Allied victory in the Persian Gulf War against Iraq helped raise Bush's popularity ratings to an all-time high for a sitting President. The end of communist rule in Eastern Europe and the breakup of the Soviet Union greatly eased tensions between the world's two military superpowers.

Bush's popularity declined rapidly, however, because of domestic problems that began in the second half of 1991. A lingering recession and Bush's decision to ignore his own strongly worded 1988 pledge not to raise taxes resulted in a challenge to the president by conservative forces within his own party. Although he won every primary contest, the intra-party opposition hurt Bush politically. In the general election, Bill Clinton's charge that George Bush was out of touch with the economic problems of middle-class Americans appeared to take hold. As a result, despite all of his government experience and the fact that two years into his term he enjoyed historically high approval ratings, Bush was defeated in his bid for a second term.

The election of Bill Clinton as the forty-second president of the United States was only the second Democratic presidential victory since 1968. Clinton, who had served as Governor of Arkansas for more than ten years, came to the presidency with a reputation as a skillful (to his opponents, "slick") politician, a capable governor, and a Washington outsider. To secure the Democratic nomination, Clinton had survived a series of difficult party primaries marked by frequent questions about his personal life and character. Choosing Senator Al Gore, from the neighboring state of Tennessee, as his running mate was shrewd politically even though it violated traditional notions of geographically balanced national tickets. The Clinton–Gore ticket, with the candidates often campaigning together around the country, proved to be an attractive political union and represented the ascendence to power of the post-World War II, "baby-boom" generation.

As president, Bill Clinton faces a number of serious challenges. The economy remained sluggish through all of 1992 and large numbers of voters, as evidenced by the support for independent candidate Ross Perot, are suspicious of politicians. Moreover, Clinton put great pressure on his administration to deliver on his campaign pledges to develop an "industrial policy" to help bolster American competitiveness in world markets, to establish a universal health-care system, to cut the budget deficit in half within four years, and to help generate economic growth and create jobs. Although Clinton entered office with the traditional good will of the American people and a Congress controlled by his own party, the road ahead will not be easy.

Selected Additional Readings

Bond, Jon R. and Fleisher, Richard. *The President in the Legislative Arena.* Chicago: University of Chicago Press, 1990.

Campbell, Colin and Rockman, Bert A. *The Bush Presidency.* Chatham, N.J.: Chatham House, 1991.

Kellerman, Barbara and Barilleaux, Ryan J. *The President as World Leader.* New York: St. Martin's Press, 1991.

Neustadt, Richard E. *Presidential Power and the Modern Presidents.* New York: The Free Press, 1991.

Orman, John. *Presidential Accountability: New and Recurring Problems.* New York: Greenwood Press, 1990.

CASE HISTORY : S u p e r f u n d

The Presidency

On December 11, 1980, President Carter signed into law the Comprehensive Environmental Response, Compensation and Liability Act of 1980 (CERCLA, popularly known as the "Superfund" law), which had been passed by an overwhelming majority of Congress the week before. This is the first of four end-of-chapter segments documenting the national government's participation in that historic legislation and its reauthorization in 1986 and 1990. Each segment deals with the role of the institution that is the focus of the chapter to which it is appended. Notations in the margins refer the student to those points in the text that develop and explain the powers or activities documented in the case history. Our treatment of one case history in four segments is intended to help students realize the interrelated nature of the institutions under consideration in this text.

Part I: The President

In 1976 the U.S. Environmental Protection Agency (EPA) and the New York State Department of Environmental Conservation (DEC) initiated an investigation of purported chemical contamination at the Love Canal site in Niagara Falls, New York. Within two years, New York's Commissioner of Health had declared a health emergency at the site, 237 families were evacuated, and the nation learned that past practices in the toxic and hazardous waste disposal promised to haunt the country well into the next century. In fact, the Surgeon General of the United States said toxic chemicals would pose a major health threat during the 1980s. By 1986, the EPA announced it expected the total number of sites around the country that could eventually "leak" toxic chemicals into the environment could exceed 22,000.

31–35   This chapter has emphasized that no president exercises power in a vacuum. Instead, he responds to and assists in the initiation of the political climate where his actions take shape and have their meaning. Carter's assessment of the hazardous-materials disposal problem was based on EPA reports and on the growing popular concern that abandoned waste sites might exist in many communities. His own involvement in the Love Canal problem began when he declared it a national disaster in August 1978. Tons of toxic chemicals were dumped at Love Canal in the 1940s, primarily by the Hooker Chemical Company, which later gave the land to Niagara Falls. The county subsequently built an elementary school directly over the location where toxic substances lay buried. A community of more than 200 homes grew up around the school. By the mid-1970s, the residents were experiencing health problems and abnormal births. New York State spent $23 million to help relocate the families and control the spread of chemicals.

27-29   By early 1979, President Carter asked Douglas M. Costle, the EPA administrator, to prepare a bill for submission to Congress addressing the cleanup of abandoned hazardous-waste sites. A special EPA task force drafted the legislation. By early June, this proposed legislation was on Carter's desk, and on June 13, he sent it to Congress.

27-28   On August 2, 1979, Carter sent a special "Environmental Message" to Congress. He called for passage of the bill, which would permit identification of hazardous sites across the country, establish a uniform system of reporting oil spills and releases, provide for federal emergency response authority to clean up or contain and mitigate the effects of such releases when those responsible were either unwilling or unable to do so, provide stronger authority to compel the responsible party to take action, provide for monetary compensation in limited cases, and establish fees for industry and state cost-sharing provisions complementing the federal government's tax contributions. The bill would have established a $1.6 billion fund (dubbed "superfund" because of its size), to clean up abandoned hazardous-waste sites.

Through the remainder of 1979 and virtually all of 1980, Carter's bill was completely stalled in Congress. The case study at the end of the next chapter details the development and substitution of different bills for the Carter proposals.

31-32   As noted, the president's power is not absolute; rather, he depends on his persuasive abilities. He ignores signs that others are not disposed to do his will at his own peril, as the case of the Carter Superfund proposal indicates. Carter's bill was aimed at cleaning up both abandoned hazardous-waste sites and oil spills, but linking these two problems in the same piece of legislation was unpopular in Congress. A 1978 oil spill liability bill died in the final days of the 95th Congress when the House refused to accept a Senate proposal including chemical spills in the same bill.

In the end, Congress exerting its own leadership potential, proposed several versions of the Superfund bill, and passed one of these, which it sent to the president on December 3, 1980. The president signed the legislation eight days later, and the Comprehensive Environmental Response, Compensation and Liability Act of 1980 (CERCLA) became law.

When a bill is signed into law, the president's responsibilities regarding its implementation begin. Under ordinary circumstances, legislation passed by Congress empowers "the president" to take certain action. There are times when federal officials other than the president are mentioned in legislation, but these are clearly exceptions. For example, Section 106 (c) of CERCLA specifies that "the Administrator of the Environmental Protection Agency shall . . . establish and publish guidelines . . . to effectuate the responsibilities and powers created by this Act." However, most of the powers granted in this and other legislation are not so specific. Rather than authorizing the "Administrator of EPA" to act, most of the provisions of CERCLA and of other laws authorize "the president" to take specific actions. The president delegates to subordinate federal officials in various agencies the powers Congress originally assigned to him. This delegation of authority, accomplished by executive order, can be a powerful political tool in the hands of any administration. When Carter signed the Superfund legislation into law, he was already a "lame duck" president, having lost the election to Ronald Reagan, who would assume the presidency on January 20, 1981. Unless an executive order delegating the president's authorities as outlined in CERCLA was issued by the White House before January 20, none of the federal agencies implementing the new law would be certain of the extent of their authority. They would be unable to take any new actions in the area of hazardous-waste cleanup other than implementing those sections of the law that, like Section 106 (c), specified action by a particular federal official other than the president.

50–52　　Senior management and staff from several affected federal agencies worked closely with the White House staff during the waning days of Carter's administration trying to iron out the details of an executive order in regard to CERCLA. Finally, on January 19, 1981—the day before he left office—Carter signed Executive Order 12286, delegating authority to various federal agencies to implement CERCLA.

29　　An executive order is a political tool in the hands of an administration. If a president favors a particular federal agency, he is able to make considerable delegations to it, thereby increasing the agency's role in implementing federal legislation and concomitantly increasing the agency's size, power, and prestige. Conversely, if an agency is "out of favor" with the White House, the president may delegate authority to others and leave the errant department with little to do. If it has no functions, no authority to act, a federal agency will shrivel and die; its personnel lose their jobs or are absorbed by other agencies.

58　　Under Executive Order 12286, Carter assigned a central role in implementing CERCLA to the Council on Environmental Quality (CEQ). When the new administration took over on January 20, 1981, it was soon apparent that some of President Reagan's advisers and White House staffers were unhappy with Carter's "lame-duck" executive order. On August 14, 1981, Reagan signed Executive Order 12316, which rescinded the Carter order.

53–54　　Two features of EO 12316 demonstrate the political nature of executive orders—the role of the Office of Management and Budget and the absence of CEQ. Under the Reagan order, all regulations and guidelines regarding the implementation of CERCLA must be approved by OMB. This is consistent with the general shift of power to that office noted earlier in this chapter. In addition, some of the new president's close advisers were mistrustful of CEQ, considering it duplicative of functions performed in other federal agencies and having "liberal leanings." By the time the new executive order was signed, CEQ was being reorganized and weakened considerably, with many CEQ staff positions eliminated. Under EO 12316, the authority to revise and republish the regulations relating to CERCLA's response capabilities was taken away from CEQ and delegated to EPA, after review and approval by OMB. Executive orders, originating from the president, do not require congressional approval. During his first term, Reagan's involvement with Superfund would be substantial, and it would be the basis of one of the longest-running scandals of his first administration, with charges of mismanagement and antienvironment bias. One key element of the scandal was the claim, made by EPA Administrator Anne M. Gorsuch in 1982, that certain Superfund records held by the agency would not be provided to Congress because they dealt with "sensitive enforcement matters" and were therefore covered by the doctrine of "executive privilege." On December 16, 1982, the House of Representatives voted to hold Gorsuch in contempt of Congress for her refusal to deliver the requested documents. Although the contempt charge was dropped in August 1983, it was instrumental in causing her resignation, the firing or resignation of at least twenty-four other senior-level policymaking and political appointees at the agency, the conviction of one former assistant administrator of perjury, and the concentration of public attention on the agency's activities (especially Superfund) for several years.

27   Partially as a result of the scandal involving EPA's handling of the popular Superfund program, Reagan announced in his State of the Union address in January 1984 that his administration would seek reauthorization and expansion of CERCLA when it expired in September 1985. On February 22, 1985, President Reagan sent Congress a $5.3 billion, five-year reauthorization proposal that would pay for the program by continuing the tax on chemicals and petroleum and by passing a new tax on hazardous waste. Although Reagan had just been reelected by a large margin, he did not assume the primary leadership in the reauthorization. President Reagan had little enthusiasm for large, national environmental programs. Both he and Congress knew that Congress would reauthorize the popular program because strong Democratic and Republican majorities in both chambers wanted it to continue and supported funding at a level substantially above the $5.3 billion in the president's proposal.

28   Facing broad support for Superfund, the White House still tried to influence Congress, threatening a presidential veto. Reagan warned Congress that he would not sign a bill either authorizing too much money or including a broad-based business tax. He and his key advisers feared that an excise tax, even one with a low rate and tied to Superfund, might eventually lead Congress to consider passing other excise taxes. Despite enormous federal budget deficits, the president opposed additional taxes.

When Congress finally did send President Reagan a Superfund reauthorization bill, it authorized $8.5 billion, of which $2.5 billion would come from a broad-based tax on businesses. The senior White House staff group recommended a veto, with members most concerned with financial matters, Treasury Secretary James A. Baker III and OMB Director James C. Miller, strongly advising this action. The question was whether their views would be more convincing than those of Lee M. Thomas, administrator of the EPA, who urged the president to sign the bill into law.

The timing of the action was probably crucial to the president's decision. Congress sent Reagan the bill on October 9, 1986, less than one month before the November congressional elections. Although most representatives and senators wanted Congress to adjourn so they could return home to campaign, the leadership indicated that Congress would stay in pro forma session if necessary for ten days, thereby preventing the president from exercising a "pocket veto" on the bill. Because the House had passed the bill 386–27 and the Senate had approved it 88–8, the two-thirds majority of votes needed to override a veto seemed easily available.

There was no White House signing ceremony for the Superfund Amendments and Reauthorization Act of 1986 (SARA). President Reagan signed the bill into law October 17 on Air Force One while en route to campaign in North Dakota. On learning this, Senator Robert T. Stafford (R.-Vt.) summarized the views of many: "The president appreciated that there was strong national support for the bill, that people were scared and wanted something done. And I think his political advisers told him that it was the wise thing to do, both morally and politically.''

When he took office in 1989, President Bush inherited the expensive but popular Superfund program. In 1991, the tax was due to expire again. Neither the president nor Congress, however, wanted to face the same difficult issues as in 1985 and 1986, this time only one year before a presidential election. They avoided a bruising public conflict by including a reauthorization of the Superfund taxes in the 1990 giant reconciliation bill. Although neither the House nor the Senate bills had included a Superfund reauthorization, the conference committee quietly added the measure with the support of the White House. There was little notice of the Superfund provision when President Bush signed the reconciliation bill in 1991. The reauthorization is through 1995, when the tax again expires.

2

THE CONGRESS

The twentieth century saw world power shift to presidents, premiers, and prime ministers. Despite the consequent weakening and demise of many legislatures, the U.S. Congress remains an essential force in governmental policymaking. Congress may not be as powerful in relation to the presidency as it was in the age of Daniel Webster, but it retains a central role in the government. As Richard Neustadt writes, "A President will often be unable to obtain congressional action on his terms or even to halt action he opposes. The reverse is equally accepted: Congress is often frustrated by the President. Their formal powers are so intertwined that neither will accomplish very much, for very long, without the acquiescence of the other."[1]

> Congress and the president are dependent on each other.

The presidency changes, sometimes abruptly, as each incumbent stamps it with his own personality. Congress, however, has demonstrated continuity in its procedures, rules, and general nature regardless of who is elected and which party controls the congressional leadership. Of course, Congress has changed since its beginnings as a tiny body of twenty-six senators and sixty-five representatives, but the changes have been much more evolutionary than revolutionary. It seems safe to predict that the Congress of the year 2000 will fundamentally resemble the Congress described in this chapter.

> Congress changes more slowly than the presidency.

CONSTITUTIONAL PREROGATIVES

The Authority to Legislate

> The Constitution grants Congress the authority to legislate, to police itself, and to impeach and try errant national officials. Table 2.1 summarizes Congress's constitutional duties.

Power to enact legislation Article I of the Constitution states "all legislative Powers herein granted shall be vested in a Congress of the United States, which shall consist of a Senate and a House of Representatives." This clause does not grant Congress the right to pass any law it deems wise, but only those pertaining to the specific powers "herein granted," which Section 8 of this same article spells

[1]Richard Neustadt, *Presidential Power* (New York: Wiley, 1960), p. 37.

TABLE 2.1   The Congress: Constitutional Prerogatives and Powers

Authority to legislate	Power to enact legislation (Art. I, Sec. 1) . . . expanded by commerce clause (Art. I, Sec. 8) . . . expanded by "elastic clause" (Art. I, Sec. 8) Power to override presidential vetoes (Art. I, Sec. 7)
Authority to impeach and try	Power to impeach and try (Art. I, Secs. 2 & 3)
Authority to police itself	Power over its own operations (Art. I, Sec. 5) Power over electoral procedures (Art. I, Sec. 4)

Most government tasks were initially left to state and local governments.

out. The Constitution provides for a national government performing specifically designated functions (coining money, establishing post offices, maintaining the armed forces, and so forth), thereby leaving most governmental functions to the states (for example, building schools and maintaining police forces).

Since the writing of the Constitution the U.S. has developed an intricate, highly industrialized society requiring many services at all levels of government. The Constitution provides sufficient flexibility for Congress to adapt itself in response to modern national needs. In particular, the commerce clause and the "elastic" or "necessary and proper" clause in Section 8 permit Congress to broaden its legislative scope.

Minimum wage legislation is an example of how the commerce clause permits broad congressional activity.

The commerce clause   The commerce clause states that Congress shall have power "to regulate Commerce with foreign Nations, and among the several States, and with the Indian Tribes." This clause is the constitutional justification of much economic legislation including minimum wage, labor, and antimonopoly legislation. Thus, although without explicit authority to prescribe working conditions or set a minimum wage, Congress enacted the Fair Labor Standards Act of 1938. Passage of this act eliminated child labor in factories and mines, mandated overtime pay after forty-four hours at the regular wage, and set a minimum wage of twenty-five cents per hour. Fred W. Darby, an employer in the lumber industry, claimed Congress lacked such authority. However, the Supreme Court ruled (in *United States* v. *Darby*, 312 U.S. 100 [1941]) that Darby's lumber products were shipped in interstate commerce, giving Congress the authority to set working standards, making it a crime to send products made in violation of those standards into another state. Because so much activity directly or indirectly involves interstate commerce, the commerce clause allows Congress to legislate in almost any economic realm it chooses. Indeed, the commerce clause has been broadly applied to more than just economic matters. Much of the civil rights legislation regarding public accommodations was based on Congress's power to regulate interstate commerce.

The "elastic clause"   The "elastic clause" states that Congress may "make all Laws which shall be necessary and proper for carrying into Execution the foregoing Powers." Limiting Congress to the specific, delegated powers of Section 8 (establishing post offices, coining money, and so on), would severely constrain the power of the national government. Instead, Justice John Marshall ruled in *McCulloch* v. *Maryland* (4 Wheaton 316 [1819]) that the "necessary and proper" clause should be interpreted as allowing Congress "implied powers" (powers not specifically delegated, but reasonably implied in the execution of those delegated powers). Thus, Justice Marshall ruled that Congress could incorporate a national bank (even though the Constitution mentions neither banks nor incorporation) as an implied constitutional power derived from the enumerated powers to tax, to borrow money, and to regulate commerce. His decision established legal grounds for congressional legislation in a wide range of areas not mentioned in the Constitution. Such legislation is viewed as a "necessary and proper" extension of Congress's constitutional prerogatives.

> Congress can pass laws "necessary and proper" to carry out its specific powers effectively.

In the twenty decades since the Constitution's writing, the United States has become characterized both by substantial cultural diversity and by a highly integrated economy. Because of these interrelated factors, few problems or situations are matters of purely local or state concern; almost everything has national implications—from a strike of migrant workers in California to a cutback in production of a logging company in Maine. The Constitution provides Congress with the specific right to pass legislation relating to commerce, war, and finances, and this right has been broadly interpreted by Congress in the extension of its legislative prerogatives. This interpretation, upheld by the courts, places only one limitation on the legislative power of Congress: It may not infringe on the rights of states and individuals explicitly granted elsewhere in the Constitution.

> Congress now has the right to legislate in all areas, but its laws cannot take away rights the Constitution explicitly grants to states and individuals.

Power to override presidential vetoes   Although all bills must be passed by Congress to become law, the Constitution does not place the entire legislative process in the hands of the Congress. Thus, it is important to explore the relationship between congressional actions and presidential vetoes. After a bill passes both the House and the Senate, it is sent to the president, who has three alternatives: He can sign it, he can veto it, or he can do nothing. If he signs it, the bill becomes a public law. If he vetoes it, the bill is returned to Congress, which may modify the bill in light of the president's wishes or may attempt a difficult override of his veto. The difficulty arises from the constitutional provision (Article I, Section 7) requiring a two-thirds majority in each house to override a presidential veto.

> Overriding a presidential veto requires a two-thirds majority in each house of Congress.

Relying on his battery of persuasive tactics, a president can usually persuade either one-third of the senators or one-third of the representatives to support his veto; hence, overridden vetoes are rare. From the administration of George Washington through that of George Bush, only 101 presidential vetoes were overridden by Congress. Not surprisingly, the president who most often found his vetoes overridden was the impeached (and almost convicted) Andrew Johnson. Congress overrode fifteen of his twenty-nine vetoes. Gerald Ford, another president who fought bitterly with Congress, found twelve of his sixty-six vetoes overridden. Ronald Reagan had nine of his seventy-eight vetoes overridden. During the 1988 to 1992 term of George Bush, the veto was used thirty-seven times with only one override.

Congress rarely overrides a presidential veto.

When the party controlling the presidency also controls both houses of Congress, successful overrides by Congress are even rarer than during periods of split party control. Of the more than 600 vetoes by Franklin D. Roosevelt, the Democrat-controlled Congress managed to override only nine. Congress overrode none of John Kennedy's twenty-one or Lyndon Johnson's thirty vetoes and only two of Jimmy Carter's thirty-one.

If a president does not sign or veto a bill within ten working days after receiving it from Congress, the bill automatically becomes law.

The president's third course of action on a bill is to sit back and do nothing with it for ten days. Ironically, it is not the action of the president but the condition of the Congress that determines the fate of the bill in this instance. If Congress remains in session, the bill automatically becomes law at the end of the ten-day period. Presidents often use this tactic, "permitting" the bill to become law without actively supporting its passage. It is thus a demonstration to Congress that the president is not pleased with the legislation but that his opposition to it is either too mild to warrant a veto or futile in face of a larger than two-thirds majority in both houses.

If Congress adjourns within ten days after sending a bill to the president and he does not sign it, the bill is "pocket vetoed."

Pocket vetoes If Congress adjourns within ten days of sending a bill to the president, the bill does not become law unless the president signs it. Presidential inaction while Congress is not in session results in a "pocket veto." Congress's adjournment prevented the president from returning the bill (which he presumably "stuffs in his pocket" and quietly ignores). It is therefore only at the end of a congressional session that a president can veto a bill by his inaction. In the flurry of legislative activity that usually marks the end of the term, many bills are passed that subsequently face pocket vetoes. Forty-two percent of presidential vetoes have fallen into this category and have contributed significantly to the low success ratio of congressional overrides mentioned earlier. Of Franklin Roosevelt's 631 vetoes, 261 were of the pocket variety, by far the largest number of any president.

To avoid a veto, Congress often changes a bill to reflect the president's wishes.

This record will probably stand, because recent presidents have made less use of the pocket veto. Richard Nixon used it only nineteen times, Ford twenty-two, Carter eighteen, Reagan thirty-nine, and, from 1988 to 1992, Bush only five. This reduced use indicates the persuasive capability of the modern presidency. By threatening to veto a bill while it is still under congressional consideration, the president is often able to persuade Congress to change those features of the bill he finds objectionable. No one is more aware of the difficulties inherent in overriding a presidential veto than the members of Congress, who seek to avoid the prospect whenever possible. A president is not at all reluctant to brandish an impending veto if the bill in question is not modified to reflect his views. Thus, in the face of Reagan's threatened veto in 1981, Congress changed the bill funding the Legal Services Corporation, removing those elements that most displeased him.

Item vetoes Although the Constitution does provide the president with veto power, it does not provide him with an *item* veto. The president must either sign an entire bill or veto an entire bill; he cannot sign certain sections of the bill while vetoing others. This lack of an item veto encourages Congress to propose *riders* (legislation not necessarily germane to its affixed bill) that may displease the president.

The president cannot veto part of a bill; he either signs the entire bill or vetoes it.

Thus, Congress, will attach legislation that, in isolation, the president would veto, to bills he particularly favors. He is unable to separate the rider from the bill it is attached to and must therefore sign or veto it in its entirety. A powerful president will, as noted in the last chapter, have enough support in Congress to avert the attachments of riders to his proposed legislation.

The Authority to Impeach and Try

Although Congress has the right to impeach and remove derelict officials of the executive and judicial branches, it rarely does so.

Besides granting Congress the right to legislate, the Constitution also grants the right to remove national officials judged guilty of "high crimes and misdemeanors." The House of Representatives *impeaches*—a misunderstood term meaning to bring to trial for consideration for removal. Following a successful impeachment by the House, the Senate acts as jury in the trial proceedings, which requires a two-thirds vote to remove the offending public official from office. Impeachment proceedings rarely take place, for the threat of it is usually sufficient cause for the tainted official to submit his resignation, as in Richard Nixon's case.

The Authority to Police Itself

Congress can deny a seat to a member chosen in a fraudulent election but generally accepts the judgment of state authorities.

Power over its own operations Constitutional prerogatives also include Congress's right to determine its own internal procedures and the legitimacy of its members. Although this latter prerogative permits it to deny a seat to a member whose election involved irregularities, Congress generally accepts without investigation winners declared by state authorities.

This authority to police itself includes the right to set salaries ($125,100 in 1992) and benefits, including a generous pension plan. In 1981, Congress greatly expanded its members' remuneration by legislating a tax deduction for all expenses incurred while in Washington and by providing for automatic raises pegged to the inflation level. In 1982, public outcry forced it to rescind the special tax deduction. In 1989, in the face of even more heated public outcry, Congress refused to give itself a 50 percent pay raise. In 1991, Congress voted itself a salary increase and accepted limitations on the outside income available to members.

Congress sets limits on the conduct permitted members. Members must make full financial disclosures of assets and liabilities. They cannot keep unofficial office accounts ("slush funds" whose sources and distributions are unreported) and cannot receive gifts valued over $100 from lobbyists. In addition, members are prohibited from "lame-duck" travel (trips taken at government expense by legislators about to retire). Because Congress has shown past reluctance to investigate the ethics of its members, the rigor of enforcement of these rules is in doubt.

Despite the existence of ethics codes, scandals continue to generate negative publicity for Congress. In 1989, Speaker Jim Wright and Majority Whip Tony Coelho resigned from Congress in response to allegations that they had violated congressional standards of ethics. In 1991, members were embarrassed by news stories of unpaid bills at the House cafeteria and ignored parking violations. And in 1992, the disclosure that a number of members had consistently overdrawn their checking accounts at the House bank and the allegations of misconduct by employees of the House post office severely damaged the reputation of the House leadership. The Senate too has experienced ethical lapses. In 1991, five U.S. senators were rebuked, one more seriously than the others, by the Senate Ethics Committee for exerting pressure on federal bank regulators on behalf of thrift operator and campaign contributor, Charles Keating. And that same year, Senator Alphonse D'Amato (R.-N.Y.), although cleared of more serious charges, was criticized by the Ethics Committee for "conducting the business of his office in an improper and inappropriate manner." The negative publicity surrounding the "Keating five" and Senator D'Amato hurt the image of the Senate.

> In spite of ethics codes, scandals continue to occur, although only a small number of legislators have been involved.

Congress also exercises its power over its own operations by requiring lobbyists in Washington to register. Because the First Amendment to the Constitution prohibits Congress from restricting lobbying ("Congress shall make no law . . . abridging . . . the right of the people . . . to petition the Government for redress of grievances"), reformers instead seek to control the excesses of pressure groups by restricting gift giving (as with the $100 restriction) and by requiring public disclosure of lobbying activities. The Lobbying Disclosure Act of 1946 requires all Washington lobbyists to specify their employers and their legislative interests, providing the public with information on who is lobbying for what. Not surprisingly, the highest-paid and most influential lobbyists are often former members of Congress; their contacts and access to the floor (open to all former members) make them highly sought after as lobbyists.

> The most successful congressional lobbyists are often former members of Congress.

Power over electoral procedures Finally, the Constitution provides that Congress can determine "the Times, Places, and Manner of holding Elections." In the absence of congressional action, each state legislature makes these determinations for the election of its U.S. senators and representatives. Congress has exercised its option to standardize electoral procedures by mandating single-member districts (only one winner in each district) for representatives, the secret ballot (also called the Australian ballot), and the time of the election (the Tuesday after the first Monday in November). In 1940, Congress passed the Hatch Act, prohibiting federal government employees from participating in political campaigns. There have been efforts to reform this act so that federal employees might enjoy the same political rights as other Americans. However, concerns that poorly written reforms might subject federal employees to the kinds of political pressures that characterized the spoils system have hampered these efforts.

> For federal elections, Congress mandates secret ballots, single-member districts, and a common date (the Tuesday after the first Monday in November).

In 1992, fourteen states joined Colorado by enacting term limitations for their congressional delegations. The movement to limit congressional terms had been slowed somewhat in 1991 when voters in the state of Washington rejected an initiative that would have limited the terms of their elected officials. State-imposed term limitations on federal officials represent a basic challenge to congressional control of electoral procedures. The issue is a classic illustration of the tensions in a federalist system, and, because it may well be settled in the courts, is also a clear example of separate institutions sharing power (see the Introduction).

> State-imposed limitations challenge congressional control over elections.

Article I, Section 4, permits Congress to pass legislation prohibiting corporations and unions from making campaign contributions and limiting the size of individual contributions. The law has a loophole that permits the creation of political action committees (PACs), through which corporations and unions funnel large sums into political campaigns. Although critics argue that the great influence of PACs perverts democratic norms of elected officials responsible only to their constituents, Congress shows little interest in reforming the campaign finance laws. In part, Congress's tolerance of PAC spending may be a consequence of the tendency of most PACs to give their money to incumbents rather than to challengers.

PACs buy influence through campaign contributions.

CONGRESSIONAL LEADERSHIP

The formal powers granted Congress by the Constitution give Congress an opportunity for leadership.

Noting that the Constitution grants Congress prerogatives enabling broad legislation, impeachment, and control over its own elections and membership shows that Congress has the potential for real leadership, but tells little about whether Congress chooses to exert this leadership. As in the case of the presidency, one must look beyond the Constitution to view Congress as leader.

The Roles of Congress

Can Congress really lead the American people in the sense that the president can fulfill a leadership role? Congress differs from the presidency speaking not with one voice, but with a chorus composed of 435 representatives and 100 senators. Congress cannot unanimously urge the adoption of a single, coherent, integrated program of government, but it can execute adeptly five functions that, taken together, give it an immense capacity for leadership. These functions are (1) representation, (2) issue creation and clarification, (3) oversight of the executive branch, (4) lawmaking, and (5) legitimation of government policies. In performing these functions, Congress not only provides and acts on alternatives to specific executive proposals but also guides the general direction of national policy. When it does so with clarity and vigor, the result is congressional leadership.

Congress can do more than just react to executive-branch initiatives.

Representation The president and vice-president are the only elected officials with a nationwide constituency and therefore can claim to represent the interest of all Americans. In representing all Americans, however, they cannot grant a special voice to the farmers of Kansas or to the lobster fishermen of Maine. Senators and representatives are expected to provide such a voice and to be supportive of the needs of their respective constituents. Thus, the senators and representatives from Maine are expected to be knowledgeable about lobster industry problems and to press for national efforts to alleviate them, while the members from South Carolina are expected to present the position of the textile interests. Congress is a place where the diverse interests of this large nation are given open representation. This does not necessarily mean Congress will pass legislation favorable to lobstering or to the textile industry, nor does it mean that all local interests are

Local interests have their views aired by their representatives.

A member of Congress, garners support for bills concerning his or her constituents by supporting the particular concerns of other members in return for their votes; vote trading, also called "logrolling," occurs most often in "pork-barrel" votes.

represented (local interests in the same district often oppose each other, with the representative supporting one interest and ignoring the other). However, most interests (at least those supportive of a particular representative in the district) will likely receive a public presentation of their views in Congress.

This situation, in which some issues carry regional significance for some representatives and are not salient at all for other representatives, allows bargaining among members of Congress. Because textiles are not salient to the representatives from Maine, they might be willing to trade their vote on a textile bill in return for the South Carolina representatives' support on a lobster bill. This form of vote trading is most common in "pork-barrel" legislation (bills involving public works projects).

Congress performs this representative function without many of its members seeing themselves as instructed delegates mirroring the will of the majority of their constituents. In fact, there is rarely a dilemma between voting one's own judgment and voting constituents' opinion. On most issues, voters exhibit neither knowledge nor concern. Even when a majority of voters have an opinion on a two-sided issue, a given constituency may be equally divided on both sides. There is also the question of whether senators and representatives accurately know the views of their constituents. Members of Congress do not usually take periodic, professionally prepared surveys of their districts. Rather, they depend on mail questionnaires, which are notoriously biased, partly because conservatives respond more frequently than liberals. So, not knowing how their constituents really stand on issues, most members of Congress assume (often correctly) that they themselves reflect the actual views of their constituency. They see no conflict between voting their own opinions and voting according to constituency opinion back home.

The electoral process enhances the extent to which individual members represent the majority sentiment in their districts. Conservative districts elect conservative representatives who, by voting conservatively, have no conflict with their constituents' views. Similarly, liberal districts elect liberal representatives, who only rarely find themselves at odds with their constituents.

On most issues, constituents either lack firm opinions or are divided.

Because most districts elect representatives who agree with the predominant constituency sentiment on issues, most representatives rarely face the dilemma of voting their conscience versus constituency opinion.

Issue creation and clarification   A second congressional function is the creation and clarification of issues, with Congress providing a forum for the public expression of diverse views. It acts as a sounding board for new ideas, many of which later are enacted into law.

In the public nature of almost all its debate, Congress differs considerably from the executive branch, where private debate beforehand usually enables it to present a united front to Congress. Although Congress formerly conducted many of its important debates in closed committee meetings, new rules passed in the mid-1970s made public all but the small number of meetings concerned with national security matters. Even markup sessions (when bills are actually drafted) are now open to the public. Of course, debate on the floor remains open.

Hearings are ostensibly investigations gathering information for writing approved legislation, but they also focus public attention on problems or new issues. In 1991, an extraordinary weekend of hearings by the Senate Judiciary Committee,

Congress opens almost all committee meetings.

looking into charges made against Supreme Court nominee Clarence Thomas, publicized the issue of sexual harassment on the job. In 1987, the Iran-Contra hearings focused national attention on the tensions between Congress and the executive branch on foreign policy matters. Early in the 1970s, hearings examined the campaign abuses of the Nixon administration. In the 1960s, Congress instigated national debate through its hearings on the Vietnam War. The Senate Foreign Relations Committee hearings largely began the nationwide questioning of the wisdom and morality of U.S. involvement in that tragic war.

Hearings often publicize problems and issues.

Oversight of the executive branch Congress's third function is that of "watchdog" or "overseer" of the executive branch. Each substantive committee is expected to oversee the activities of the executive branch that fall within its subject area. For example, the Armed Services Committees in both houses are expected to maintain vigilance over military activities. Reports that Congress was weak in its oversight function led to the House's 1974 requirement that substantive committees develop plans specifying how they will fulfill their oversight function for each two-year period. As a safeguard, the House Committee on Government Operations (in addition to its own broad oversight activities) supervises and coordinates the oversight activities of the substantive committees.

Every substantive committee is responsible for oversight activities in its area of specialization.

Committees use their powers of investigation to review executive actions. Administrative officials and other interested parties are required to attend hearings where they must answer questions put to them by legislators. Subjects of investigation in the early 1990s have included the savings and loan bailout and the restructuring of the U.S. banking system by the House Banking, Finance and Urban Affairs Committee and the Department of Housing and Urban Development's (HUD) proposal to sell public housing to tenants by the subcommittee of the Senate Appropriations Committee responsible for HUD funding. These and similar investigations helped Congress learn about many executive-branch activities.

Committee hearings often investigate executive-branch behavior.

Oversight also is performed as an unintentional outgrowth of the casework that members perform for constituents. Annually, each member's office handles thousands of requests from constituents who seek information or assistance in dealing with the federal bureaucracy. Through these communications members discover problem areas in the federal program implementation.

Casework provides oversight information to members.

Congress also fulfills its oversight function through the General Accounting Office (GAO), which audits the executive branch, conducts inquiries, and gathers information at the request of Congress or even of individual members. Headed by Comptroller General Charles A. Bowsher whom President Reagan appointed for a fifteen-year term with Senate approval in 1981, the GAO is designed primarily to provide nonpartisan information on the spending behavior of the executive branch. The GAO works closely with the Congressional Budget Office, supplying the Budget Committees with up-to-date information on how money is spent.

The GAO audits the executive branch and performs inquiries requested by Congress.

Congress's control of appropriations is its real strength in carrying out its oversight responsibilities. Congress takes its oversight responsibilities seriously because members know that they have the power to reduce or even to stop the funding of programs they find inefficient. The executive branch, knowing Congress

Congress's control of appropriations is the key power that makes oversight important.

has this power, tries to convince the legislators that programs are being effectively administered in line with congressional intentions. The oversight function is thus a never-ending review of executive branch performance where the stakes are the expansion, reduction, and elimination of federal agencies and programs.

Lawmaking Congress's fourth, most obvious function, is that of lawmaking. Congress considers thousands of bills each year, enacting only a small number into law. Congress's lawmaking function involves not only passing bills but modifying and rejecting them as well. Although major legislation increasingly originates in the executive branch, Congress rarely accepts the executive's versions without making important substantive revisions. Sometimes, as in this chapter's case study, Congress substitutes its own version of a bill for the one offered by the president, and it often rejects executive proposals entirely. In fact, some of Congress's finest hours have come in its rejection of politically popular but ill-conceived bills. Annually, for example, Congress rejects bills infringing on the constitutional rights of unpopular minorities, such as the American Communist party, the Ku Klux Klan, and the Gay Activist Alliance.

Congress rejects most bills that are offered.

People feel a responsibility to obey federal laws because Congress is a representative institution whose members are freely elected.

Legitimation of government policy A fifth and final systemic function of Congress is legitimation of government policies, the result of the other four. If people believe that governmental policies are passed by a fairly elected legislature, they are very likely to believe that the policy decisions of the government are legitimate, that the government has a right to do what it is doing. Because people believe that most of the policy decisions of the government are arrived at "justly" through a representative institution, they usually then feel obligated to obey those decisions—even those they would otherwise consider absurd. Thus, Congress aids in the peaceful resolution of conflicting interests. A citizen who disagrees with governmental policies knows that a peaceful remedy (electing members of Congress who agree with him or her) is available. The existence of this electoral remedy, which is not available in nations such as Cuba and Libya, legitimates the regime.

The previous chapter stressed that one cannot think of the president as "switching" from one role to another in the process of leadership. His roles often overlap and merge with each other, and congressional functions should be reviewed in a similar light. Thus, the national budget, involving the expenditure of nearly $1.5 trillion, might be referred to as an important "law" that the Congress must pass every year; yet the process by which the Appropriations Committee of the House reviews the budget requests of the various agencies, bureaus, and departments of the executive branch forms an integral part of the budgetary process as well. This close scrutiny represents at least two congressional functions—overseeing the executive branch and enacting legislation.

Congressional actions often involve more than one function.

These five roles do not equal the leadership potential of the president, but congressional leadership potential is nonetheless immense. When Congress maximizes its leadership capabilities, it represents a wide variety of interests, clarifies important issues, carefully oversees the executive branch, passes relevant legislation, and legitimates government actions. When Congress fails in its leadership

TABLE 2.2   House–Senate Differences

House	Senate
Larger (435 members)	Smaller (100 members)
Two-year term of office	Six-year term of office
More centralized power	Less centralized power
Acts more quickly	Acts more slowly
More rigid rules	More flexible rules
More impersonal	More personal
Policy specialists	Policy generalists
Smaller constituencies	Larger constituencies
Less prestige	More prestige
Younger	Older
Wider minority representation	Narrower minority representation
Less reliance on staff	More reliance on staff
More committees	Fewer committees

Congress has the potential for leadership.

responsibilities, it ceases to represent many Americans, confuses and badly articulates issues, gives unbridled rein to the executive branch, fails to justify government policies adequately, and passes inadequate laws. It is extremely important that Congress fulfill its leadership roles vigorously.

ELECTORAL PROCEDURES

Apportionment

Senators and representatives are elected for different periods of time to bodies of different sizes. These differences of tenure and size cause operational differences between the two houses, some of which are outlined in Table 2.2.

Each state, regardless of size, has two senators.

Senate apportionment There are 100 senators, two from each state. This method of Senate apportionment gives each state equal representation, regardless of its population. Thus, the composition of the Senate ignores the democratic premise of one-person, one-vote. The senators from California, for example, represent over 29 million Americans in 1992, whereas the senators from Alaska represent just over a half-million. The Founders, however, believed that this "undemocratic" apportionment of the Senate was so important that its constitutional provision cannot be amended. Article V, which describes the amending process, states "no State, without its Consent, shall be deprived of its equal Suffrage in the Senate."

House apportionment The House of Representatives comprises 435 members elected under the one-person, one-vote rule, with the added stipulation that each state must have at least one representative. Congress itself determines the size of the House, which started with 65 members in 1790 but has remained at 435

Each state has the number of representatives proportionate to its population.

since 1912. Every ten years, each state legislature redraws congressional district boundaries so that its districts contain close to the same number of people, approximately 600,000 in the 1990s. Of course, the six states with only one representative (Alaska, Delaware, North Dakota, South Dakota, Vermont, and Wyoming) face no redistricting tasks. In those states (and in Washington, D.C., which has one nonvoting representative), House candidates must run statewide.

In 1964, the Supreme Court applied the principle of "one person, one vote" to congressional districts.

Until the 1960s, there existed substantial discrepancies (malapportionment) in congressional district size, with some members of Congress representing one million constituents while others represented fewer than 200,000 people. In 1946, the Supreme Court ruled in *Colegrove* v. *Green* (328 U.S. 549) that apportionment was strictly a legislative matter. However, beginning with *Baker* v. *Carr* (369 U.S. 186 [1962]), the Court reversed its previous view and began considering apportionment cases. In *Wesberry* v. *Sanders* (376 U.S. 1 [1964]), the Supreme Court ruled that "as nearly as is practicable one man's vote in a congressional election is to be worth as much as another's." This ruling acted to equalize the population of congressional districts by ending the practice of malapportionment. The Court's decision caused a sharp decrease in rural area representation and a substantial increase in the number of members from suburban congressional districts.

House and Senate compared   The smaller size of the Senate gives each senator more prestige than each representative, as 1/100th of a legislative body rather than 1/435th. The Senate's smaller size also permits it to be less formal and more personal than the House, which needs more rigid rules to avoid chaos. Senators are usually generalists who try to learn a little about many policy areas; representatives often focus on a smaller number of issues of particular interest to them or their constituents. The larger size of the senatorial constituency, an entire state, makes it less likely that a senator will represent the parochial interests of a subregion or have a narrow, localized viewpoint.

The Senate runs itself more informally than does the House.

Single-Member Districts and Plurality

As mentioned in the introduction, both senators and representatives are elected from single-members districts. (Although each state's two senators share the same "district," they are not elected simultaneously.) These districts operate on a "winner-take-all" plurality basis. This means that each district elects only one representative, the candidate who receives the greatest proportion of the votes, regardless of whether this proportion is a majority. In an election with four candidates receiving, respectively, 35 percent, 30 percent, 25 percent, and 10 percent of the votes cast, the candidate with 35 percent of the votes would be elected with no runoff election between the first two finishers. In this election system, a minor party can win 25 percent of the vote in every congressional district and still fail to send even one of its candidates to Congress.

Each district elects only one person to Congress. A plurality wins, meaning no runoff elections.

Alternatives   If the electoral system were changed to require an absolute majority for election, a system of runoffs (or successive ballots) would be initiated.

Voters would know that on the first balloting they could vote for a minor-party candidate without "wasting their votes," with the likelihood that neither major-party candidate would win 51 percent of the vote on the first ballot. Voters would then still have a vote in the second balloting between the two "real" candidates. If an absolute majority were required for election, the proportion of votes going to minor parties would be higher than the proportion minor parties receive under the current electoral system. This would encourage minor parties and at the same time weaken the dominance of the two major parties.

Tenure

Senators have six-year terms.

Senate tenure Senators are elected for six-year terms, staggered in such a way that every two years one-third of the senators are up for reelection. A senator elected in 1992 does not have to face reelection until 1998, an appealing prospect to politicians accustomed to running for office every other year.

Representatives have two-year terms.

House tenure Representatives are elected for two-year terms, so most of them are thinking seriously about the next campaign by the day they are sworn into office. Incumbent representatives rarely lose their bids for reelection. While in office, most legislators make skillful use of franking privileges (free mailing), casework opportunities (information and assistance to individual constituents), and media communications to their districts. In the past decade over 90 percent of House incumbents who sought reelection were successful, and most of the contests were not close: In 1990, only 11 percent were won by less than 55 percent of the vote. In contrast, in the 1980s incumbent senators—whose stands on controversial issues are more visible—were victorious in only two-thirds of their races; and over one-third of the winners squeaked by with less than 55 percent of the vote.

House members usually are reelected; only two-thirds of Senate incumbents win their races.

In 1992, there were significant changes in the membership of Congress due to incumbent retirements and electoral defeats. Indeed, that year witnessed a fifty-year high in the number of members who retired from both their House seats and from public life. The dramatic changes in 1992 are attributable to a variety of factors including member frustration with the political conflicts inherent in divided government; public anger at government generally and the Congress in particular; and the effects of the decennial redistricting which changed a number of members' districts.

SENATORS AND REPRESENTATIVES

Characteristics

In terms of age, race, sex, and wealth, members of Congress are not representative of the American people. Instead, they resemble middle- to upper-level managers found in American corporations.

Age Not surprisingly, members of Congress are older than most Americans. The average age of members of the 103nd Congress (1993–1994) was fifty-three.

Congress in the 1990s was younger than it was in the 1960s and 1970s. This change reflects the increasingly competitive nature of elections in the South (which regularly sent many septuagenarians and octogenerians to Congress) and the decision of many older incumbents to take advantage of the generous pension benefits that Congress made available to its retirees.

The leadership of Congress is older than the rank-and-file membership. In 1993, Speaker of the House Tom Foley (D.-Wash.) was sixty-three; Senate Majority Leader George Mitchell (D.-Me.) was fifty-nine. The average age of committee chairpersons, powerful leaders in Congress, was sixty-two. In general, the top leadership of Congress resembles that of the executive branch and large corporations, with white men in their late fifties and early sixties predominating.

Gender and race   In 1993, there were only forty-eight women in the House (11 percent of the membership) and six in the Senate. Thus, Congress is largely composed of middle-aged men. Moreover, Congress is for the most part white. In 1993, there were thirty-nine African-Americans in Congress, including Eleanor Holmes Norton, the nonvoting delegate from Washington, D.C. With the exception of Senator Carol Moseley Braun (D.-Ill.), the other thirty-eight were representatives, composing 9 percent of House membership.

Occupation and wealth   Members of Congress are not only older and more likely to be white and male than the general population, but there are also disproportionately higher numbers of lawyers and businesspeople in Congress than among the general citizenry. In 1992, 46 percent of the members of Congress were lawyers and 36 percent were bankers or businesspersons.

The Ethics in Government Act of 1978 requires members to disclose (within broad categories) their investments and sources of unearned income, such as stock dividends. Although it is impossible to know exactly how wealthy our legislators are, we do know that approximately 10 percent are millionaires. Most members invest in stocks or bonds, and 63 percent of representatives and 75 senators have real estate investments besides their personal residences or vacation homes. Although a few members have not amassed great savings, most have well surpassed the wealth of working-class and middle-class Americans.

The typical member   The typical member of Congress is roughly fifty years of age, Protestant, white, male, a lawyer, and an investor in real estate and stocks. Less affluent people are rarely found in Congress, and women and blacks have only token representation. That these groups often feel unrepresented and left out of congressional decision making is not surprising. After all, the vast preponderance of the verbiage in Congress is by affluent white males.

Activities

How does the typical member of Congress spend his or her time? The image of long hours spent in debate on the floor of Congress is inaccurate. Instead, senators

Few women and few blacks are in Congress.

Nearly half the members of Congress are lawyers.

Most legislators have accumulated substantial wealth.

The typical member is a middle-aged, white, male, affluent lawyer.

and representatives have harried schedules involving committee work and constituent service in addition to floor action. The typical member reaches the office quite early in the morning to review the mail and do legislative homework before committee meetings begin, usually around 10 A.M. Although members have staffs who open the mail and respond to many constituent requests, each legislator prepares the daily schedule, involving some difficult and conflicting decisions. Should he or she speak before the Rotary Club back in the district at its annual "Hurrah for Capitalism!" luncheon in two months, or will Congress still be in session (possibly holding an important vote), or should that time be spent with an often-neglected family?

Most members spend little time debating issues on the floor.

Legislative homework   A member may also spend morning time gathering information on bills, especially those under consideration in the committees to which he or she is assigned. In addition, a member is likely to find lobbyists waiting to talk with him or her on these same bills. Although the lobbyists are not likely to change his or her vote on pending legislation, they gladly provide members with information that they believe necessary to do the job.

Considerable work on writing and evaluating bills is done prior to formal committee meetings.

Committee meetings   At 10 A.M., the member likely attends a committee meeting in which several proposals to amend a bill originating in the executive branch may be discussed and voted on. Most committee meetings adjourn just before noon, when the House usually convenes. While the House is in session, the few members actually in attendance will not usually pay much attention to the debate, because the real work of Congress is done in committees. Instead, the typical member probably converses with lobbyists in the lobby next to the floor (whence the word *lobbyist* was derived), speaks with constituents visiting Washington, meet with office staff, or listens to a party leader attempting to persuade him or her to side with the leadership on an upcoming vote.

Most serious work in Congress occurs in committee.

Floor appearances   When the bells in the House office buildings ring, signifying a floor vote, the typical member joins fellow legislators, who temporarily leave their other duties and appear in the chamber. Previously briefed by staff on the nature of the proposed legislation, the member will not cast his or her vote capriciously. Thus, the member has made optimum use of his or her time, not "wasted" it on the floor.

Constituent service   After the House adjourns for the day, the member is likely to return to the office to catch up with work. He or she may contact supporters in the district to determine whether rumors of a tough primary election challenge are true. The member may return a call from a financial backer in the district who is upset over the member's recent voting record and must be assuaged. Then there are the ever-present groups of tourists visiting Washington who want to be assured that "their" representative in Washington is working for them. Before leaving the office, the representative may attempt to intercede with officials on behalf of a constituent. This might mean several calls to the Department of Veterans'

Members of Congress and their staff devote major efforts to helping individual constituents deal with the federal bureaucracy.

Affairs, for example, to remedy the inexplicable termination of disability payments due a constituent who lost his foot in Vietnam.

Public appearances   Quite often, the typical member's day is still not finished. The member's schedule may reveal he or she has committed to speak briefly at a banquet convention of the National Association of Beet Growers, because there are important beet farmers in his district. He is subjected to a meal of questionable chicken (served, of course, with beets), after which he delivers an impassioned plea for legislation proclaiming the beet our national vegetable. When the member returns home after the speech, he or she probably reads memos prepared by his or her staff on the merits of amendments to legislation coming up for a vote the following day.

> Campaigning, in the form of speaking before interested groups, never stops.

To be done competently, the job of the representative requires enormous amounts of energy and work. The representative is further pressed when the demands of the job in Washington are supplemented by almost-weekly travel back to the district to attend town meetings or for similar occasions. Because so many legislators are independently wealthy and have professional abilities that are attractive to private employers, perhaps it is surprising that more of them do not quit their often-frustrating jobs. Instead, most members leave Congress either by involuntary retirement by the voters or after reaching their sixties, seventies, or eighties.

Personal staff and activities   The increasing complexity of the issues facing Congress and the increasing demands on members' time have necessitated substantial growth in personal staffs. In 1900, there were fewer than fifty full-time personal staff assistants in Congress, and they were all in the Senate. In 1947, the House and the Senate employed slightly over 2,000 as personal staff assistants. Today, nearly 11,000 people act as personal staff for members of Congress. These increases in personal staff enable members of Congress to maintain closer ties with their constituents and to research complex issues more thoroughly.

> The roles of personal staff include researching pending legislation and keeping legislators abreast of current developments.

Personal staff serve a variety of roles. Staff members organize and coordinate the legislator's offices in Washington and back in the home district. They engage in constituency service, enabling the legislator to assist the "folks back home" in a personal and direct fashion. Staffers research pending legislation, analyze important issues, and keep legislators abreast of current developments. They meet with lobbyists and transmit their concerns to the legislator. Staffers also handle public relations for the legislator, making sure that positive news concerning him or her is carried by district media outlets.

THE LEADERS OF CONGRESS

Each house has its own leaders and its own leadership system. The power of the leadership in the House in relation to rank-and-file members is greater than the power of the leadership in the Senate in relation to rank-and-file senators. In both houses, the leadership may be conveniently defined as elected party leaders and committee chairpersons. Table 2.3 lists elected party leaders in both houses.

TABLE 2.3   Leaders of Congress, 103rd Congress (1993–94)

Democrats	*Republicans*
Senate	
	President* Daniel Quayle
President pro tempore* Robert Byrd, W.Va.	
Majority Leader George Mitchell, Me.	Minority Leader Robert Dole, Kan.
Majority Whip Alan Cranston, Calif.	Minority Whip Alan Simpson, Wyo.
House	
Speaker Thomas Foley, Wash.	
Majority Leader Richard Gephardt, Mo.	Minority Leader Robert Michel, Ill.
Majority Whip David Bonior, Mich.	Minority Whip Newt Gingrich, Ga.

*Largely symbolic; there is very little power in these offices.

Leaders of the House

Speaker of the House The Speaker of the House is elected by House members in a straight party vote, the only vote that determines the party identification of members for organizational purposes. Each party caucus (the assembly of all members of the party in the respective houses of Congress) nominates one of its members for the speakership, with the majority party of course able to elect its nominee. Between 1890 and 1910, the Speaker was immensely powerful, controlling appointments to committees as well as chairing the powerful Rules Committee. Democrats and dissident Republicans revolted against this concentration of power in the hands of Thomas B. Reed and Joseph G. ("Uncle Joe") Cannon and succeeded in removing many formal powers from the Speaker. Control of the House shifted from the Speaker to committee chairpersons, who reached their positions through operation of the seniority rule. According to the seniority rule, the member of the majority party with the longest service on each committee becomes its head and gains broad powers of control over the actions of the committee. From 1910 until the 1970s, power in the House of Representatives was decentralized to committee chairpersons.

At the turn of the century, the Speaker ruled the House. The 1910 revolt against Speaker Cannon shifted power to committee chairpersons.

The Speaker did retain some powers: presiding over sessions and assigning bills to committee.

During this period of weakened speakership, the Speaker, whose office is provided for in the Constitution ("The House of Representatives shall choose their Speaker and other Officers," Article I, Section 2), nonetheless remained an important officer. He presided over the House, recognized or ignored members wishing to speak, appointed members of special or select committees, and assigned bills to committees. This last power sometimes enables a Speaker who favors a bill to send it to a committee also likely to favor it rather than to one likely to kill the bill. The content of some bills is sufficiently broad, enabling the Speaker to choose between at least two committees.

The Speaker has great influence on the Democratic Steering and Policy Committee.

The Speaker nominates the members of his party who serve on the powerful Rules Committee.

By the mid-1970s, House Democrats came to believe that a strong, more centralized leadership would allow Congress to deal more effectively with the president. They created the Democratic Steering and Policy Committee, chaired by the Speaker, and assigned it the responsibility of making committee assignments for Democrats. (These appointments had formerly been made by the Democratic members of the Ways and Means Committee.) The Speaker not only chairs the Steering and Policy Committee but also directly appoints eight of its thirty-one members.

The Speaker was also given the right to nominate all of his party's members, including the chair, of the powerful Rules Committee, which greatly influences the flow of legislation in the House. In addition, the Speaker's power was enhanced by the expansion of the Democratic whip system, a useful tool in the Speaker's efforts to effect legislation. Finally, the new budget process (discussed at the end of this chapter) gives the Speaker an opportunity to coordinate and oversee the behavior of House committees. By granting the Speaker these new powers with the Steering and Policy Committee, the Rules Committee, the whip system, and the budget process, the Democrats strengthened his leadership role.

The Speaker is elected to office by a secret ballot of the majority caucus, which has been Democratic since 1955. Tom Foley assumed the speakership in 1989 following the resignation of Jim Wright (D.-Tex.). Wright had assumed the office in 1987 upon the retirement of Tip O'Neill (D.-Mass.). This was a continuation of a tradition in which the majority leader succeeds to the speakership.

The majority leader coordinates party strategy and tactics with the Speaker; normally, the majority leader succeeds the retiring Speaker.

House majority leader   The majority party also selects, in caucus, a House majority leader, who functions as a key party strategist. Together with the Speaker and the members of the Rules Committee, he schedules debate and negotiates with both the opposition party and committee chairpersons on procedures. Since World War II, the majority leader traditionally ascended to the speakership upon the retirement of the Speaker. Thomas Foley (D.-Wash.) became majority leader in 1987 and was chosen Speaker in 1989.

House majority whip   The third leader of the majority party in the House of Representatives is the majority whip, a word derived from the British "whipper-in" (the chap in the fox hunt who attempts to restrain the hounds from straying). In the House, the whip rounds up members for votes. He also conducts "straw ballots" (polls to determine voting intentions) for the leadership. These straw ballots affect both bargaining efforts and the timing of legislation on the floor, so that only bills favored by the leadership will be enacted. The Speaker in conjunction with the majority leader nominates the whip, a chief deputy whip, and three other deputy whips, who must then be approved by the entire caucus. The leadership also appoints regional whips, each of whom has responsibility for a state or group of states. David Bonier (D.-Mich.) became majority whip in 1991 after the incumbent whip, William Gray III (D.-Pa.), resigned to become head of the United Negro College Fund.

The whips gather information for the leadership on how party members intend to vote.

House minority leader The organization of the leadership in the minority party closely parallels that of the majority party, except the minority party lacks a Speaker. For instance, the 1993 Republicans have a minority leader who would become Speaker should the Republicans gain control of the House (an event not experienced since 1954). When the president and the minority leader in the House are members of the same party, the latter is expected to support the president's program and work toward its enactment. In 1981, the Republicans elevated their whip, Robert H. Michel (R.-Ill.), to replace retiring minority leader John Rhodes (R.-Ariz.).

The minority leader heads the minority party in the House.

House minority whip The duties of the minority whip are the same as those of the majority whip. In today's Democratic-controlled House, he is responsible for finding out how Republicans in the House plan to vote, information he relays to the minority leader. The minority whip is aided by regional and assistant whips. The assistant whips report to the regional whips, who in turn advise the leadership of the expected voting patterns of minority-party members.

The minority whip heads the whip organization of the minority party.

Leaders of the Senate

President of the Senate The Senate's structure of leadership parallels the House's, with important differences. The vice-president holds the constitutionally delegated office of president of the Senate, with authority to preside over debate, an impotent prerogative. The Senate's rules developed in such a way that the presiding officer is denied even the power to structure debate. The position is so meaningless that the vice-president usually yields the gavel to one of the freshman senators, who are expected to devote a certain amount of their time to presiding. The only important function fulfilled by the president of the Senate is to vote in the event of a tie (a rare occurrence), to which the vice-president is quickly alerted by the leadership.

The president of the Senate has little involvement in Senate activities, except to cast tie-breaking votes.

President pro tempore The president pro tempore of the Senate, a constitutionally provided position, has little real power because the office is largely ceremonial in nature. Its weakness stands in stark contrast to the very powerful position of Speaker of the House. Elected by the majority party, the president pro tempore is traditionally the majority party member with the greatest seniority.

President pro tempore of the Senate is an honorary position.

Senate majority leader   The real power of the leadership in the Senate is found in the offices of the majority and minority leaders. The majority leader schedules floor action on pending legislation. If the Senate is controlled by the president's party, as it was between 1981 and 1986 when Howard Baker (R.-Tenn.) and then Robert Dole (R.-Kan.) were majority leaders, the majority leader will schedule floor action so issues come up at the most propitious time for the administration. If the Senate is controlled by the opposition party, as it has been since 1987, when first Robert Byrd (D.-W. Va.) and then George Mitchell (D.-Me.) held that position, the majority leader's decisions on scheduling will often depend on negotiations with the White House and the minority leader.

> The majority leader schedules bills for consideration on the floor. The office legitimates efforts by the majority leader to persuade other senators in his party to vote as he suggests.

The majority leader's other powers arise from the responsibility for making committee assignments, coordinating party policy positions, and representing the Senate majority in the media. How a majority leader uses these positions is a matter of personal choice and style. Just as with the presidency, although the office provides significant resources to an individual who wants to use them to exert strong leadership, only the occupant of the office can determine how best to use its opportunities for persuasion. In 1989, the Democrats selected George Mitchell (D.-Me.) majority leader.

Senate minority leader   The Senate minority leader presents his party's program to the Senate. If the Senate minority leader is from the president's party, as he has been since 1987 with Robert Dole (R.-Kan.) holding the position, the minority leader works closely with the White House pushing for the administration's legislative program. If the minority leader is from the opposition party, as he was from 1981 to 1986 with Robert Byrd (D.-W. Va.), he criticizes and presents his party's alternative to the president's program, attempting to influence specific legislative proposals (especially on issues where the majority party is divided). Such a role, similar to that of the "loyal opposition" in Great Britain, is required of the "out" party when the other party controls the executive.

> The Senate minority leader leads the "loyal opposition."

Senate whips   The whip organization of both parties in the Senate parallels the House's, although the job is easier in the Senate because there are fewer members to survey. In 1993, the Senate majority whip has to know the voting positions of only 57 Democratic senators, in contrast to the Democratic votes his counterpart in the House has to ascertain.

Senate whip positions seem to offer entry to higher positions of Senate leadership. Byrd had been whip at the time he was elected Democratic leader in 1977. Ted Stevens (D.-Alaska), the Republican whip in the previous Congress, lost the race to become Republican leader in 1985 to Dole by only three votes. In 1992, the whips were Alan K. Simpson (R.-Wyo.) and Alan Cranston (D.-Calif.). Part of the rationale for their elections was to provide geographical balance with their respective majority and minority leaders. Considerations of ideological and geographical balance are common in choosing whips.

> Whips often provide geographical and ideological balance with other party leaders.

The Senate and the House: Leadership Compared

Senate leadership depends on strong interpersonal skills. House leadership comes more with positions.

In the smaller and less formal Senate, leadership is less a matter of holding a position (the Speaker of the House is almost certain to be very powerful) and more a matter of strength of personality and individual will. Senators can be prima donnas successfully led only by accomplished students of human nature who tailor their approaches to the whims, needs, and pathologies of individual senators. The majority and minority leaders are viewed by their colleagues as senators who have special coordinating and spokesperson roles. In contrast, colleagues view the Speaker as much more than just another representative with some special responsibilities. Symbolic of the Speaker's high position is the custom of his not voting except to break a tie. Party leaders in the Senate, in contrast, vote along with all other senators.

Trends in the House have been toward increasing power in the speakership. Trends in the Senate have been toward increasing the roles of individual members.

As stated in the discussion of the speakership, 1970s House reforms both increased the power of the Speaker and decreased the power of committee chairpersons. The net effect centralized power in the elected leadership and expanded the roles of individual members. Reforms in the Senate followed one of these trends but not the other: The roles of individual members were expanded at the expense of committee chairpersons, but the centralized leadership was not significantly strengthened. The Senate was formerly dominated by a small group of committee chairpersons; it is now a much more egalitarian institution.

The party caucus is the assembly of all members of the party in the respective houses of Congress. Membership is determined by party self-identification, with members very rarely excluded even when their activities have been supportive of the other party.

In meetings of the caucus (or the Republican term, conference), party policy is debated and positions taken, even though members are not bound to vote the party's positions. This inability to bind caucus members to the party line led former Speaker Sam Rayburn to characterize caucus meetings as "a waste of time."

Caucuses elect party leaders and committee chairpersons, though most of the work of Congress is done in committee.

This unflattering characterization may still hold for the majority of caucus meetings. The exceptions are the organization meetings conducted at the start of each two-year Congress. These meetings are clearly important in both the Senate and the House. The majority party, meeting in caucus, determines committee chairpersons and committee structures by which each chamber organizes its work. In approaching the legislature's task, both chambers make the committee the chief workplace.

Committee Chairpersons as Leaders

Congress and congressional leadership cannot be understood without referring to the chairpersons of the twenty-two standing committees of the House and the fifteen standing committees of the Senate. A strong committee system is the only way Congress can handle the more than 10,000 bills introduced each two-year period. Committee decisions to report out some bills (a committee vote permitting the bill's passage on to the entire House or Senate for consideration) and kill others are generally respected by the chamber as a whole.

Powers of chairpersons The committee chairpersons usually have great influence in their respective committees. In addition to presiding over meetings, they (more than any other committee members) influence the scheduling of meetings, determine which bills are considered and when, and appoint and direct the committee's staff. Most chairpersons have a broad knowledge of the subject area within the jurisdiction of their committees, an expertise usually respected by committee members.

Chairpersons preside over meetings and strongly influence how committees deal with bills.

Congressional reformers in the 1960s felt some committee chairpersons were misusing their powers by failing to respond to their committees' wills. For instance, some chairpersons refused to hold hearings on bills they viewed negatively or stacked the hearings so only one side's position was presented. Committees passed committee "bills of rights" in the 1960s, guaranteeing minimal standards of procedural fairness. Chairpersons must now regularly schedule meetings, hold hearings on bills when requested by a majority of the committee, and share with committee members the hiring and utilization of committee staff.

Committee "bills of rights" help ensure that committee chairpersons respond to the wills of their committees.

Characteristics of chairpersons In the 102nd Congress, all chairpersons in both the House and the Senate were Democrats. Although no written rule requires this, long tradition dictates the majority party in each chamber controls all the committee chairs. Thus, the Democratic capture of the Senate in 1986 unseated all the Republican chairpersons, who secured the positions in 1980. Except for the exclusion of Republicans from chairs, the committee chairpersons (listed in Tables 2.4 and 2.5) do not stand out as greatly distinct from the general membership of Congress. This is quite a change from similar data for the 1960s and 1970s, when chairpersons were substantially older than their colleagues and much more likely to be Southerners. Chairpersons are still older (for the 102nd Congress, an average of sixty-two years of age for Senate chairpersons, compared to sixty-one for the House), although the differences, especially in the Senate, are not large. These changes reflect the increasingly competitive nature of statewide elections in the South and the increase in older members choosing retirement. Tables 2.4 and 2.5 also indicate the experience of chairpersons, listing the year each was first elected to the House or Senate. Seniority dictates that chairpersons be experienced members of Congress.

The majority party in each chamber elects committee chairpersons.

Chairpersons are somewhat older than rank-and-file members.

Selection of chairpersons by seniority The nature of future committee chairpersons can be accurately predicted because of the means by which they are usually selected. One becomes a chairperson through *seniority,* an important concept for understanding Congress. The majority party member who has served continuously on a given committee longer than any of his or her colleagues can expect to become the chairperson. This practice, not found in any written rule of Congress, is followed by both parties. Thus, any member knows that remaining on the same committee year after year and remaining in office long enough will probably result in

The member of the majority party who has been on a particular committee the longest normally becomes its chairperson.

becoming committee chairperson when his or her party controls the house of Congress. By the same token, a competitive district, which sometimes elects Democrats and sometimes Republicans, will never have its representative become a committee chairperson.

Critics have argued that the seniority system promotes members not on the basis of their abilities and performances but solely on the basis of time on the committee.

Criticisms of seniority system   Critics have long argued that the seniority system sometimes results in chairpersons who are unresponsive to committee majorities and almost incompetent in the handling of committee business. The critics point to examples of the chairpersons who have been alcoholics, senile, or just inept. Defenders of the seniority system point to the many talented chairpersons and argue that any other means of selecting chairpersons would involve a large expenditure of valuable time in rancorous deal making and other politicking, upsetting the harmony of Congress. The rationale is that the enormity of the task facing Congress requires that conflict among members be minimized, even at the cost of sometimes having feeble or reactionary chairpersons.

In response to critics, Congress now submits each nominee for committee chairperson or ranking minority member to a secret ballot vote of the nominee's party caucus in the House or Senate.

Chairpersons now know that they must be responsive and fair to the members of their committees or face possible removal from their leadership positions.

Modification of seniority system   Partly as a response to the criticisms of reformers, the seniority system has been modified. Although it is still assumed the most senior majority-party member on a committee will become its chairperson and the most senior minority-party member on a committee will become its ranking minority member, the seniority system no longer operates automatically. Every nominee now must undergo a vote of the full party caucus by secret ballot. In 1975, the House Democratic caucus selected new chairpersons of the Agriculture, Armed Services, and Banking committees over the opposition of incumbent chairpersons. In 1985, the House Democratic caucus ousted the incumbent chairperson of the Armed Services Committee. And, in 1991, the House Democratic caucus replaced the incumbent chairpersons of the Public Works and House Administration Committees. In each case, Democratic leaders were quick to state the actions were exceptions to the unwritten rule that seniority is an important criterion when selecting committee chairs.

Although all of the preceding examples and the denials of chairs to most senior members came from the House Democratic caucus, House Republicans as well as Senate Democrats and Republicans all vote in caucus for their head committee positions.

Leadership by Tradition

Seniority   The unwritten rule of seniority is part of the informal structure, a series of customs followed by all but a few members. Seniority is more than just the way committee leaders are chosen. It includes the notion that new members especially should respect the institution and its ways of doing things. In rhetorical exchanges they should avoid insulting language, instead referring to each other in glowing terms, such as "The distinguished senior senator from New York who has often enlightened us. . . . " This broadened concept of seniority also includes notions of deference to more senior members and an appropriate term of apprenticeship

TABLE 2.4 House Committees, 103rd Congress (1993–1994)

	Committee		Chairperson	State	First Elected
Exclusive	Appropriations	A member of any one of these is not permitted to serve on any other committee.	William Natcher	Kentucky	1953
	Rules		John Moakley	Massachusetts	1972
	Ways and Means		Dan Rostenkowski	Illinois	1958
Major	Agriculture	A member of any one of these is permitted one other membership, which must be on a nonmajor committee.	E. de la Garza	Texas	1964
	Armed Services		Ronald V. Dellums	California	1970
	Banking, Finance, and Urban Affairs		Henry Gonzalez	Texas	1961
	Education and Labor		William Ford	Michigan	1965
	Foreign Affairs		Lee Hamilton	Indiana	1965
	Energy and Commerce		John Dingell	Michigan	1955
	Judiciary		Jack Brooks	Texas	1952
	Public Works and Transportation		Norman Mineta	California	1975
Nonmajor	Budget	Members may serve on two (or occasionally three) of these.	Martin Olav Sabo	Minnesota	1978
	District of Columbia		Fortney "Pete" Stark	California	1972
	Government Operations		John Conyers	Michigan	1964
	House Administration		Charles Rose	North Carolina	1973
	Interior and Insular Affairs				
	Merchant Marine and Fisheries		George Miller	California	1975
	Post Office and Civil Service		Gerry Studds	Massachusetts	1966
	Science and Technology		William Clay	Missouri	1969
	Small Business		George Brown	California	1963
	Standards of Official Conduct		John LaFalce	New York	1974
	Veterans Affairs		Louis Stokes	Ohio	1969
			G. V. (Sonny) Montgomery	Mississippi	1966

TABLE 2.5 Senate Committees, 103rd Congress (1993–1994)

		Chairperson	State	First Elected
Major	Agriculture, Nutrition, and Forestry	Patrick Leahy	Vermont	1974
	Appropriations	Senators may serve on two of these committees.		
	Armed Services	Robert C. Byrd	West Virginia	1958
	Banking, Housing, and Urban Affairs	Sam Nunn	Georgia	1972
		Donald Riegel	Michigan	1976
	Budget	Jim Sasser	Tennessee	1976
	Commerce, Science, and Transportation	Ernest Hollins	South Carolina	1966
	Energy and Natural Resources	J. Bennett Johnston	Louisiana	1972
	Environment and Public Works	Max Baucus	Montana	1978
	Finance	Daniel Moynihan	New York	1976
	Foreign Relations	Claiborne Pell	Rhode Island	1960
	Governmental Affairs	John Glenn	Ohio	1974
	Judiciary	Joe Biden	Delaware	1972
	Labor and Human Resources	Edward M. Kennedy	Massachusetts	1962
Nonmajor	Rules and Administration	Senators may serve on one of these committees.		
	Veterans Affairs	Wendell H. Ford	Kentucky	1974
		John D. Rockefeller	West Virginia	1984

Seniority also means respecting congressional traditions and deferring to more experienced legislators.

before assuming public leadership positions on issues. These seniority norms have weakened a great deal in the Senate in recent years, as Senate membership turned over rapidly and brash new senators are not reluctant to speak out. The idea that new senators should be seen but not heard is no longer widely shared in the Senate. In the House, although the seniority tradition has weakened somewhat, a strong degree of deference to more experienced representatives is still the norm.

For low-level federal appointments the president must get the approval of the senators or senator of the president's party from the state to which the appointment is made.

Senatorial courtesy One unwritten rule maintaining full force in the Senate is the practice of senatorial courtesy. The Senate will refuse confirming a presidential nomination for lower offices such as district court judge or United States marshal unless the nomination is first cleared with the senators of the president's own party from the state to which the appointment is made. Thus, when President Ford nominated William Poff of Virginia to a district judgeship in 1976, Ford sought the approval of the Republican senators from Virginia; and when Senator William Scott (R.-Va.) informed the Judiciary Committee that he disapproved of the nomination, the committee failed to recommend Poff to the entire Senate, thereby killing the nomination. This was done as a matter of courtesy to the objecting senator. This practice of senatorial courtesy began in 1789 with the rejection of the nomination of Georgia's Benjamin Fishbourne for the post of naval officer of Savannah's port. Georgia's senators persuaded the Senate to reject the nomination made by Washington. Since that time, presidents, mindful of the power of senatorial courtesy, have sought the approval of the appropriate senators before making nominations. Senatorial courtesy, in effect, gives any senator of the president's own party veto power over federal job vacancy appointments within his or her state. The practice does not extend, however, to Supreme Court appointments or to cabinet departments serving more than one state.

CONGRESSIONAL COMMITTEES

Woodrow Wilson wrote in 1885 that "Congress in session is Congress on public exhibition, whilst Congress in Committee rooms is Congress at work." Although somewhat overstated, Wilson's characterization is still largely valid for the U.S. national legislature.

House Committees

The previous section was about chairpersons, for they are indeed leaders of Congress. Although all chairpersons are powerful within their committees, not all committees are equally important. In the House of Representatives, three committees—Rules, Appropriations, and Ways and Means—stand out. These committees are considered so prestigious that membership on one of them precludes membership on any other standing House committee.

Rules, Appropriations, and Ways and Means are the most powerful House committees.

House Rules Committee The House Rules Committee is one of four nonsubstantive standing committees (a committee that does not consider the actual substance

Bills go from substantive committees to the Rules Committee. The nature of the "rule" given a bill by the Rules Committee influences how it may be amended as well as its ultimate passage or defeat.

of legislation) in the House. The Rules Committee decides which bills get to the floor for debate. When a substantive committee reports out a bill, it goes to the Rules Committee, which may kill the bill (recently an infrequent occurrence) or give it a "rule"—that is, set the time allowed for floor debate, the terms of the debate, and the degree to which the bill may be amended on the floor. It is the Rules Committee that consistently decides not to allow tax bills to be amended on the floor, a decision prohibiting recorded votes on tax loopholes.

The debate over the rule granted to the 1981 budget reconciliation bill illustrates the control the Speaker has gained over the Rules Committee and the critical importance of the rule assigned in the passage or defeat of bills. As part of the budget process in 1981, Congress voted instructions to fifteen House committees to make budget reductions. The resulting bill was the most comprehensive budget provision ever passed by Congress. The members of the Rules Committee were divided on what sort of rule would garner the most support for substantive changes in the bill on the floor. Speaker O'Neill finally persuaded the committee to adopt a modified closed rule that would permit separate votes on several amendments. Realizing they did not want to face individual votes on cutting popular programs such as Social Security and student loans, Reagan and House Republican strategists favored a rule that would accept or reject the entire budget cuts package in a single vote. Republicans challenged the rule adopted by the Rules Committee when the bill reached the floor of the House. By a 217 to 212 vote, with twenty-nine conservative Democrats voting with the Republicans, the committee-assigned rule was overturned and replaced with a "closed" rule that required an "up" or "down" vote on the entire package, with no amendments. If the Republicans had not won this procedural vote, the outcome of the 1981 budget battle could have been dramatically different, for some of the massive cuts in popular programs probably would have been scaled back. After winning the procedural vote, the Republicans had little difficulty winning acceptance of the president's entire package.

Rules given to bills by the Rules Committee can be challenged, although such occurrences are rare.

House Ways and Means Committee A second powerful House committee is the Ways and Means Committee, concerned with all revenue bills. All measures for tax law changes originate in this committee according to constitutional mandate (Article I, Section 7) stating "all bills for raising Revenue shall originate in the House of Representatives." Although the executive branch and the Senate Finance Committee are also heavily involved in tax legislation, and tax bills require full House and Senate approval just like other legislation, the Ways and Means Committee is the traditional key battleground on taxes. Because seemingly innocuous changes in obscure sections of the complex tax code can mean billions of dollars to individual industries and companies, lobbyists exert great energies to influence committee members. The extent of these efforts is seen in the case study at the end of this chapter.

Congressional action on all tax bills originates in the Ways and Means Committee.

House Appropriations Committee The third of the powerful House committees is Appropriations. Bills dealt with in substantive committees, passed by Congress, and signed by the president become laws; yet these laws do not actually appropriate funds. Funding is accomplished only when the budgetary process is completed (discussed fully later in this chapter). Each item in the budget, which is several thousand pages in length, is reviewed by a subcommittee of Appropriations and then by the committee as a whole. The committee members believe strongly that they must preserve the watchdog function of Congress, guarding the treasury against bureaucratic waste. The committee calls many witnesses, especially executive-branch officials, who are asked to justify items in the president's budget or the conspicuous absence of items. During the conservative Reagan administration, executive officials were often asked to explain why the president's proposed budget did not include sums sufficient to administer adequately programs Congress mandated. Scrutinizing the budget constitutes almost all of the activity of the Appropriations Committee. It is such an enormous task that committee members have the reputation of being among the hardest-working members of Congress.

The Appropriations Committee reviews the annual federal budget in detail. Subcommittees of the Appropriations Committee hold hundreds of hearings, at which administration officials are asked to justify the president's proposed budget.

Other House committees Rules, Ways and Means, and Appropriations are exclusive committees; members of any one of these committees are, with rare exceptions, not permitted to serve on any other committee. The House also has eight major committees, which limit membership on additional committees but does not exclude it (Table 2.4). The eleven remaining committees are nonmajor, and members usually serve on two of these. All major and nonmajor committees are substantive, with the exceptions of Budget and Standards of Official Conduct. This last committee proposes standards of ethics for passage by the entire House and occasionally conducts inquiries into alleged breaches of those standards.

Members may serve on only one of the eight "major" committees.

Usually the competition for assignments to exclusive and major committees is stiff. One recent exception is assignment to the Judiciary Committee. Many members of Congress seek to avoid service on this committee, which traditionally handles highly controversial matters, such as federal criminal code reform, gun control, and abortion.

Much of the work assigned to House committees is decentralized further to the 140 subcommittees. During the 102nd Congress, every committee except Standards of Official Conduct had at least two subcommittees; Appropriations topped the list with thirteen. The subcommittees act as miniatures of the larger committees, complete with powers of investigation. However, subcommittees do not report their actions to the Speaker or the Rules Committee, but back to the full committee for further action. The many subcommittees mean large numbers of subcommittee chairpersons who hold hearings and deal with bills. Because committee chairpersons usually have little control over their subcommittees, subcommittee proliferation has further weakened the power of committee chairpersons.

The proliferation of subcommittees in the 1970s further weakened the power of committee chairpersons.

Senate Committees

The Senate's smaller size results in fewer committees and subcommittees, but senators will serve on two major committees and up to eight subcommittees (Table 2.5). These limits were established in 1977 when the Senate also set the maximum number of subcommittees a senator could chair at three. The reforms

Senators serve on two major committees and up to eight subcommittees. Limitations on the number of committee assignments and chairs each senator can hold ensure that even the most junior senators get some choice assignments.

opened up some choice committee seats and subcommittee chairs to junior senators—seats previously held by senior senators serving on more than three committees or holding more than three subcommittee chairs. As in the House, power has been decentralized in the Senate.

There are no committees in the Senate that are exactly comparable to the Rules, Ways and Means, and Appropriations Committees of the House. The Senate Rules and Administration Committee is a minor committee; in the Senate, bills are not given a "rule" because they come directly from substantive committees to the floor, where debate and amendments are always in order. The Senate counterpart to the House Ways and Means Committee is the Finance Committee, an important committee but one that lacks the constitutional authority to originate tax bills. The Senate Appropriations Committee is ostensibly the counterpart of the House Appropriations Committee, but the Senate committee lacks the size needed to scrutinize carefully the entire budget. The Senate Appropriations Committee therefore limits its activities primarily to reviewing the actions of the House and to attempting reinstatement of funds for a few pet projects or the removal of funds from less favored ones.

Staff does considerable work for senators at subcommittee meetings.

Subcommittees proliferated in the Senate in the 1970s, as they had in the House. During the 102nd Congress, the fifteen Senate standing committees had more than 100 subcommittees, a particularly large total when one recalls there are only 100 senators. With senators serving on up to eight subcommittees, subcommittee meetings frequently have only one senator in attendance. The absent senators generally send staff members who report back on subcommittee activities.

Committees are more important in the House, because the smaller Senate does more of its work on the floor.

The smaller Senate does not defer to committee decisions as much as the House. Accordingly, although still essential to the legislative process, the committee system is somewhat less important in the Senate. Most bills die in committee, where fundamental modifications of administration bills also occur. In the Senate, as in the House, Congress in committee is Congress at work.

Appointments to Committees

Committee seats are divided between the parties in proportion to their overall strengths in each chamber.

Size of committees The size of committees varies by chamber (House committees are larger) and by workload (in 1992, House Appropriations, with fifty-nine members, was the largest). The division of committee seats between Democrats and Republicans in the Senate is made on the basis of party proportions. For example, the 102nd Congress had ten Democrats and eight Republicans on the Foreign Relations Committee, proportions reflecting the Democrats' fifty-seven to forty-three advantage in the entire Senate. The same procedure applies in the House, except that the majority party controls two-thirds of the seats on the Rules Committee. Thus, the Democrats in the 102nd Congress had 61 percent of the seats in the House, and nine of the thirteen members of Rules were Democrats.

House appointments Committee assignments in the House are decided by each party's Committee on Committees. For the Democrats, the Steering and Policy Committee (composed of the Speaker; ten other Democrats with official positions,

Each party has a commit-
tee that determines which
party members will serve
on which committees.

such as chairs of important committees; eight members appointed by the Speaker; and twelve members elected by regional caucuses) acts as the Committee on Committees at the start of each Congress. The composition of the committee ensures that appointments will be responsive to the desires of the Democratic leadership. For the Republicans, the minority leader appoints the members of the Committee on Committees (one from each state that has at least one Republican representative), which functions to ratify appointments made by its own executive committee. In the executive committee, members of large states dominate because each is allotted the number of votes equal to the number of Republican representatives from his or her state. For example, in 1991 the executive committee member from California had nineteen votes because nineteen of California's forty-five representatives at that time were Republicans.

Seniority, of course, remains the key to assignment; freshman members are rarely appointed to Rules, Ways and Means, or Appropriations. However, once assigned to a committee, a junior representative will not be dropped if a senior representative seeks the seat. The only time members are bumped from committees is when their party loses seats in an election, with the result that the party also loses proportional seats on each committee. Then straight seniority operates, and the least-senior members are automatically removed. Even when a party loses many seats, members are rarely bumped from their committees since it is likely that one or two other committee members are not returning, either voluntarily or through election defeat.

More senior members get
the more prestigious com-
mittee assignments.
Members, building up ex-
pertise, often remain on
the same committees for
many years.

Seniority aside, other considerations come into play in making committee assignments, particularly when assigning freshman members. The Committee on Committees takes into account party standing (party dissidents do not do well in committee assignments), geographical balance on committees with vacancies, and interests of the applicant's district. When Shirley Chisholm, a black Democrat from Brooklyn, was initially elected to Congress, she found herself appointed to the Agriculture Committee—an assignment that helped the geographical balance of the committee but did little to relate to the interests of her constituents. In a rare instance of willingness to reverse its decision, the Democratic Committee on Committees transferred Chisholm to the Veterans' Affairs Committee after she agreed to support the leadership's choice for majority leader.

Senate appointments The Democrats use their Senate Steering Committee, chaired by Daniel Inouye (D.-Haw.), to decide which Democrats will serve on which committees. The Republicans set up their Committee on Committees, composed of about fifteen members who get on the committee either by holding high party office or by appointment by the Republican conference chairperson. In 1991, the Republican conference renamed Trent Lott (R.-Miss.) conference chair. Among his first important actions was appointment of Republican senators to their Committee on Committees. Both parties have adopted rules ensuring each senator a prestigious committee appointment before any senator receives a second-choice appointment. This tradition began in the 1950s under Democratic Majority Leader Lyndon Johnson. Although the Senate does not have committees as exclusive as

House Rules, Ways and Means, and Appropriations, there is a recognized hierarchy from the prestigious Foreign Relations Committee to the minor committees such as Rules and Administration or Veterans' Affairs.

Senate committee appointments follow the same general norms as House appointments, with every senator assured at least one choice committee appointment.

The Foreign Relations Committee is a particularly choice appointment, in part because of the Senate's special responsibilities in ratifying treaties and in part because of the overwhelming importance of foreign affairs in the nuclear age. The 1980s saw debates in the Foreign Relations Committee focusing attention on Central American strife and on disarmament agreement proposals with the Soviet Union.

Other Committee Features

Almost all committee and subcommittee meetings are open to the public.

Open committee meetings Reformers in Congress long sought to open committee meetings to the public. By the mid-1970s, "sunshine" resolutions passed in both chambers, so that now only a few meetings (generally dealing with national security) are closed to the public. Even markup sessions, when bill modifications are discussed prior to subcommittee or committee voting, are open. The reformers in the 1960s and early 1970s expected the press, public interest watchdog groups, and interested citizens would attend open meetings. Instead, many meetings are attended primarily (if not entirely) by special interest lobbyists concerned with the bills under consideration. Nevertheless, Congress in committee is visible to anyone who wants to observe. On any day Congress is in session, a visitor to Washington can watch a committee or subcommittee at work—one of the capital city's free and often entertaining shows.

Joint committees have specialized objectives ranging from studying a particular problem to administering the Library of Congress.

Joint committees Joint committees, composed of members from both chambers, perform studies and routine oversight activities. The 102nd Congress had four joint committees. The Joint Economic Committee supervised economic studies; the Joint Taxation Committee functioned as the formal "home" for staff working for both chambers' tax-writing committees; the Joint Library Committee supervised the Library of Congress; and the Joint Printing Committee directed the Government Printing Office. Although these joint committees have long histories, other joint committees are organized to investigate a particular problem and exist only long enough to hold investigatory hearings and report their findings.

Select committees usually coordinate policy recommendations for groups (for example, the aged or Native Americans) over which no single standing committee has jurisdiction.

Special or select committees Special or select committees are usually temporary bodies formed to investigate a particular problem. For example, the Senate Select Committee on Presidential Campaign Activities, popularly known as the Watergate Committee, examined the campaign abuses of the Nixon administration. Some select committees, such as the Senate Select Small Business Committee, Senate Select Committee on Intelligence, and the House Select Committee on Narcotics Abuse and Control, have lasted for several years. Differing from standing committees, they lack the authority to handle bills directly and may only investigate and make recommendations to the standing committees.

Every committee has the power to subpoena witnesses for information gathering for legislative purposes.

Subpoena power All congressional committees have the right to subpoena witnesses for investigative purposes in preparing legislation. Reluctant witnesses may be granted varying levels and types of immunity from prosecution in the courts, thereby forcing testimony by removing the Fifth Amendment option—a respondent's refusal to answer questions on the grounds that such responses may tend to incriminate him or her. A witness who, granted immunity, still refuses to testify (as did Watergate burglar and conspirator G. Gordon Liddy in 1973 before the House Armed Services Committee) may be cited for contempt of Congress and immediately imprisoned.

Scores of staffers, both professional and clerical, are assigned to every committee.

Staff Although the 6,000 committee staffers are a smaller crew than the 11,000 personal staffers hired by individual senators and representatives, they are a strong and valuable resource. Divided into Republican and Democratic staffs on each committee, congressional committee staffers include secretaries as well as professionals such as doctors, scientists, and lawyers. They research, arrange hearings, draft bills, and keep committee members informed. The enormous demands on elected members mean staffers play a crucial role, enabling committees to perform their legislative tasks. Professional committee staff often serve for many years, providing the "institutional memory" of the committee on the laws over which the committee has jurisdiction.

This relatively short book on the nuts and bolts of American politics devotes an entire section to committees, and a large part of its section on congressional leaders concerns committee chairpersons. This is because the leaders of committees are leaders in Congress, for the key locus of power is the committee. This situation is even more obvious in the forthcoming descriptions of how a bill becomes a law and of the budgetary process.

HOW A BILL BECOMES A LAW

Bills can be blocked at several points on the route toward passage.

Of the more than 10,000 bills and joint resolutions introduced during a typical two-year session of Congress, roughly 7 percent are enacted into public law. To become a law, a bill must pass through the series of roadblocks shown in Figure 2.1, any one of which may kill it. It is indeed a hazardous route from introduction to final passage. Not every congressional pronouncement is a bill; congressional action also takes the form of simple, joint, or concurrent resolutions (Table 2.6). However, because the treatment of a resolution in each house is the same as that of a bill, this section will follow a bill's progress through Congress. The great majority of major legislation is introduced in the form of a bill.

Only a member can formally introduce a bill.

Most bills have similar versions introduced in both houses, and any member of either house can introduce a bill. Although most bills have their origin in the executive branch, only members of Congress may introduce a bill. The administration usually seeks powerful leaders on committees relevant to the substance of a bill to handle its introduction. Members of the executive branch cannot themselves introduce a bill, nor can they seek recognition even to speak on the floor.

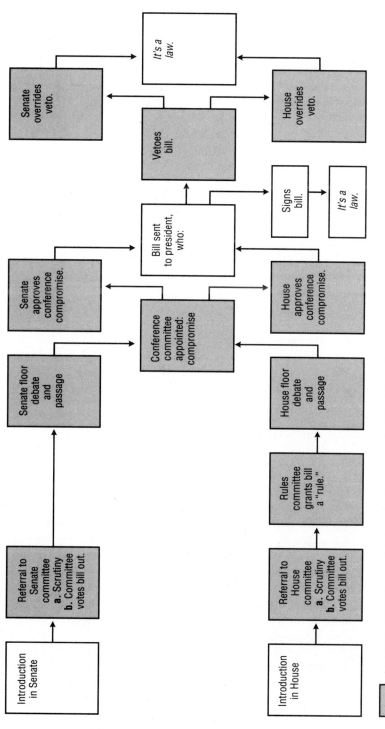

Legislative roadblocks: points in the legislative process at which a bill may be killed.

FIGURE 2.1 How a bill becomes a law

TABLE 2.6   Congressional Bills and Resolutions

Measure	Nature	Necessary for Passage	Force of Law?
Bill	Broad, general legislation such as the Superfund Act of 1980	Majority vote in both houses and the president's signature	Yes
Simple resolution	Changes in the rules of one chamber or expressions of sentiment, such as the determination of the daily meeting time in the Senate	Majority vote in one house	No
Concurrent resolution	Changes in the rules of Congress or expressions of sentiment, such as a proclamation of congratulations to an astronaut	Majority vote in both houses	No
Joint resolution	Limited, specific legislation, such as a special appropriation for flood victims	Majority vote in both houses and the president's signature	Yes
Joint resolution to amend the Constitution	Changes to the Constitution, such as the Twenty-second Amendment (limiting any president to two terms)	⅔ vote in both houses and ratification by ¾ of the states	Yes

Referral to Committee

Most bills die in committee.

Once a bill is introduced, it is assigned a number and referred to a committee, the place where most bills die. In the House, the bill is referred to a substantive committee by the Speaker; in the Senate, referral is by agreement between the majority and minority leaders. This right of referral is a source of some power, for the Speaker may kill a bill or greatly enhance its chances of passage by his choice of committee. As this chapter's case study will show, committees can claim jurisdiction over a bill, but the Speaker reserves the authority to refer bills to committee. However, in most instances the bill's subject matter gives the Speaker little leeway in referral.

Subcommittee scrutiny   After a committee receives a bill, it usually refers it to a subcommittee, which studies the bill and often holds open hearings on its provisions. The subcommittee (or the committee as a whole if the bill is not referred to a subcommittee) usually requests comment on the bill from executive branch

Subcommittees perform much of the detailed review of bills.

agencies the proposed legislation affects. The subcommittee then reports its recommendations back to the full committee, including proposed amendments to the bill. If the bill is substantially amended, the committee often discards the original, replacing it with a "clean bill" (complete with a new number) incorporating all the proposed changes.

If committees refuse to report out bills, those bills die. Committees are the graveyard of proposed legislation.

The committee then decides whether to report out the bill. Although a bill may be reported out unfavorably, or with no committee or subcommittee recommendation, most bills passing this stage have the support of a majority of the committee. The bill is reported out with amendments (without amendments if it is a "clean bill") and with a report detailing the committee's justifications for supporting the bill. A minority report stating the opposing committee members' reasoning usually accompanies the positive report. Of course, the chances are the committee will never report out the bill, because 90 percent of all bills are killed in committee.

Discharge petitions Disgruntled Congress members with pet bills bottled up in committees will try informally to influence the committee to report out the bill. There is a way of discharging a committee from its jurisdiction over a bill, but the method is rarely successful. In the House, a member may file a discharge petition if a committee fails to report out a bill within thirty days. Such a petition requires that its sponsors obtain 218 signatures—a formidable task in a chamber whose members have a very strong respect for the judgments of committees. Since the House adopted the discharge procedure in 1910, fewer than thirty bills have been discharged, and only two of these became law. The discharge procedure is mainly a threat to encourage reluctant committees to report out bills.

A total of 218 representatives can pry a bill out of committee if they sign a discharge petition, but this procedure is rarely used.

In the Senate, the motion to discharge a committee from its jurisdiction over a bill may be made by a single senator, but senators are even more likely than representatives to reject discharge. In the history of the Senate, only fourteen bills were pried from committees through discharge motions, and only six of these bills were subsequently passed by the Senate. Only one actually resulted in a law; it permitted the government to mint a special medal commemorating a state of Florida celebration in 1964—hardly a landmark piece of legislation.

Bills Reported Out of Committee

Calendars are lists of bills awaiting action on the floor.

House bills reported out of committee are placed on one of five calendars (lists of bills pending floor action). As Table 2.7 shows, the Union Calendar (money matters) and House Calendar (other major proposals) contain the major bills. Bills on the House Calendar pass through the Rules Committee, which gives the bill a "rule" setting the limits of the bill's amendability and the length of its debate. Bills on the minor calendars (Private and Consent) do not need a rule, and bills on the Union Calendar are given special status, by which both Appropriations and Ways and Means can bypass the Rules Committee and send their bills directly to the floor. This prerogative is rarely exercised, because both committees prefer the Rules Committee to limit amendability and debate time.

TABLE 2.7   Congressional Calendars

	Name	Nature of Contents	*Vote on Floor Necessary for Passage*
House Calendars	Union	Monetary considerations (revenue and appropriations, such as tax bills)	Majority
	House	All major nonmoney matters (such as anti-drug legislation)	Majority
	Private	Individual claims (such as bills to permit particular persons to immigrate)	Unanimous
	Consent	Noncontroversial matters (such as naming a government office building in honor of a distinguished citizen)	Unanimous
	Discharge	Successful discharge petitions (very rare)	Majority
Senate Calendars	Regular	All legislative matters	Majority
	Executive	Treaties and presidential nominations	Treaties: ⅔ Nominations: majority

The Rules Committee organizes floor proceedings, working closely with the House majority leadership.

The Rules Committee is an arm of the leadership. However, if the Rules Committee refuses to grant a rule, the bill could be pried from the committee by means of a discharge petition (this has never been done) or by a mechanism known as "Calendar Wednesday." On Wednesday, the list of substantive committees is read so that any of their bills on the House or Union Calendars may be immediately considered, bypassing the Rules Committee. The availability of Calendar Wednesday procedures encourages the Rules Committee to grant a rule to almost any bill.

Bills held up in the Rules Committee are those with lukewarm support and those on which the leadership and many representatives do not want to have to take a public stand through a vote on the floor. The private death of a bill in the Rules Committee allows House members to equivocate on their position on an issue without the embarrassment of a public vote.

In the Senate, bills go directly to the floor after being reported out by committees; the majority party leadership determines when bills are scheduled for floor actions.

The Senate has only two calendars; the Regular Calendar, composed of all bills voted out by committees, and the Executive Calendar, containing all nonlegislative measures, such as treaties and presidential nominations (Table 2.7). As previously mentioned, the Senate does not have a rules committee so all bills go to the floor open to amendment and limitless debate. The only exception to this direct referral occurs when another committee also claims jurisdiction over a bill and wishes to hold hearings. Although he often confers with the minority leader, the majority leader decides the order in which bills are considered on the floor of the Senate.

Floor Action

House floor procedures Debate on the floor of the House usually involves only a small number of representatives until there is a vote or quorum call, at which time members rapidly file into the chamber. A quorum is 218 members, an unwieldy number for the transaction of business when one considers the myriad demands on a representative's time.

To avoid the unreasonable quorum and at the same time permit interested or affected representatives a chance to debate the merits of a bill, the House "dissolves itself" into the Committee of the Whole House. There are no assignments to the Committee of the Whole; the quorum is reduced to 100 members, and any interested representative may request debate time. When debate is in the House sitting as the House of Representatives, the length of debate is determined by the rule; if there is no rule, one hour is allocated to each member. When debate is in the Committee of the Whole, the debate's length is agreed on and divided equally between supporters and opponents of the bill. After general debate is completed, the bill is read section by section for amendment. Each proposed amendment is debated for ten minutes, with time divided equally between its supporters and opponents.

After the Committee of the Whole debates and possibly amends the bill, it dissolves itself by "rising" (thereby reestablishing the larger quorum) and reporting its recommendations to the entire House. The House, sitting now as the House of Representatives, then begins its considerations of the bill by voting on each of its provisions, section by section (and therefore on any amendments adopted by the Committee of the Whole). The House then votes on the bill as a whole, either sending it back to a substantive committee (thereby effectively killing it) or passing it. Votes on minor and procedural matters on which there are few disagreements are usually by voice vote, in which members shout "yea" or "nay" in chorus. Votes on important procedural questions and major bills and their amendments are usually recorded by electronic voting devices. On demand of forty-four members (one-fifth of a quorum), any vote must be electronically recorded, thus exposing the members' voting decisions to public scrutiny.

Senate floor procedures Floor procedures in the Senate reflect its relatively small size. Debate and amendability are unlimited, giving minority opponents the opportunity to attempt talking a bill to death by not permitting it to come to a vote. The use, or threatened use, of this tactic (called *filibustering*) by Southern senators in the 1950s and 1960s led to the defeat of many civil rights bills. These senators knew that if the bills came to a vote, they would pass with solid majorities. Once recognized by the chair, a filibuster talks for a couple of hours, then yields the floor to a fellow filibuster, who yields only to another filibuster, and the process continues.

A filibuster can be broken only when sixteen senators petition for a vote of *cloture,* which halts debate, bringing the bill to a vote. Proponents of the bill must then win the support of at least sixty senators on the cloture vote. If they fail to

Most floor debate is tightly structured by the "rule" granted each bill by the Rules Committee.

Noncontroversial votes are often by voice; other votes are almost always electronically recorded and then published so that citizens may know how members are voting.

Senate floor procedures are less structured, with unlimited debate permitted.

Filibusters are broken when sixty senators vote for "cloture."

invoke cloture after a couple of attempts, the proponents must resign themselves to the success of the filibuster; the bill will not be put to a vote.

Before 1975, cloture required support from two-thirds of the senators present and voting. This difficult standard and the Senate's traditional respect for the rights of strong-willed legislative minorities meant that between 1917 and 1975 only 21 of 100 cloture attempts were successful. Successful cloture votes include the Civil Rights Act of 1964 and 1968 and the Voting Rights Act of 1965, all dramatic victories by liberal reformers. Since 1975, almost half the cloture attempts were successful, and liberals often find themselves on the side of the filibusters. For example, in 1981 and 1982, Senate liberals filibustered to defeat bills promoting school prayer and the end of federal involvement in school desegregation efforts.

The final vote in the Senate is by voice, by division (members supporting a bill stand and are counted, then the process is repeated for opponents), or by roll call. Only roll-call votes, which may be demanded by 20 percent of the senators present, record the vote of every senator for the public record.

Senate voting resembles House voting, except that the smaller body conducts roll calls by reading through the list of senators rather than electronically tabulating votes.

Conference Committees

A bill passed by both the House and the Senate is still not ready to be sent to the president. Most bills are modified during the consideration process, meaning the House and the Senate rarely pass the same version of a bill. If the House and Senate versions differ, the bill is sent to a conference committee composed of members of both chambers selected by the presiding officer of each chamber. Usually, senior members of the relevant substantive committees are appointed to the conference committee, which normally arrives at a compromise bill. The committee writes an explanatory report noting changes from each house's version and justifying these changes. The Senate and the House then vote separately, either accepting or rejecting the conference committee report. (They cannot amend it.) If the report is accepted, the bill is sent to the president, and the conference committee dissolves. If either chamber rejects the report, the conference committee tries again to prepare a compromise bill able to pass both bodies.

When the House and Senate pass different versions of the same bill, a conference committee reconciles differences.

Final Action

Once both chambers pass identical versions of the bill, it is sent to the president. If he decides to veto the bill, he returns it to the chamber of origination, along with a message outlining his objections and the reason for rejection. Party leaders may not schedule an override attempt if they know they lack the votes. If party leaders in either chamber believe they can muster the necessary two-thirds majority, they schedule an override attempt. If successful, the bill is sent to the other chamber, where another successful override vote would make it a law. Unless both houses vote to override the veto, the bill is dead and can be revived only as a new bill requiring the same lengthy process of analysis as any other new bill.

To become laws, all bills must either have the president's signature or must pass by two-thirds margins in both chambers to override presidential vetoes.

THE BUDGETARY PROCESS

Appropriations

The budgetary process is an extremely important aspect of the government's work. A president who wants to help handicapped youngsters may introduce a bill for this purpose into Congress. The bill may then pass into law. The legislation authorizes expenditures of up to a certain amount, but not a penny will be spent unless Congress subsequently *appropriates* money for the law's purpose in the annual budget. There are many laws authorizing the government to spend millions on programs for which little or no money is ever appropriated. Thus, an interest group arguing on behalf of handicapped youngsters must do more than persuade the president and Congress to pass legislation authorizing a new program; the interest group must make certain that the program, once authorized, is actually funded.

General laws authorize expenditures but do not actually appropriate money; the annual budget is the law that actually provides the authority for the Treasury to release funds.

The authorization process involves the substantive committees (for example, Agriculture or Armed Services) that decide if a program is desirable. The appropriation process involves the Appropriations Committees and the Budget Committees that determine to what extent programs already authorized can be afforded within the budget.

The Current Congressional Budget Process

Congress appropriates approximately $1.5 trillion in the budget, which is the one piece of legislation Congress must pass every year. Three laws guide the Congress in its consideration of the annual budget. One, the Budget and Impoundment Control Act of 1974, established the framework for the current congressional budget process; another, the Balanced Budget and Emergency Deficit Control Act of 1985 (as amended in 1987) institutionalized federal deficit controls; and the third, The Budget Enforcement Act of 1990 revised the method of deficit control included in the 1985 act.

The 1974 Budget Act forced Congress to consider the budget as a whole.

Before passage of the Budget and Impoundment Control Act of 1974, Congress approached the budget in the same way as it does most bills: The process was handled by various committees, with little centralized coordination. The 1974 legislation attempted to provide that needed coordination and to control the practice of executive impoundment of funds. The act forced Congress to focus on the budget as a whole by creating budget committees in each chamber charged with drafting an annual budget plan for consideration by the full House and Senate. Unlike other congressional committees, which consider only policy-specific budget issues, the budget committees emphasize the whole budget and its effects on the national economy. The act also created the Congressional Budget Office (CBO), a legislative counterpart to the executive branch's Office of Management and the Budget (OMB), providing Congress with economic forecasts, updated information, and expert advice concerning fiscal issues. The act also instituted a congressional budget timetable designed to complete the process of budgetary review by the start of the nation's fiscal year on October 1.

Seemingly runaway federal deficits resulted in the Balanced Budget and Emergency Deficit Reduction Act of 1985. The 1985 act, known popularly as the Gramm-Rudman Act after its sponsors, Senators Warren Rudman (R.-N.H.) and Phil Gramm (R.-Tex.), set targets for deficit reduction through fiscal year 1991 and provided an automatic deficit reduction process if Congress and the president failed to reach the deficit target for a particular fiscal year.

Gramm-Rudman sets targets for deficit reduction.

In 1986, the Supreme Court, exercising its power of judicial review (see Chapter 3), ruled in *Bowsher* v. *Synar* (478 U.S. 714) that the automatic deficit reduction component of Gramm-Rudman was unconstitutional because it gave executive power to the Comptroller General, a congressional appointee. Congress responded with the Balanced Budget and Emergency Deficit Control Reaffirmation Act of 1987 which assigned the Office of Management and the Budget (an executive office) the power to implement automatic deficit reductions.

In 1990, with the budget further from balance than when the Gramm-Rudman Act was first passed and with an economic downturn threatening additions to the deficit, Congress once again responded with legislation. After a particularly intense political battle which included open rebellion against the House and Senate leadership, Congress passed and the president signed the Omnibus Budget Act of 1990, which included the Budget Enforcement Act of 1990. The Budget Enforcement Act, in force through fiscal year 1995, separated discretionary spending (spending Congress has direct control over) from entitlement programs (programs which automatically extend benefits to anyone meeting their criteria).

In terms of discretionary spending, the 1990 act established spending caps for each of three general policy areas: domestic programs, foreign aid, and military spending. It also provided that any increased spending proposal in a particular area above the provided cap was out of order for floor consideration. In relation to entitlement programs, the 1990 act mandated that bills increasing spending on entitlements be "deficit-neutral," that is, balanced by accompanying entitlement cuts or revenue increases. (This "pay as you go" process also applies to all tax cut proposals.)

The Budget and Deficit Reduction Timetable

The congressional budget process focuses on producing a national budget while controlling spending. The 1974 Budget Act, the 1985 Gramm-Rudman Act as amended, and the 1990 Budget Enforcement Act established a timetable (outlined in Table 2.8) designed to ensure that Congress has sufficient time to work on each stage of the budget. In February, the Senate and House budget committees hold hearings on the president's budget, which is submitted to the Congress in January. These committees also collect reports from standing committees on budget matters relevant to their jurisdictions and receive CBO's report on the nation's economic outlook. The budget committees are charged with incorporating all of this material

---

TABLE 2.8   Congressional Budget and Deficit Reduction Timetable

Deadline	*Action to Be Completed*
First Monday after January 3	President submits budget to Congress.
First Monday in February	Initial OMB sequester preview
February 15	CBO issues annual report to Budget Committees.
February 25	Congressional committees submit estimates to Budget Committees.
April 1	Senate Budget Committee reports budget resolution.
April 15	Congress completes action on concurrent resolution on the budget.
May 15	Annual appropriations bills may be considered in the House.
June 10	House Appropriations Committee reports last annual appropriations bill.
June 15	Congress completes action on reconciliation legislation.
June 30	House completes action on annual appropriation bill.
August 15	CBO updates sequester preview.
August 20	OMB updates sequester preview.
October 1	Fiscal year begins.
Ten days after adjournment	CBO final sequester report
Fifteen days after adjournment	OMB sequester report; president issues sequester order.
Thirty days later	GAO sequester compliance report

Sources: Adapted from U.S. Congress, Senate, Committee on the Budget, *Budget Process Law Annotated,* 102nd Congress, 1st. sess., April 1991, pp. 41–44; and *Congressional Quarterly,* November 3, 1990, p. 3712.

---

into budget resolutions (also known as concurrent resolutions on the budget) and reporting these resolutions to their respective legislative bodies by April 1.

The budget resolutions contain three basic parts: budget totals, including revenues, expenditures, and resulting deficits; spending broken down among 21 different functional areas, such as national defense, agriculture, and health; and a procedure known as *reconciliation,* which directs the substantive committees of each house to propose legislation decreasing spending or increasing revenues by specified amounts to bring federal spending in their particular functional areas within the overall budget guidelines. Congress is mandated to adopt a budget resolution that, under Gramm-Rudman, should meet the deficit reduction target for that year by April 15.

Congress completes reconciliation by June 15.

The process is designed so that Congress completes its reconciliation process by June 15. Following reconciliation, the House and Senate appropriations committees translate the budget authorizations into budget appropriations, with the House Appropriations Committee report required by June 30 and the Senate

Appropriations Committee report due before the start of the fiscal year on October 1. The appropriations committees are divided into numerous subcommittees with budgetary responsibilities for specific areas, and much of the work is completed there. The levels of spending agreed upon in the budget resolutions act as constraints on the subcommittees considerations.

The 1990 Budget Enforcement Act attempts deficit reduction by placing caps on spending and establishing "pay as you go" budgeting.

Prior to the 1990 Budget Enforcement Act, if Congress could not meet the Gramm-Rudman deficit targets, automatic deficit reduction procedures (known as sequester calculations) went into effect. Complex rules for sequestering or reducing budget allocations included the requirement that one-half of the deficit excess must come from defense and one-half from nondefense programs. Many indexed retirement and disability programs were exempt from sequestration. Under this system, a single target for the budget deficit was assessed at the end of the federal fiscal year. If the deficit-reduction target was not achieved, there would be automatic spending cuts in all nonexempt programs in the federal budget.

The Budget Enforcement Act made important changes in the budget process. Under the procedures adopted in 1990, sequester previews are updated periodically throughout the year rather than just at the end. Moreover, the 1990 act mandates three possible sequesters if spending exceeds statutory spending limits: one involves discretionary spending based on the spending caps; one focuses on entitlement programs and is based on the deficit neutrality requirement; and the third involves all nonexempt programs, and is based on overall deficit-reduction targets. In the event that an increase in any spending category exceeds the cap or is not deficit neutral, the director of the Office of Management and the Budget (OMB) implements sufficient cuts in that category to offset the increase. Within thirty days of OMB's action, the General Accounting Office (GAO) must issue a report certifying sequester compliance.

The budget process illustrates that Congress can choose to ignore its own rules. In 1988, for only the first time since the Budget Act passed in 1974, Congress completed action on all spending bills by the October 1 deadline. Many observers contend that such timeliness was only possible in 1988 because of a budget summit conducted between the White House and the bipartisan congressional leadership in November 1987. In previous years, Congress failed to pass one or more of the thirteen regular appropriation bills by the start of the fiscal year. When this happened, Congress passed *continuing resolutions* (stopgaps that keep government agencies in operation for short periods until regular appropriation bills are passed).

Continuing resolutions are sometimes used for spending decisions.

At times, even when Congress adhered to the "letter" of its budgetary rules, it did so only by bending their "spirit." For example, military paydays were changed from the last to the first day of the month, effective September 1988, thereby moving the salary appropriations necessary for September 30 into an entirely new fiscal year (October 1).

At other times, Congress has had difficulty sticking to the long-term commitments in its rules. Although the Budget Enforcement Act of 1990 provided that the three discretionary budget areas would be consolidated in fiscal year 1994 permitting fiscal reallocations among them, some members of Congress argued that a proportion of the unexpected savings in military spending following the Soviet Union's collapse should be reallocated to domestic spending for fiscal year 1992. Whatever the merits of such a proposal, it seeks to revise a five-year agreement reached less than one year earlier.

The current fiscal situation forces members of Congress to confront politically unpalatable budget options. During periods of substantial economic growth like the 1960s, budgeting can be both politically manageable and satisfying. Members of Congress use budget allocations to firm up their existing political support and even reach out to new constituents. However, during times of slow or moderate economic growth coupled with great pressure for maintenance of most government programs and increases in others, congressional budget making becomes a struggle. Congressional budgeting in the 1990s is a clear example of such a struggle.

CONCLUSION

Reforms in the 1970s strengthened the ability of both the leadership and individual members to participate fully in legislative tasks.

Congress moves with great deliberation. Major new ideas receive detailed scrutiny and require a strong consensus before they are enacted into legislation. In the early 1970s, reformers who believed the snail's pace of Congress kept it from dealing responsibly with national problems led a struggle to change Congress. Although the reformers were not entirely successful in getting everything they wanted, many substantial reforms were enacted. The net effect increased both the power of the party leadership (especially in the House) and the ability of younger members (especially in the Senate) to participate fully in the legislative process. Conversely, the reforms decreased the power of committee chairpersons in the House and the "inner club" of senior senators who formerly ran the Senate. The budgetary process reforms added to Congress's ability to systematically tackle the annual budget, and, by substantially increasing its professional staff, Congress enhanced its ability to process information relevant to its legislative tasks.

Bills are still blocked at several points in the legislative process. The incoherent nature of much public policy reflects the absence of a congressional consensus on what should be done; when such a consensus exists, however briefly (for example, in 1981), Congress acts swiftly and boldly.

The effects of these reforms can be overstated. The leadership is stronger, yet a bill's path to law still involves many roadblocks, any one of which can prove fatal to a bill. Congress is a rubber stamp for no one, including its own leadership. If there is no consensus among legislators on the resolution of public problems (or, for that matter, no consensus on what constitutes public problems), it is difficult to see how any set of reforms will produce consistent and coherent public policies. Congress is a representative body, its policies reflecting a lack of harmony when its members sharply divide along several dimensions. Conversely, Congress can act quickly and decisively when consensus exists. In 1981, strong presidential leadership combined with conservative majorities in both the House and Senate enacted significant changes in fiscal policy. The political strength of President Reagan and his allies in Congress overcame structural obstacles to massive changes in spending and taxing. In Congress, however, the policy process never ends. The degree to which these new policies satisfy the American people's expectations will largely determine the president's political popularity and thereby delimit his ability to get what he wants from Congress. Politics and structure will continue interacting and producing public policy.

Selected Readings

Davidson, Roger H. ed. *The Postreform Congress.* New York: St. Martin's, 1990.

Kornacki, John J. *Leading Congress: New Styles, New Strategies.* Washington, D.C.: Congressional Quarterly, 1990.

Peterson, Mark A. *Legislating Together: The White House and Capitol Hill from Eisenhower to Reagan.* Cambridge: Harvard Press, 1990.

Thurber, James A. *Divided Democracy: Cooperation and Conflict Between the President and Congress.* Washington, D.C.: Congressional Quarterly, 1991.

CASE HISTORY : Superfund

The Congress

98–99   On June 13, 1979, President Jimmy Carter sent Congress a proposal to establish a $1.69 billion "Superfund" to handle the problems of oil and chemical spills and the cleanup of abandoned hazardous-waste dump sites. In the Senate, the bill (S 1341) went to the Environment and Public Works Subcommittee on Environmental Pollution. In the House, because the bill (HR 4571) covered both oil and hazardous substances, it fell under jurisdictions of three committees—the Public Works and Merchant Marine committees (both of which handle oil legislation), and the Commerce Committee (which has jurisdiction over hazardous wastes). This multijurisdictional problem was the first of many roadblocks that affected, and ultimately defeated, the president's proposal.

71–74   As emphasized throughout this chapter, Congress has the ability to exert considerable leadership in its own right if it chooses. To be sure, that leadership potential is often linked to the presidency—especially if Congress and the presidency are controlled by the same political party. This linkage often means that congressional and presidential powers complement one another rather than conflict with each other. In the case of oil spill and hazardous-waste legislation, Congress was actually out in front of the president.

By the time Carter's proposal reached Congress, both houses were already considering Superfund legislation, and the extent of the ongoing machinations in various committees virtually assured Congress would continue to debate its own bills. At least four bills were already introduced, each designed by committee and subcommittee chairpersons to limit jurisdiction to their own committees and to deny jurisdiction to "rival" committees.

100   The bills embodying the Carter proposals, S 1341 and HR 4571, were both shelved in committee for the remainder of the legislative session. By mid-1980, the media gave considerable attention to hazardous-waste disposal. Communities across the country victimized by past improper and unsafe disposal practices continued to suffer the consequences, and public opinion polls showed a dramatic increase in the importance the American people accorded this problem. An ABC News-Louis Harris Poll on July 8, 1980, found an amazing 86 percent of the public favored "giving the problem of toxic chemical dumps and spills a very high priority for federal action." Congress, while not ready to accept Carter's proposal was nonetheless grappling with the issue.

99   The principal Superfund bill in the House, HR 7020, was being considered by the Commerce Subcommittee on Transportation. Originally proposed by its chairperson, Jame J. Florio (D.-NJ), in the previous session as HR 5790, the bill had a stormy history demonstrating the collegial nature of Congress. Florio proposed the bill the previous year as a $1.3 billion measure handling only the cleanup of hazardous-waste sites, not oil or chemical spills. This exemption ensured that only Florio's committee would have jurisdiction over the bill. But Florio failed to consult with the members of his subcommittee before proposing and pushing the bill, which they perceived as heavy-handedness. As a result, the subcommittee "stonewalled" its chairperson and refused to permit the bill to be brought up for a vote. By early 1980 Florio mended his fences and was working closely with the members of his subcommittee. The old bill had been scaled down and replaced with a compromise version, HR 7020 (also written by Florio), which the subcommittee was willing to consider.

HR 7020 provided for a $600 million fund for the cleanup of hazardous-waste dumps. It was reported out of the subcommittee favorably on April 30 and the full committee passed it by a vote of twenty-one to three on May 13. Thus, HR 7020, as well as one of its rival bills concerned with both oil and chemical spills (HR 85), awaited floor action, but other roadblocks remained.

91   On May 8, Al Ullman (D.-Ore.), chairperson of the House Ways and Means Committee, asserted his committee's jurisdiction over both HR 7020 and HR 85 on the grounds that Ways and Means had authority not only over all legislation containing tax revenue provisions but over "revenue measures generally." On June 13, the Ways and Means Committee approved HR 85. The Ways and Means Committee, however, can amend bills it considers, just like any other substantive committee of the House. Among the changes to HR 85 proposed by the committee was an increase in the amount of money available to the oil and chemical spill fund, from $300 million to $750 million over a five-year period. In a similar move, the committee approved HR 7020 on June 18, this time increasing the amount of money available to clean up hazardous dump sites from the $600 million approved by the Commerce Committee to $1.2 billion. In addition, the Ways and Means Committee increased the percentage of the fund provided by a tax on industry.

99–100   After Ways and Means Committee passage, the bills were still not ready for floor action; each needed to be granted a rule by the Rules Committee. For this reason, the Ways and Means Committee held conferences with all committees that previously handled the bills, seeking concurrence on the latest version of each prior to Rules Committee consideration. This maneuver helped ensure the granting of a rule acceptable to all the committees concerned and reduced the probability that a displeased committee chairman would oppose the bill on the floor.

101   With the Ways and Means, Rules, and all substantive committees that had dealt with the legislation in agreement, HR 85 and HR 7020 were finally ready for floor action, but lobbyists had also been busy. At each successive stage of the development of the bills, environmental groups, federal agencies, oil and chemical companies, residents living near and affected by hazardous-waste dumps, members of Congress, state and local officials, and a host of private citizens lobbied members of the House incessantly regarding these bills. No matter how this legislation was written, someone somewhere would be dramatically affected by the outcome, whether the bill passed or failed.

As HR 85 and HR 7020 moved through successive stages of consideration by the various House committees holding jurisdiction over them, lobbying by both sides intensified. In the end, compromises considerably weakened the provisions proposed in the original versions. Most observers agree that industry lobbyists won more than they lost during these compromise sessions. The Chemical Manufacturers' Association (CMA) representative called the final product "a constructive compromise" and "a substantial improvement" over the earlier version proposed by Florio. However, Marchant Wentworth of Environmental Action noted: "Industry got what they wanted. The bill is a mere shadow of its former self." Similarly, Swep Davis, the Environmental Protection Agency's Associate Administrator for Water and Waste Management commended: "If I were the industry, I'd go out and have a party." By the middle of September, the House approved both measures by overwhelming majorities—HR 85 on September 19 (288-11) and HR 7020 on September 23 (351-23).

While the House bills underwent considerable weakening in the long compromise process through final passage, a measure that originated in two Senate Environment and Public Works subcommittees had been moving slowly through the Senate. The Bill (S 1480) had been sponsored by Edmund S. Muskie (D.-Me.), chairperson of the Environmental Pollution Subcommittee, and John C. Culver (D.-Iowa), chairperson of the Resources Protection Subcommittee. Unlike either of its House counterparts, S1480 covered any release into the environment (i.e., into any medium, not just water) of virtually any toxic substance, including nuclear wastes. The precedent-setting bill would have established a $500 million annual fund (based on industry fees) and would have compensated victims, permitting them to sue in federal court, and liberalize rules of evidence admissible in such cases.

Despite the concentrated opposition of industry lobbyists, who considered it completely unacceptable, by May 22, 1980, both subcommittees favorably reported out S 1480, sending the measure to the full Environment and Public Works Committee, which began hearings on June 4. In six working sessions on the bill, the Environment Committee adjusted the bill a bit more to industry's liking. On June 27, the Environment Committee voted ten to one to send the bill to the Senate floor. Nevertheless, industry still opposed the bill, initiating a nationwide lobbying effort to defeat S 1480. As one Shell Oil lobbyist put it, "We are opposing it with everything we've got."

71-72   Chemical companies wrote to their shareholders, characterizing the bill as "overkill" and a "radical rewriting of all environmental legislation." More than 40,000 shareholders of Monsanto alone sent letters to the Senate. Curtis Moore, minority counsel for the Senate Environment Committee, stated, "This campaign is much more sophisticated, much more effective than a postcard campaign." Its effectiveness stemmed in part from the type of person writing the letters; engineers, attorneys, architects—professionals accustomed to influencing policy.

101-102   Senators who favored S 1480 began to fight back. On July 11, twenty-five senators (an unusually high number) signed a letter addressed to Majority Leader Robert Byrd (D.-W. Va.) and Minority Leader Howard Baker (R.-Tenn.) urging them to schedule floor action

93   on the bill. However, just as HR 7020 and HR 85 had been referred to the Ways and Means Committee in the House because of revenue implications, the Senate Finance Committee, under Russell B. Long (D.-La.), insisted that it had jurisdiction over S 1480.

Senate-watchers widely believed that the referral of S 1480 to Finance would kill the bill. For one thing, during the preceding three years Long received over $25,000 in campaign contributions from chemical-industry political action committees, and he was facing a primary election on September 13. Long, however, was also under pressure from constituents to favor the bill. Several then-recent incidents in Louisiana involving chemical and toxic substances caused considerable concern in that state, as Long was forcefully reminded. Bending to these pressures, he announced on August 22 that he was confident a bill would pass during that session of Congress and that he expected "to help pass the bill." After holding hearings on September 11 on those portions of the bill that imposed new taxes, however, the Finance Committee was still not ready to report the bill back to the Senate. Although Long had earlier predicted passage, he did nothing to move the bill forward. When Congress recessed in early October for the upcoming elections, S 1480 was still bottled up in the Finance Committee.

85–86   The 1980 presidential and congressional elections had a dramatic effect on the outcome of the Superfund proposals. By the time Congress reconvened in lame-duck session, the entire fabric of national politics had been substantially altered. Ronald Reagan had captured the White House, and for the first time in decades, the Republican party controlled a majority in the Senate. This meant that in the new Congress that would take its seat in January there would be split-party control, and that the Senate would likely be allied closely with the White House against the Democratic-controlled House of Representatives. Although Reagan had not taken a stand on the Superfund issue, industry representatives felt confident that any Superfund measure proposed by his administration would be "better" (from their point of view) than either the House-passed HR 7020 and HR 85 or the still unpassed S 1480. In short, industry wanted all action on Superfund postponed until the new Congress convened. Republican leaders in the Senate concurred. Baker, who would become the majority leader in the new Senate, said he favored some kind of Superfund legislation but thought the new Congress could do a "better job" on the bill.

86–87   "Politics" had also altered some of the key players in the move to pass Superfund. Neither Muskie nor Culver (the originators of S 1480) would be in the new Congress. Muskie gave up his seat earlier to become secretary of state under Carter, and Culver was defeated in his reelection bid. When Muskie left the Senate, Jennings Randolph (D.-W. Va.), took his place as chairperson of the Senate Environment Committee. The ranking Republican on the committee was Robert Stafford (R.-Vt.), who was slated to take over the chair. Both Stafford and Randolph were convinced that the only chance of getting a meaningful Superfund law on the books lay with the lame-duck Congress. Neither believed the new Congress would produce anything even remotely acceptable to those with environmental concerns, because industry influence would expand with Republican control of the White House and Senate. What had begun as a Muskie-Culver proposal now depended on the success of a Randolph-Stafford compromise. On November 14, a $2.7 billion compromise was worked out. Stafford regretted the need to compromise but agreed to eliminate some of the more controversial liability and compensation provisions in the hope of getting the bill to the floor of the Senate, where he believed there would be sufficient votes to pass it.

84   The Finance Committee, however, still had S 1480 bottled up. Bowing to intense pressure from the senators who had worked out the compromise, the committee reported the bill to the floor, but without recommendation. Supporters of the compromise believed they had enough votes for passage. On November 20, Majority Leader Byrd tried to call up the bill, but Baker objected, arguing the compromise was unacceptable to his side of the aisle. Byrd withdrew the bill from the floor so that proponents would have further opportunity to effect an acceptable compromise. Later that day, Baker joined in the negotiations on the compromise version and predicted a "favorable outcome" by the end of the session. By the time Byrd called the bill up to the floor on November 24, Stafford was ready with the new compromise.

101   The bill that was called up to the floor, however, was the version sent over from the House (HR 7020). Stafford moved to have the contents of HR 7020 replaced with the compromise version he and the other senators had worked out. The Senate accepted the new compromise version of HR 7020 as a substitute for the House-passed measure by a vote of seventy-eight to nine. This vote substituted the language of the compromise for the language of the bill passed by the House, so that the new HR 7020 was now ready for a final vote in the Senate. Given the size of the vote to substitute, the bill passed by a simple voice vote.

By November 24, then, the House and Senate had passed widely differing versions of HR 7020. In fact, earlier in the month, eight House members wrote to Senators Byrd and Baker, urging them to push for Senate acceptance of the original House versions of both HR 7020 and HR 85 so that the need for the lengthy conference committee procedure could be avoided. The House was not even back from its election recess and would not reconvene until December 1. With adjournment scheduled for December 5, it was highly improbable that a compromise could be worked out in conference and passed by both houses before the end of the session.

The Democratic leadership in the House began to lobby House members to accept the Senate version of HR 7020, but there were considerable obstacles to overcome. For acceptance, the language of the Senate-passed HR 7020 would have to be substituted for the language of the HR 7020 previously passed by the House and voted on "under suspension of the rules," requiring a minimum of 246 votes for passage.

The House leadership decided to risk calling the bill up for consideration under suspension of the rules. The debate would take place on the floor of the House. Edward R. Madigan (R.-Ill.), still incensed that the oil provisions had been excluded from the Senate version, declared: "We have been left at a take-it-or-leave-it situation, and I rise to recommend to the House that we leave it." Others disagreed. Bob Eckhardt (D.-Pa.) asserted that "unless we move on swell of tide to deal with the question of hazardous waste today, it is not that we will do it three months from now, it may be that we will not do it for seven years from now." John LaFalce (D.-N.Y.), whose district contained the infamous Love Canal, continued the argument: "Mr. Speaker, it is Wednesday night, December 3. We adjourn on December 5, this Friday. The time is now, or not maybe later. The time is now or never."

The time was now. On the evening of December 3, 1980—less than forty-eight hours before adjournment—the House passed a "new" HR 7020. Its language was identical to the language of the version of HR 7020 that had been passed by the Senate on November 24.

The Comprehensive Environmental Response, Compensation and Liability Act of 1980 (CERCLA) was on its way to the desk of Jimmy Carter. He signed the bill on December 11, and the country finally had a Superfund law.

74   Congress's lawmaking function does not stop with the passage of legislation. Laws are expanded, limited, or even nullified in subsequent sessions in response to the nation's experience with their implementation. Unlike many other laws, CERCLA would terminate because the taxing authority to put money into the Superfund would expire on September 30, 1985, if Congress did not reauthorize the act. Superfund could then survive only until it ran out of money.

86   In early January 1984, anticipating the president's State of the Union address, Representative Florio released to the press an internal EPA report putting the eventual cost of Superfund cleanup between $8 and $16 billion. Using this leverage, Florio again engineered the development of a Superfund bill, with an $11 billion price tag over five years. As he had neglected to do four years earlier, Florio again did not seek the support of his subcommittee, which "stonewalled" the bill. The subcommittee substituted a much weaker bill, and Florio was forced to adjourn the subcommittee markup session or the new, weaker bill would have passed.

Eventually Florio again mended his fences, and the subcommittee voted out a strong bill, but Superfund reauthorization proponents lost valuable weeks in 1984. Proposed legislation did not pass through the full Commerce Committee until mid-June, leaving little time for the House Ways and Means Committee to consider the bills' monetary aspects. Proponents pushed diligently, and the House, on the eve of its recess prior to the Republican National Convention in August, passed a Superfund reauthorization bill, 323-33.

In the interim, the Senate Environment and Public Works Committee, chaired by Stafford, worked toward a Superfund bill restoring many of the elements "compromised out" of the 1980 legislation. Stafford, too, could not expand the law's authorities greatly but he dramatically increased funding levels of Superfund; a $7.5 billion package went to the Senate Finance Committee on September 13, 1984, by a committee vote of seventeen to one. Unlike Long, who was forced to report out the original Superfund bill in 1980, Robert Dole (R.-Kan.), the new chairperson, successfully rebuffed pressures, and Superfund reauthorization died in the 98th Congress. Essentially, in 1980 President Carter wanted the Democratic-controlled Senate to pass the proposal; in 1984 President Reagan wanted the Republican-controlled Senate to let it die. Reagan feared that, in an election year, environmentalists would have the upper hand in strengthening the popular Superfund program.

With all the staff work completed in 1984 and the tax due to expire on September 30, 1985, quick enactment of a Superfund reauthorization act was expected in 1985. However, the Superfund Amendments and Reauthorization Act (SARA) was not passed until October 17, 1986. Passage was delayed in 1985 and 1986 not because of interference from the White House, but from difficulties reaching agreements among committees and between chambers.

In 1985, a major dispute between the two House committees, the Energy and Commerce Committee and the Public Works and Transportation Committee, delayed House passage for months. The Public Works version, favored by environmentalists, was stricter on cleanup standards and schedules and also provided standing for citizens to sue polluters for cleanup costs. On December 10, the House passed a bill that largely adopted the Public

Works Committee version, with authorized expenditures of $10 billion for five ears. Meanwhile, since the Superfund tax had expired on September 30, new work on Superfund projects had ceased almost entirely.

In September 1985, the Senate passed a Superfund reauthorization, but its bill was quite different from the House's version. The Senate's version included a broad-based excise tax and a total authorization of only $7.5 billion. The Senate bill was favored by oil-state legislators, whereas the House's version, which paid for Superfund through a combination of petrochemical-industry taxes and general revenues, was opposed by oil-state representatives and senators. President Reagan opposed both versions, arguing that less money was needed and that the new broad-based tax might lead Congress to pass other similar taxes he opposed.

67–68   Senator Bob Packwood (R.-Ore.), the chairperson of the Senate Finance Committee, and his oil-state allies attached the Superfund bill to the giant $74 billion deficit-reduction package. By doing this, they hoped that after both chambers agreed upon a common bill, the bill would be "veto-proof" because President Reagan would be unwilling to veto a bill with large deficit reductions, regardless of his views on the Superfund issue. It is not known whether this strategy would have worked, because Congress never sent a bill to the president in 1985. Packwood was successful in the conference committee in getting the broad-based tax accepted. The Senate then voted 78-1 to accept the conference committee report. All that remained to reauthorize Superfund was the House's approval and the president's signature.

102   By a vote of 205-151, the House voted on December 19 to reject the broad-based tax and to stick with the chemical and petroleum taxes. Each chamber, then, rejected the other's position in a parliamentary test of wills lasting well into the early morning hours of December 20. After the Senate sent the bill back to the conference committee, the House adjourned for the year without acting. Superfund, despite its broad support, would not be reauthorized in 1985.

Because Congress changes its membership only after election years (such as 1990, 1992, and 1994), work on renewing Superfund in 1986 picked up where the legislators left off in 1985. Both chambers passed bills, but no agreement was reached on a conference committee compromise. On February 18, 1986, EPA Administrator Lee Thomas sent Congress a message that he would have to start dismantling the program April 1 unless Congress acted by that date. He included a draft interim financing bill that would fund the program for one year while the legislators worked out their differences. Members of the Senate Environment Committee and others attacked the idea of a one-year extension because it would relieve the pressure on Congress to reauthorize Superfund during an election year. They said that the delay until 1987 would make it easier for President Reagan to veto the bill, since he would be much more reluctant to do so in the 1986 election year. The president, they argued, would not want to hurt the electoral chances of Republican candidates by vetoing a bill reauthorizing the popular Superfund program. The conference committee began its work on February 26 with a strong commitment to reach agreement.

On March 21, Congress sent President Reagan an interim extension of the Superfund tax, but only for two months. They intended to save the program from dismantlement, but keep the pressure on the conferees.

85   On April 30, a group of dissident Democrats left a caucus of House conferees, charging that the negotiation position backed by House Energy Committee Chair John D. Dingell (D.-Mich.) gave in too readily to less progressive Senate positions. This was a rematch of the 1985 dispute between the House Energy and Public Works Committees, largely won by the Public Works Committee, as the House adopted its position. The new dispute raised the question of whether the House as a whole would support the bill that would eventually emerge from the conference committee. By failing to act by May 31, Congress again heard from Lee Thomas that EPA would be forced to reduce Superfund cleanup activities to an absolute minimal level.

102   On July 31, the conference committee reached agreement on the content and cost ($9 billion for five years) of the program. All that remained was to decide the mix of taxes to pay for the program. On August 15, Congress passed a special stopgap appropriation of $48 million, designed to keep Superfund intact until October 1. By that date, Congress expected either to have passed a Superfund reauthorization or to have adjourned to campaign for the November elections.

The conference committee continued to fail to reach agreement on taxing. On September 22, Lee Thomas wrote to Representative Dingell, "Should adjournment occur before the reauthorization is accomplished, there will be no Superfund program when Congress returns next January." On October 2, the conference committee agreed on a $8.5 billion program—with $2.75 billion to come from petroleum taxes, $1.4 billion from chemical feedstocks, $2.5 billion from a broad-based tax, $1.25 billion from general revenues, and $0.6 billion from interest and costs recovered from polluters. Both the American Petroleum Institute and the Grocery Manufacturers Association, the leader of a coalition of interest groups opposed to the broad-based tax, denounced the compromise. Senate Finance Committee Chair Bob Packwood noted with satisfaction that the criticisms by both lobby groups indicated the compromise probably was fair to everyone.

The Senate agreed to the conference report by an 88-8 vote on October 3, 1986, and the House approved it 386-27 on October 8. The president signed the bill into law on October 17. After literally years of struggle to renew Superfund, Congress was relieved to limit its role to oversight and to leave Superfund for the courts to interpret and the bureaucracy to implement, at least until next legislative round, when the tax would expire in 1991.

73–74   Congress used the General Accounting Office to help oversee the Superfund program in the years after the passage of SARA in 1986. In both 1988 and 1989 the GAO issued reports critical of EPA's Superfund implementation. The GAO found that contractors, who do most of the actual on-site cleanup work, were not adequately supervised by EPA officials. In October 1991 the GAO issued another report, *Superfund: EPA Has Not Corrected Long-Standing Contract Management Problems* requested by Representative John Dingell (D-MI) and Senators Frank Lautenburg (D-NJ) and David Pryor (D-AR). The Subcommittee on Investigation and Oversight of the House Public Works and Transportation Committee then held hearings at which EPA Administrator William Reilly responded to the GAO criticisms. Even though Congress approved an extension of Superfund in 1990, oversight continued and will continue through the life of the program.

Just as the Congress sometimes fights long and hard over an important issue, at other times the Congress is adept at quickly reaching compromises. As the 1991 expiration of the Superfund taxes approached, Congress wanted to avoid the wrenching experience of 1985 and 1986. As one House aide, remembering the earlier battles, put it, ''It was real messy and no one wanted to go through that again.''

There were two other reasons Congress wanted to settle the Superfund extension issue quickly and with little rancor. One is Congress can only deal effectively with a limited number of environmental issues at any one time. The Resource Conservation and Recovery Act, the complex law regulating hazardous waste management, expired in 1988, and Congress was committed to review and renew the act during 1991 and 1992. Congress was unsure it could effectively review Superfund at the same time. In addition, 1991 was only one year before the 1992 elections. Both proponents and opponents of strengthening Superfund worried that presidential electoral politics would not be a good environment for careful review of Superfund.

The difficult battle that produced the tax and budget compromise of 1990 provided the means to extend the Superfund taxes through 1995. Although neither the House nor the Senate had any hearings on the Superfund taxes, the conference committee handled the overall reconciliation bill quietly adding the extension of the Superfund taxes. The rest of the bill, with its new taxes and spending cuts, was so controversial that the Superfund extension received little attention. Neither the House nor the Senate voted directly on the Superfund extension, but only on the overall reconciliation bill.

THE FEDERAL JUDICIARY

The federal judiciary has an important role in the political process, but it operates in conjunction with the other branches of government.

Congress is not entirely independent of the executive branch, because the president is indeed the chief legislator. Similarly, the president is not entirely independent of the legislative branch; his programs require legislative approval, his treaties and many personnel nominations need senatorial confirmation, and his execution of the laws is under constant surveillance and oversight by Congress. Likewise, the federal judiciary is not entirely independent of the other branches of government. All federal judges are nominated by the president and then confirmed by the Senate. The jurisdiction (what kind of cases are handled) of the judiciary, as well as its size and the remuneration of judges, is determined in part by Congress. Federal judges are not elected and often portray themselves as "above politics," but the judicial branch of our national government is very much part of the political process.

This chapter concerns the federal judiciary, with the Supreme Court of the United States at its pinnacle. The chapter does not describe the fifty systems of state courts that combine with the federal system in a dual system of courts. State court systems primarily enforce state and local laws and include a state's highest court, usually called a state supreme court, which handles appeals from lower courts (for example, municipal, county, and magisterial courts). Of the more than fifteen million cases tried annually in the United States, most are tried in state courts and involve state and local laws. Judges in these state courts are recruited by various means, including election. They are required in all cases to apply national law if a question involving national law or the Constitution arises, even if national law contradicts a state constitution or state law.

CONSTITUTIONAL PREROGATIVES

The two types of federal courts are judicial and administrative.[1] As Table 3.1 summarizes, judicial courts are established under the judiciary article of the Consti-

[1]Many authors discussing these two types of courts label judicial courts *constitutional courts* and administrative courts *legislative courts*. To minimize confusion, this chapter uses the accurately descriptive labels *judicial* and *administrative*.

TABLE 3.1   Judicial and Administrative Courts

	Judicial	*Administrative*
Authority for	Art. III—Judicial article	Art. I—Legislative article
Functions of	Judicial	Judicial, quasi-judicial, administrative
Advisory Opinions?	No	Yes
Tenure of Judges	Life	At discretion of Congress
Examples	Supreme Court Courts of appeals District courts	Court of Military Appeals Territorial courts Tax Court

tution and include the Supreme Court, courts of appeals, and district courts. Administrative courts are created by Congress under its power "to constitute Tribunals inferior to the Supreme Court" (Article I, Section 8), granted in the legislative article, and include the Tax Court, territorial courts, and the Court of Military Appeals. Whereas the judicial courts are limited to deciding cases and controversies, the administrative courts perform quasi-judicial and administrative tasks as well. Administrative courts are often asked for advisory opinions; for example, rulings on the legitimacy of possible government actions in the absence of an actual case or controversy. Judicial courts cannot render such rulings. In addition, the judges on administrative courts may be removed by simple majority vote of Congress for any reason. In contrast, judges on judicial courts have lifetime tenure, subject only to impeachment.

> Judicial courts decide only cases based on existing law. Administrative courts perform whatever services Congress assigns them.

Constitutional Authorization

> The Constitution established the Supreme Court; Congress set up all the lower courts.

Judicial courts   Article III, Section 1, of the Constitution states "the judicial Power of the United States, shall be vested in one Supreme Court and in such inferior Courts as the Congress may from time to time ordain and establish." Thus, there must be a Supreme Court, but the rest of the judiciary's structure is determined by Congress and is therefore beyond the judiciary's control. Although the Supreme Court cannot control the lower courts' structure, it dramatically influences the politics of those courts. For instance, when the chief justice addresses a group such as the American Bar Association (ABA), the media give his remarks wide circulation, and they are likely to influence judicial actions even at the local level.

The Judiciary Act of 1789 established thirteen district courts, each with a single judge, and three circuit courts, each consisting of two judges (one from the Supreme Court and one from a district court). At that time, district courts handled mainly admiralty and maritime cases, and the circuit courts functioned as the basic trial system. Over time, Congress adopted a three-tiered system, with the district courts acting as the basic courts originating almost all federal cases. Cases are appealed

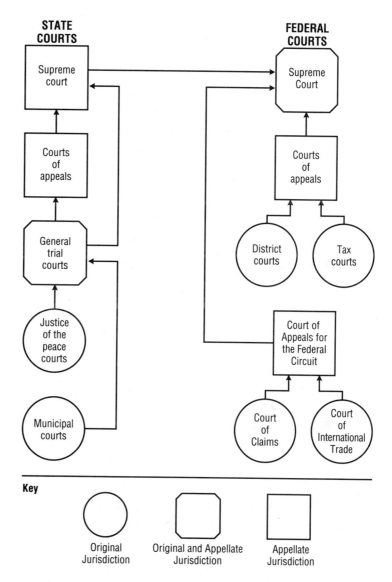

FIGURE 3.1 United States judicial systems. On occasion, the Supreme Court hears a case appealed directly from a lower state court. This may happen if a federal question is involved and the state denies the litigant the opportunity to appeal to a higher state court. (The structure of state court systems may vary.)

from a district court to a circuit court of appeals and finally to the Supreme Court. This three-stage system, still in effect, is shown in Figure 3.1. As the nation expanded, however, the number of district courts grew to ninety-four, and the number of circuit courts of appeals, with their own full-time judges, reached thirteen.

All federal judges in the judicial courts have lifetime tenure.

Tenure   The Constitution states "the judges, both of the supreme and inferior Courts, shall hold their Offices during good Behavior," a lifetime tenure provision. This constitutional guarantee protects judicial court judges from hostile majorities, a security unknown to either legislators or the president, who must face the voters periodically. Judges are not selected by the citizens and, once in office, can be removed only by time-consuming, multistaged, and rarely used impeachment proceedings in Congress. The only Supreme Court justice ever impeached was Associate Justice Samuel Chase in 1804, and he was acquitted by the Senate and remained on the bench. Many Americans may be angered by Supreme Court decisions, but they are powerless to remove offending justices. This constitutional provision has enabled the Supreme Court to defend the rights of speech, fair trial, and the equal protection of the laws when applied to unpopular actions by disliked or even broadly despised groups and individuals.

Administrative courts   Administrative courts come and go at the will of Congress. They are set up to remove some of the workload from the crowded judicial courts as well as to efficiently handle specialized needs. For example, the United States Court of Military Appeals is an administrative court handling court-martial appeals involving military personnel. The United States Court of International Trade, known before 1980 as the United States Customs Court, was an administrative court until Congress made it a judicial court in 1956. In 1988, Congress voted to create a Court of Veterans Appeals, the final arbiter in veterans'-benefit rulings. The court is composed of three to seven judges, appointed by the president for fifteen-year terms. Although Congress has the constitutional authority to establish administrative courts empowered to hear cases in many areas, it has not made extensive use of administrative courts except in the area of military justice. Hence, this chapter's main focus is on the politics and structures of judicial courts.

Congress has not made extensive use of specialized administrative courts.

Congressional Limitations

Original jurisdiction and appellate jurisdiction   Congress can limit the powers of the judiciary. With administrative courts, Congress can change jurisdictions, fire judges, and even abolish any administrative court. With judicial courts, Congress can take cases out of the courts and limit the size and number of courts, but it cannot replace judges who have incurred its wrath. In the case of the Supreme Court, the Constitution provides that the Court shall have original jurisdiction (the right to hear a case directly, not on appeal) only in rare cases involving ambassadors and those in which a state is the litigant. Cases with a state as a party generally involve interstate questions such as water rights (for example, a dam in one state reduces the flow of water into a downriver state), and are often settled out of court. In the entire history of the Supreme Court, in fewer than 150 instances the Court has exercised its original jurisdiction. Thus, the majority of Supreme Court cases involve its appellate jurisdiction (cases heard on appeal). In all other cases (not involving an ambassador or state), the Constitution provides that "the supreme Court shall have appellate Jurisdiction, both as to law

The Supreme Court has little original jurisdiction.

and Fact, with such Exceptions and under such Regulations as the Congress shall make."

Congress has the authority to limit the appellate jurisdiction of the federal courts but has rarely done so.

If the Supreme Court greatly angers Congress, the legislature can deny the Court its usual appellate jurisdiction. In fact, after the Civil War, Congress did not permit the Supreme Court to review any of the Reconstruction laws. In recent years, some members of Congress have tried to strip the federal courts of their jurisdiction over cases involving school prayer, abortion, and busing to achieve racially integrated schools.

In response to an unpopular Court decision, Congress can initiate the process of amending the Constitution.

Constitutional amendments   Congress, in conjunction with state legislatures, also has the constitutional prerogative to overrule the Supreme Court by amending the Constitution. Two-thirds of each house of Congress can endorse a proposed amendment, which then requires ratification by three-fourths of the states. The Eleventh, Fourteenth, Sixteenth, and Twenty-sixth Amendments reversed specific Supreme Court rulings. The Sixteenth Amendment, for example, ratified in 1913, was a response to the Court's ruling that a progressive income tax was unconstitutional (*Pollock* v. *Farmers' Loan and Trust Company,* 158 U.S. 601 [1895]). Similarly, the Twenty-sixth Amendment, ratified in 1971, was in response to the Court's ruling that Congress lacked the authority to mandate that states permit eighteen-year-olds to vote in state and local elections.

Legislation   Amending the Constitution is difficult. A much easier way for Congress to reverse a Supreme Court ruling is through simple legislation. A reversal through legislation is not possible when the issue is the constitutionality of congressional action. When Congress's complaint, however, is that the Court interpreted a law contrary to congressional intent, clarifying legislation can reverse the Court's decision. For example, in 1984, the Supreme Court limited the coverage of Title IX of the 1972 Education Act Amendments, which barred discrimination on the basis of sex in educational programs (*Grove City College* v. *Bell*, 465 U.S. 555). The Court ruled the act did not apply to all school activities, but only to specific programs receiving federal funds. This meant a college could discriminate in those programs that did not receive federal funds, yet still receive funds for other programs. Many in Congress argued that Title IX was intended to make the entire college subject to the act's antidiscriminatory provisions. On March 22, 1988, Congress passed the Civil Rights Restoration Act over President Reagan's veto. Similarly, the Civil Rights Act of 1991 reversed a number of Supreme Court decisions that narrowly interpreted civil rights laws.

Congress can create new courts and increase the number of judges on existing courts, including the Supreme Court.

Size of the judiciary   Congress can also control the size of the judiciary, including the number of justices of the Supreme Court. The lifetime tenure provision prohibits Congress from penalizing the Supreme Court by reducing its size; reduction can be accomplished only by Congress's specifying that new vacancies will not be filled until the Court reaches the desired smaller size.

No provision prohibits Congress from immediately increasing the Court's size. Franklin D. Roosevelt favored this plan in 1937, when he schemed to increase the

Court's size, to enable him to add members sympathetic to his views. Roosevelt's proposal would have given the president the right to appoint an additional justice for every justice on the Court aged seventy or older. The plan would have expanded the Court to fifteen members, likely changing the many five-to-four decisions against New Deal legislation into ten-to-five decisions validating Roosevelt's programs. During the plan's heated debates in Congress, the Court reversed its stand and began to validate New Deal legislation. Justice Owen Roberts switched his voting habits, thereby turning five-to-four votes voiding New Deal legislation into five-to-four votes sustaining the laws. Roosevelt's bill died in Congress, a surprising loss for a president who had just won the biggest landslide in modern U.S. electoral history—a clear demonstration of the Supreme Court's prestige.

The Supreme Court has remained at nine judges since 1869 and is not likely to change.

In 1984, Justice William Rehnquist suggested that President Ronald Reagan might propose an increase in the number of Supreme Court justices to create a court more to the president's liking. Perhaps remembering Roosevelt's defeat, Reagan did not pick up on the idea.

Jurisdiction

The Constitution and statutes specify the types of cases handled by the federal judiciary. Besides the two areas of original Supreme Court jurisdiction, the federal courts have jurisdiction over cases involving federal crimes (for example, crossing a state boundary with a stolen vehicle), claims against the United States (for example, a suit to recover for overpayment of taxes), suits between citizens of different states, any federal question (for example, a patent dispute), and any constitutional issue. In civil cases (those involving relations between individuals or organizations), unless at least $50,000 is involved, the case is decided by state courts, applying their own state laws. Of the 265,831 cases that commenced in the district courts in 1990, 217,980 were civil suits. The rest were criminal cases (those involving crimes against society, such as airplane hijacking) involving federal laws.

Criminal cases in the federal courts involve violations of federal laws. Civil cases in the federal courts involve citizens of different states suing each other for at least $50,000.

Cases involving constitutional questions often begin in the state courts, reach the highest state court, and then are appealed directly to the Supreme Court. Figure 3.1 clarifies the usual routes of appeal.

Thus, Articles I and III spell out the constitutional prerogatives of the federal courts. Article III authorizes federal courts to hear cases involving national law and establishes the Supreme Court with little original jurisdiction but with a possibility for appellate jurisdiction as determined by Congress. Article I grants Congress the authority to establish administrative courts whose main purpose is facilitating the administration of government programs. These constitutional prerogatives do not seem to amount to a powerful court system, but the Constitution, although it does little to help the Supreme Court develop into a very powerful institution, also does little to hinder its development. While the Constitution gives the Court few formal powers that it can develop, it also fails to list powers explicitly forbidden to the Court. In the absence of limitations on its powers, the Supreme Court has evolved into an essential part of the national government.

JUDICIAL LEADERSHIP

The Constitutional Convention never raised the question of whether the judicial branch should provide national affairs leadership. Only Chief Justice John Marshall's (1801–1835) assertion of strong judicial independence helped realize this leadership, and many succeeding Courts continued the expansion of judicial power. In the late nineteenth and early twentieth centuries, the Court asserted leadership by rejecting a number of social reforms regulating business behavior. Under Chief Justice Earl Warren (1954–1969), the Court reaffirmed judicial leadership by instigating massive social and political reform in legislative apportionment, school integration, and individual rights. In contrast, the Rehnquist Court (1986–) has more often supported the community and government preferences over the rights of individuals.

The Supreme Court can exercise leadership through three means: (1) judicial review, (2) the review of state and local statutes and practices, and (3) the interpretation of federal statutes. However, performing these judicial functions does not guarantee judicial leadership. If the Court is to lead, it must, like Congress, also provide representation, create and clarify issues, oversee government, participate in policy making, and, as a consequence of its actions, legitimate government policy.

Judicial Review of Federal Actions

Without judicial review—the right to strike down presidential or congressional actions as conflicting with the Constitution—the Supreme Court's power would be severely restricted.

The Supreme Court exerts judicial leadership through its power of *judicial review,* the right to strike down executive and legislative actions it deems at variance with the Constitution. The Constitution does not explicitly provide the Court with the authority to void congressional acts; instead, the Court itself assumed this authority through an early interpretation of its powers by Chief Justice Marshall in 1803.

Marbury v. Madison   Thomas Jefferson discovered in 1801 that his predecessor as president, John Adams, had appointed several federal judges in the waning moments of the Federalist's tenure as president. Jefferson also discovered that the commissions (the formal notifications) for some of these jobs had not yet been delivered, including one to William Marbury, Adams' appointee as justice of the peace for the District of Columbia. Jefferson ordered Secretary of State James Madison not to deliver the commission to Marbury, thereby denying Marbury the position. In response, Marbury sued for his commission under a provision of the Judiciary Act of 1789 that gave the Supreme Court the authority to issue writs compelling the delivery of the commissions. The Supreme Court ruled in favor of Madison on the grounds that the section of the Judiciary Act giving the Supreme Court the authority to issue the type of writ in question was unconstitutional.

Thus, Marshall both avoided a confrontation with the executive branch (had he ordered Madison to act, Madison might have refused, thereby precipitating a constitutional crisis, which the Court, in 1803, might well have lost) and estab-

Judicial review developed
out of politically shrewd
Supreme Court decisions,
not an explicit
constitutional grant.

lished the principle of judicial review. By establishing this principle without requiring any action on the part of the president or Congress, Marshall made it impossible for the other branches of government to deny the validity of the principle—a basis of the power of the Supreme Court—upon which he expounded. Marshall wrote, "The Constitution is superior to any act of the legislature . . . a law repugnant to the Constitution is void" (*Marbury* v. *Madison,* 1 Cranch 137 [1803]).

The Supreme Court has
used judicial review to
overturn federal laws
sparingly.

Judicial review of acts of Congress   The Supreme Court has rarely, especially in its early years, overturned acts of Congress. Although *Marbury* v. *Madison* established the principle, the second use of judicial review to overturn a federal statute occurred fifty-four years later with the *Dred Scott* decision, which hastened the outbreak of the Civil War. In sum, the Court overturned only seventy-six federal laws between 1789 and 1941, an average of one every two years. Of course, the Court's judgments of unconstitutionality have not been spread out evenly over the years but have occurred sporadically. The activism of the Hughes Court between 1934 and 1936, for example, which invalidated thirteen New Deal laws, so infuriated Franklin Roosevelt that he proposed his "court-packing" scheme.

During the post–World War II era, the Court has been less reluctant to overturn federal acts, although the acts overturned have not generally been major laws. In sixteen years (1953–1968), the Warren Court overturned twenty-one laws or sections of laws covering a wide range of issues. A typical example is the section of the Nationality Act of 1940 that provided for the loss of U.S. citizenship as a penalty for voting in a foreign election. In *Afroyin* v. *Rusk* (387 U.S. 253 [1967]), the Court ruled that Congress lacked the authority to pass laws depriving individuals of their citizenship without a hearing.

The Burger (1969–1986) and Rehnquist (1986–) Courts have been overturning acts of Congress at a rate of almost two per year, although the overturned sections are generally minor or outdated. One exception is *Buckley* v. *Valeo* (424 U.S. 1 [1976]), in which the Court overturned some significant sections of the Federal Election Campaign Act concerning campaign financing. As noted above, in 1982 the Court invalidated the bankruptcy court system that Congress established four years earlier (*Northern Pipeline Construction Co.* v. *Marathon Pipe Line Co.,* 458 U.S. 50).

The importance of judicial review extends beyond the Court actually overturning federal legislation, for it deters Congress as well. Just as Congress sometimes modifies bills in anticipation of a presidential veto, the lawmakers themselves may modify legislation anticipating a Court ruling of unconstitutionality.

Judicial review of presidential actions   Although judicial review usually involves the constitutionality of acts of Congress, it also includes determining of the constitutionality of presidential acts. In 1952, during the Korean War, President Harry Truman sought to seize and operate steel plants that were threatened with a strike. He justified the actions under his authority as commander in chief. The Court ruled his actions were unconstitutional because he did not follow congressional procedures for private property seizure during an emergency (*Youngstown Sheet* *and Tube Company* v. *Sawyer,* 343 U.S. 579 [1952]). Thus, the Court exercised judicial review, finding a presidential action unconstitutional.

Judicial review includes the right to overturn executive acts, although the Court has rarely done so.

More recently, the Court has rarely ruled that presidential actions conflict with statutes or the Constitution. One significant case is *Train* v. *City of New York* (420 U.S. 35 [1975]), that presidents must spend funds appropriated by Congress even if they dislike the funded programs. President Richard Nixon impounded funds, attempting to kill programs he thought wasteful. The Rehnquist Court has been particularly supportive of executive branch actions. For example, in 1991 the Court upheld a Bush administration policy interpreting Title X of the Public Health Service Act as barring abortion counseling at federally funded clinics (*Rust* v. *Sullivan,* 89 U.S. 1391). Opponents of the Bush policy had urged the Court to rule it an unconstitutional infringement of freedom of speech guaranteed in the First Amendment.

Review of State and Local Actions

The supremacy clause The principle of judicial review refers, then, to the Court's right to review the constitutionality of acts by the two other branches of the national government. Yet even before Marshall established the principle, the Supreme Court had the authority to consider (and did consider) the constitutionality of acts of state and local governments. Article VI states, "This Constitution, and the Laws of the United States which shall be made in Pursuance thereof; and all Treaties made, or which shall be made, under the Authority of the United States, shall be the supreme Law of the Land." This *supremacy clause* enabled the Supreme Court from its inception to strike down any local or state government acts conflicting with federal laws or the Constitution.

Most of the controversy surrounding the Court has come from its decisions outlawing actions and laws of state and local governments.

The Supreme Court's review of the constitutionality of state and local actions is an indisputable source of leadership. The Court's history includes overturning more than 1,000 state and local practices. Although each of these cases concerned a practice in a specified place, the principles laid down are applicable everywhere. For example, the decision outlawing *de jure* school segregation[2] (*Brown* v. *Board of Education of Topeka, Kansas,* 347 U.S. 483 [1954]) involved Topeka, Kansas, but the principle that *de jure* school segregation violates the Fourteenth Amendment automatically applied everywhere in the country. Thus, the Court can set national policy with a single local decision.

The Fourteenth Amendment Passage of the Fourteenth Amendment in 1869 greatly expanded the scope of the Court's role in reviewing state and local laws. Previously, the Court could not intervene in cases of alleged denials of freedoms guaranteed by the first ten amendments, the Bill of Rights. The Bill of Rights specifically bars Congress from intervening in certain areas (for example, *Congress* "shall make no law respecting an establishment of religion . . . ."). However, the Bill

---

[2]*De jure* segregation means segregation is mandated by law, not merely a consequence of residential racial distribution.

of Rights does not say that *state* or *local governments* cannot restrict freedom of religion. This same distinction can be made for any of the rights enumerated in these ten amendments (speech, assembly, and so forth).

Thus, although the Court found in 1833 (*Barron* v. *Baltimore,* 7 Peters 243) that a litigant had indeed been denied effective use of his property without just compensation (a violation of the Fifth Amendment if perpetrated by Congress), there was nothing the Court could do because the violation was committed by a locality. Chief Justice Marshall stated that the Bill of Rights protected citizens from national government excesses but did not apply to the states.

By its statement that no state shall "deprive any person of life, liberty, or property, without due process of law; nor deny to any person within its jurisdiction the equal protection of the laws," the Fourteenth Amendment enabled the Supreme Court to review the state and local denials of freedoms guaranteed by the Bill of Rights. The Fourteenth Amendment did not, however, make the Bill of Rights automatically applicable to the states. Instead, a process of selective incorporation took place, by which the Court, over time, determined that individual elements of the Bill of Rights were applicable to the states *through* the Fourteenth Amendment. The process began in 1925 when the Court first ruled that freedom of speech was a "liberty" protected from federal encroachment by the First Amendment and from state encroachment under the Fourteenth Amendment (*Gitlow* v. *New York,* 268 U.S. 652). Freedom of the press was covered in 1931 (*Near* v. *Minnesota,* 283 U.S. 697), followed the next year by the right to counsel in capital criminal cases[3] (*Powell* v. *Alabama,* 287 U.S. 45). In 1963, this right was expanded to include all criminal cases involving felony charges—that is, major crimes (*Gideon* v. *Wainwright,* 372 U.S. 335), and was further extended in 1971 to include all imprisonable crimes (*Argersinger* v. *Hamlin,* 407 U.S. 25). The other elements of the Bill of Rights (for example, the freedoms of religion and assembly and the right to remain silent to avoid self-incrimination) have similarly become applicable to the states through the Fourteenth Amendment. The only exception still outstanding is the Fifth Amendment's right to indictment by a grand jury for major crimes. (Although most states employ grand juries, trial without grand jury indictment is practiced in some states.)

Importance of state and local practice review The Court's review of state and local practices may be its most important source of leadership. When Warren retired in early 1969 after sixteen years as chief justice, he remarked that his three most important cases were *Gideon* v. *Wainwright,* which expanded the right of the accused to fair trial, *Brown* v. *Board of Education,* which helped to create the civil rights movement, and *Reynolds* v. *Sims,* which established the one-person, one-vote principle, stopping the overrepresentation of rural areas in state legislatures. None of these involved judicial review of federal legislation; all dealt with state or local actions.

Until the Fourteenth Amendment passed in 1869, the freedoms guaranteed in the Bill of Rights protected citizens only from federal government violations, not those by state or local governments.

Over time, most of the guarantees in the Bill of Rights have been applied to state and local governments.

The Warren Court of the 1950s and 1960s expanded civil rights and civil liberties by overturning many state and local practices.

[3]Cases involving a possible sentence of death.

Issues of state and local practices Current areas of Court controversy usually involve its review of state and local practices. For example, the dispute over whether the Court has gone too far in protecting the rights of the accused arose from the 1966 *Miranda* ruling. In that decision, the Court ruled that a convicted man was entitled to a new trial because the confession police used in court was obtained without informing the accused that he had the right to remain silent (*Miranda* v. *Arizona*, 384 U.S. 436). The Court ruled that the defendant's statements cannot be used against him unless he has been warned "prior to any questioning . . . that he has a right to remain silent, that any statement he does make may be used against him, and that he has the right to the presence of an attorney, either retained or appointed." As a result, police now use a "Miranda card" to read suspects their rights at the time of arrest.[4]

> The Burger and Rehnquist Courts have been more reluctant to protect the rights of persons accused of crimes.

Critics who have argued the Supreme Court has "tied the hands of the police" were heartened by some Burger Court decisions weakening the *Miranda* decision. In 1971, for example, the Court ruled that statements made by a defendant who had not been given the Miranda warnings could still be used in court to discredit his testimony (*Harris* v. *New York,* 401 U.S. 222). The Rehnquist Court has been even less willing to restrict police practices. For example, in 1991 the Court ruled that evidence introduced at trial from a coerced confession does not automatically negate a conviction (*Arizona* v. *Fulimante*, 89 U.S. 839).

Another area of state and local practice involving the Court is the emotional abortion issue. In 1973 the Court ruled that the Fourteenth Amendment guaranteed women the right to an abortion during the early months of pregnancy (*Roe* v. *Wade,* 410 U.S. 113; *Doe* v. *Bolton,* 410 U.S. 179). The decisions struck down the antiabortion laws of forty-six states as unconstitutional interferences with individual rights. In 1977, however, the Court determined that states can refuse to spend public funds on elective abortions for women unable to pay themselves (*Maher* v. *Roe*, 432 U.S. 464). Thus, the Court guaranteed a woman's right to terminate a pregnancy during the first three months, but only if she had the money to afford the operation. In 1989, in *Webster* v. *Reproductive Health Services* (109 S.Ct. 3040), the Supreme Court upheld most provisions of a Missouri law making abortions more difficult to obtain. This action signaled state legislatures that the Court might well approve other limitations on abortion rights and might even directly overturn the *Roe* v. *Wade* decision. In a 1992 decision (*Planned Parenthood* v. *Casey,* No. 91–744), by a 5–4 vote the Court upheld the *Roe* v. *Wade* decision, but ruled that states could regulate abortions so long as their requirements do not place an "undue burden" on women seeking abortions. Both "pro-choice" and "pro-life" interest groups intensified their lobbying in the wake of this decision.

---

[4]The Court did not free Miranda; he merely received a new trial and was convicted again, even without the confession. Out on parole in 1976, Miranda was stabbed to death during a dispute in a bar. The police, using a "Miranda card," read the prime suspect his rights. So it goes.

Interpretation of Federal Statutes

The Supreme Court exercises leadership through its judicial reviews of national government actions and state and local practices only when the constitutionality of a statute is challenged in court. Both these sources of leadership involve overturning a law or practice on the basis of its unconstitutionality. The interpretation of laws, the third source of judicial leadership, differs from the first two in that it does not involve findings of unconstitutionality. For example, as noted earlier in this chapter, the Rehnquist Court weakened civil rights protections by narrowly interpreting several provisions of civil rights laws. Nobody challenged the constitutionality of the provisions, just how broadly Congress intended them to be implemented.

Many Supreme Court decisions do not challenge the constitutionality of legislation but dispute how legislation should be interpreted.

As a policy, the Court tries to avoid considerations of unconstitutionality. Frequently, to avoid this question, the Court interprets a law in a manner that changes the intent of Congress or a state legislature but avoids a finding of unconstitutionality. In 1968, for example, the Court interpreted the Selective Service Act to mean a draft board could not withdraw a divinity student's draft exemption because of participation in antiwar protest activities (*Oestereich* v. *Selective Service Board,* 393 U.S. 233). Thus, although the Court made national policy by prohibiting draft boards from removing the exemptions of protesters, it did not rule the Selective Service Act, or any of its sections, unconstitutional. Two years later the Court again altered national draft policy, ruling that individuals were entitled to conscientious objector status if their objections to war came from deeply held moral standards, even if these standards did not stem from religious beliefs (*Welsh* v. *United States,* 398 U.S. 333). Although the Court interpreted the Selective Service Act in a new way, thereby effectively changing it, it did not rule any parts of the act unconstitutional.

Functions of Leadership

The judicial branch is similar to Congress in that neither can speak with one voice (as can the president), but both are capable of real leadership. Chapter 2 noted that if Congress performed five functions well, it would provide leadership. The five functions were (1) representation, (2) creation and clarification of issues, (3) oversight of government, (4) lawmaking, and (5) legitimation of government policies. To a significant degree, the Court is also capable of realizing these functions. To the degree that the Court performs these same functions, it, too, is capable of real leadership.

The Court, somewhat protected from public opinion, often provides representation to unpopular minorities.

Representation   The Court often provides a forum where minority positions receive representation—representation often already denied by the other branches of government. Sometimes these minorities are privileged; for example, in 1918, business leaders were overjoyed when the Court overturned state legislation limiting child labor (*Hammer* v. *Dagenhart,* 247 U.S. 251). In contrast, the Warren Court often represented the interests of unpopular and/or underprivileged minorities, including those of draft protesters, persons accused of crimes, and African-American schoolchildren.

Issue creation and clarification   The Court often provides leadership by creating and clarifying issues. Perhaps the most significant example of this is the *Brown* v. *Board of Education* decision (347 U.S. 483 [1954]). Prior to that decision, the problem of inferior, segregated education was not an important issue before Congress and state legislatures. Indeed, the forces of integration were so weak that legislative remedies were not even seriously debated, especially in those Southern states where conditions for African-American youngsters were most wretched. The *Brown* decision helped America to face up to its problems of racial discrimination.

> The Court often puts significant issues, such as racial segregation, on the political agenda.

Oversight   Although the Court itself cannot conduct investigations, it performs oversight functions in response to claims by litigants who believe that government's administration of programs is denying them their rights. In the draft case previously discussed, for example, the Court in effect reviewed the government's administration of parts of the Selective Service Act and ordered the executive branch to modify its behavior in line with the Court's ruling.

Policy making   The Court does not make laws in the same sense that Congress passes legislation. Yet it does make policy through its decisions, and such policy has the force of law. Most often the Court does not make an entirely new policy but rather modifies existing policies in accord with the Court's interpretations of the Constitution. Thus, the Warren Court decisions expanding the rights of the accused did not initiate entirely new policies regarding relations between the police and the accused. The decisions did not revolutionize police behavior, and even court-mandated changes were often ignored by the police.[5] Nevertheless, in the post-World War II period, the Court has had a major impact in changing national and state policies regarding legislative apportionment, the rights of the accused, abortion, and the civil rights of racial minorities.

> The Court sometimes forces significant modifications in government policies.

Legitimation of government policy   Just as governmental policy is legitimated by passing through the representational process in Congress, policy is also legitimated when it receives a "seal of approval" of constitutionality from the Supreme Court. Although the Court may seem to lead only when actively protecting the rights of citizens from government infringement, the Court is not unimportant when endorsing the constitutionality of government acts. The judiciary does provide a third arena, in addition to the legislature and the executive, for political battle. The mere existence of this third arena, with its august judges and hallowed traditions, tends to increase popular respect for the government and the legitimacy of governmental policies.

> By providing another forum in which to appeal government policies, the Court legitimates the entire policy process.

[5]An example of noncompliance with a Supreme Court decision is the persistence of prayers in many public schools in the wake of the *Engel* v. *Vitale* decision (370 U.S. 421 [1962]), barring state-imposed prayers.

JUDICIAL ACTIVISM VERSUS JUDICIAL RESTRAINT

Its power to strike down laws as unconstitutional and to interpret statutes provides the Supreme Court leadership opportunities. Still, justices on the Court must personally decide that they want to lead and that the Court should exert strong leadership. Individuals favoring a strong leadership role for the Court support the philosophy of *judicial activism*; others favoring a more limited role favor a philosophy of *judicial restraint.*

Judicial activists want the Court to move quickly to stop violations of the Constitution.

Judicial activism involves the willingness of the Court both to accept controversial cases and to find behavior by government officials—national, state, or local—unconstitutional. Thus, activism is not just a matter of the Court's willingness to disagree with other government institutions; it is primarily a matter of willingness even to accept cases. As discussed later in this chapter, in its area of appellate jurisdiction the Court is free to choose those cases it will hear. A Court dominated by a judicial restraint philosophy is reluctant to hear cases, much less rule against decisions made by elected officials.

One argument for judicial activism is that justices are appointed for life tenure specifically to insulate them from public passions so that they will protect the liberties of the less powerful or unpopular groups and individuals. This view holds that the powers of government are indeed limited by the Constitution and it is the courts' function to be wary that the government does not infringe on citizens' rights. This was generally the philosophy of the Warren Court, a philosophy that enabled it to initiate changes benefiting disadvantaged minorities.

Judicial restraint advocates want the Court not to overturn government actions unless severe and obvious violations of the Constitution are occurring.

Judicial restraint advocates, in contrast, argue that the non-elected justices are least accountable to the people and therefore should be reluctant to disallow the actions of elected officials. This view supports upholding governmental acts unless they clearly violate a specific clause of the Constitution. This point of view, by suggesting that the Supreme Court should almost always uphold governmental actions, relegates the Court to a position well short of leadership.

Areas of Confusion

Strict constructionists believe that the powers granted the federal government in the Constitution should be interpreted narrowly, limiting what the federal government can do. Loose constructionists are reluctant to limit congressional and presidential activities.

Loose and strict constructionism   The debate between judicial activism and judicial restraint is sometimes confused with the debate between loose constructionism and strict constructionism. The constructionist debate has two dimensions. The first hinges on the interpretation of the Tenth Amendment: "The powers not delegated to the United States by the Constitution, nor prohibited by it to the States, are reserved to the States respectively, or to the people." Strict constructionists prefer a literal interpretation of this amendment, an interpretation limiting the national government's powers to those explicitly granted. Loose constructionists, in contrast, argue that the "elastic," or "necessary and proper," clause (Article I, Section 8) permits the national government broad powers to carry out the explicitly stated powers. Strict constructionists, who have lost most court challenges in recent years, might argue, for example, that the national government does not have the power to force chemical manufacturers to keep records of hazardous waste disposals because the Constitution nowhere explicitly mentions hazardous waste control as a national government responsibility. Loose constructionists would argue that control of hazardous waste disposal is a logical extension of the federal government's right to regulate interstate commerce.

The second dimension of the constructionist debate refers not to the national government's powers but rather to the individual rights guaranteed in the Bill of Rights. In this debate, strict constructionists argue that the wording of the Bill of Rights must be taken literally. Strict constructionists say, for example, that the First Amendment statement "Congress shall make no law . . . abridging the freedom of speech" means that Congress shall make *no* such law regardless of the circumstances. According to this strict interpretation, all speech is protected from congressional sanction regardless of whether the speech incites to riot, advocates violent overthrow of the government, or is racist or sexist in nature. Strict constructionists argue that Congress can punish individuals for actions (for example, rioting, discrimination, or attempting to overthrow the government by violence) but not for speech. Loose constructionists argue instead that, in the instance of speech, the government has the authority to protect itself and the citizenry by prohibiting incendiary remarks, such as in the face of a clear and present danger of irreparable harm.

Strict constructionists also believe that the federal government is tightly prohibited from limiting individual freedoms such as speech and religion. Loose constructionists again are reluctant to limit Congress and the president if these elected officials believe that laws limiting civil liberties are warranted.

There is another aspect to strict interpretation of the Bill of Rights. Some strict constructionists argue that its protections are specifically enumerated and should not be extended by judicial fiat. For example, strict constructionists argue that the broad notion of a "right to privacy" that forms the basis for such important Supreme Court decisions as *Roe* v. *Wade* (410 U.S. 113 [1973]), which constitutionally protects the right to abortion, represents less an interpretation of the Bill of Rights than an unwarranted extension of those rights. Loose constructionists reply that such broad interpretations are necessary in a changing world and are constitutionally based in the Ninth Amendment to the Constitution, which states: "The enumeration in the Constitution, of certain rights, shall not be construed to deny or disparage others retained by the people."

Liberalism and conservatism The position of judicial activism argues for a Court leading the protection of minority rights, but such a position is not necessarily politically liberal or progressive. For several decades prior to 1937, the Supreme Court took an activist role in defense of a privileged minority—namely, big corporations. The Fourteenth Amendment provides that no state shall "deprive any person of life, liberty, or property, without due process of law." The Court interpreted a corporation as a "person" within the meaning of the Fourteenth Amendment and struck down a great deal of antitrust and child labor legislation as well as many other New Deal efforts.

In that era, the position of judicial restraint held by Justice Oliver Wendell Holmes, Jr., made him appear quite progressive. Holmes, although personally quite conservative and pro-laissez faire in his political views, believed that the courts should permit the government to pass whatever legislation it desired unless the legislation was obviously unconstitutional. For this view Holmes is remembered as "the great dissenter" by reason of his many disagreements with his activist colleagues on the Court, who overruled much legislation. It was not that Holmes considered the legislation wise but rather that he held to the judicial restraint position giving elected branches of government a wide range of activities. When legislatures pass much liberal legislation, a Court that intervenes to strike down such legislation is activist and conservative. When legislatures enact conservative legislation (for example, segregation laws), a Court that strikes down such legislation is activist and progressive. Given this interpretation of judicial restraint, Holmes, a progressive member of the Taft Court of the 1920s, would have been a conservative member of the Warren Court of the 1960s.

Linkage with the Political-Question Doctrine

The political-question doctrine holds that some issues are so tied to the other branches that the courts should not decide them.

Advocates of judicial restraint vigorously embrace the "political-question" doctrine, which holds that certain issues are political questions requiring executive or legislative branch decisions, not Court rulings. In the case of *Luther* v. *Borden* (7 Howard 1 [1849]), Chief Justice Roger B. Taney faced a suit charging that the chartered government of Rhode Island was not the legitimate government because it so restricted voting rights that it violated the clause in Article IV, Section 4, guaranteeing every state a republican form of government. In his decision, Taney laid down the political question doctrine, stating that such a determination could be made only by the president and/or Congress.

Until the *Baker* v. *Carr* (369 U.S. 186 [1962]) decision of the Warren Court, the political-question doctrine was applied to all cases of legislative apportionment. The Court refused to hear such cases on the grounds that they were "political questions"—that plaintiffs from underapportioned areas should seek a remedy from the legislature, not the courts. Of course, asking the residents of an underapportioned area to seek a remedy from a malapportioned legislature was similar to asking an assault victim to seek a remedy from the attacker. Once the Court's *Baker* ruling made apportionment cases justiciable (able to be decided by the courts), only two years elapsed before it ruled that both houses of all state legislatures must be apportioned on a one-person, one-vote formula. In *Reynolds* v. *Sims* (377 U.S. 533 [1964]), Chief Justice Warren ruled that "to the extent that a citizen's right to vote is debased, he is that much less a citizen." Any debasement of citizenship was viewed with alarm by the activist Warren Court.

JUDICIAL RECRUITMENT

Appointment of Federal Judges

The road to a federal judgeship, although not especially complicated, is strewn with possible pitfalls and rejection. The necessity of obtaining Senate approval of all presidential nominees for these positions is a primary source of such rejection. Congress determines not only the number of districts the federal judiciary is divided into but also the number of justices within each district. There are currently 575 judgeships in the district courts of the United States and 156 in the courts of appeals.

All recent judges have been lawyers.

General criteria Nowhere in the law is there a written requirement that the president must nominate only lawyers to be judges, but this custom developed so strongly in this century that if the president nominated a person who was not a lawyer, the outcry from the American Bar Association would be so great that the nominee would face almost certain rejection by the Senate. Although many county and local judges throughout the state systems are not lawyers, every recent federal judge has been a member of the bar at the time of nomination to the bench.

The president nominates and the Senate confirms judicial appointments.

Only the president, who nominates, and the Senate, which confirms, are formally involved in the recruitment of federal judges. Others, however, also play important roles. For instance, a deputy attorney general is usually instructed to prepare a list of potential nominees for the president.

Senatorial courtesy is involved in district court appointments.

Senatorial courtesy In preparing the list, the attorney general's office will certainly learn the wishes of the senators from the president's own party from the state with the vacant judgeship. As noted in Chapter 2, the practice of senatorial courtesy applies to district court judges, so that any presidential nominee must be approved by the appropriate senators (if both senators from a state are of the president's party) or senator (if only one of a state's senators is of the president's party). In practice, senators from the state with the vacancy usually submit a list of four or five preferred individuals, from which the president chooses the new judge. If neither senator is of the president's party, the deputy attorney general is not concerned with senatorial courtesy but instead consults with local or state party officials to identify prospective nominees.

Every president has made the great majority of appointments from among lawyers who share his party affiliation.

Although presidents often state their intentions to find the "best person for the job" and emphasize the nonpartisan nature of the work, a very substantial majority of the judges appointed in this century have been of the president's party. Among recent presidents, the only one who nominated even 10 percent of his judges from the other party was Gerald Ford, a Republican who made Democrats 21 percent of his judicial nominations.

Potential judges are identified through contacts with state party leaders, the attorney general's office, and, of course, relevant senators. A deputy attorney general then asks the FBI for a background investigation and members of the bar and judges in the affected area for their assessment of the potential nominee's professional competence and their opinion of whether he or she will likely blend well with the other members of the court. The deputy attorney general also turns over the names of all serious potential nominees to the American Bar Association's Standing Committee on Federal Judiciary which rates candidates as exceptionally well qualified, qualified, or not qualified. A low rating from the committee generally results in a decision by the president not to nominate that person. The Senate is unlikely to confirm a nominee who the ABA declares publicly is not qualified for a federal judgeship.

The American Bar Association ranks potential nominees.

Senate action   Once a nomination is made, it is considered by the Senate Judiciary Committee, which, after hearings, usually supports the president's choice—assuming, of course, that senatorial courtesy was exercised. Action on the floor generally follows in the form of almost unanimous approval of the nominee. The president is then empowered to appoint his nominee and grant the commission—that is, the authority to carry through the duties of the judgeship.

Appointment of Supreme Court Justices

The appointment procedure for Supreme Court justices is much more rigorous than for other judges, because of the great nationwide political interest in the Supreme Court. While the senators from Maine probably care very little about who is appointed district court judge in New Mexico, they are understandably concerned about nominees for the Supreme Court. Also, the president takes a much greater personal interest in the nomination. He very much wants to nominate individuals who, while on the Court, will support his position on issues, for he is well aware that the Court can make policy through its decisions.

Senatorial courtesy is not applicable to Supreme Court appointments.

Sometimes presidents miscalculate and later regret their appointments. Once a nominee is on the bench, however, a president cannot remove him or her. Conservative President Dwight D. Eisenhower reportedly described his appointment of Earl Warren as the worst decision of his presidency. Warren's record as governor of California evidenced little concern for civil rights (for example, those of Japanese Americans during World War II), but Chief Justice Warren consistently championed the causes of underprivileged minorities.

President Nixon's four appointees sometimes supported his conservative views but also frequently disagreed with his positions. Perhaps most surprising was the high activism level of the Burger Court. In spite of Nixon's statements that his appointees would limit the Court's role, the Burger Court was not reluctant to tackle issues and to rule government actions unconstitutional. On the emotional issue of abortion, three Nixon appointees (Burger, Blackmun, and Powell) voted with the Court's majority, striking down state laws prohibiting abortion in the early months of pregnancy (in opposition to Nixon's antiabortion stance). In the decision probably most resented by Nixon, his appointees voted unanimously that he had to turn over "Watergate tapes" to the special prosecutor.

President Reagan's three appointees and President Bush's two are moving the Court in a more conservative direction. In *Bowen* v. *Kendrick* (101 L. Ed. 2d 520 [1988]), the Court upheld a 1981 law allowing federal funding of religious groups counseling young people to be chaste and avoid abortion. In *Hazelwood School District* v. *Kuhlmeier* (484 U.S. 260 [1988]), the Court narrowed free speech protections by upholding censorship of high school newspapers. In *City of Richmond* v. *J. A. Croson Co.* (109 S. Ct. 706 [1989]), the Court struck down a Richmond ordinance requiring a percentage of the city's construction contracts be set aside for minority-owned businesses. As noted earlier in this chapter, recent Rehnquist Court decisions limited civil rights protections, weakened the constitutional protections for criminal case defendants, and allowed state legislatures to chip away at abortion rights guaranteed in the *Roe v. Wade* decision. In choosing between government interest and individual rights, the Court has enhanced government power. Critics fear the Court is becoming more activist in promoting a conservative social philosophy.

The Senate's record Only 20 percent of all presidential nominations for Supreme Court seats have been rejected by the Senate, but recent years contributed substantially to this percentage. President Reagan's nomination of Appeals Court Judge Robert Bork was rejected by a 58 to 42 Senate vote. Many senators voting against Bork said they thought that Bork's conservative views were so far from the mainstream that he would not have made a good Supreme Court justice. Before Reagan, the last Senate rejections were of two Nixon nominees.

With the increasing domination of the Supreme Court by conservative judges, many senators are concerned that the Court not reflect only conservative views. In 1991 George Bush nominated Clarence Thomas to serve on the Court. Thomas, an African-American who had chaired the Equal Employment Opportunity Commission during the Reagan administration, had been such an outspoken conservative that most civil rights organizations, despite their preference that a black nominee replace the retiring Thurgood Marshall, opposed Thomas's nomination. During the hearings, Thomas moderated his positions, often explaining that his earlier statements had been merely theoretical musings that would not impact his decisions. After bitter hearings that also included charges of sexual harassment, Clarence Thomas did win confirmation by a 52–48 vote, the closest in history.

Although the rejection rate has not been substantial, the threat of rejection has caused presidents to sometimes withdraw names of nominees once it became clear they were not likely to meet with Senate approval. In 1968, for example, the nomination to elevate Justice Abe Fortas to the vacant chief justice post was withdrawn by Lyndon Johnson. The Senate expressed displeasure over Fortas's social activism, the "lame-duck" nature of the appointment (Johnson would soon leave the White House), and the alleged element of "cronyism" (Fortas was a long-time personal friend of the president). In 1987, Ronald Reagan withdrew Douglas Ginsberg's nomination after Ginsberg admitted smoking marijuana while a Harvard law professor.

> The Senate scrutinizes Supreme Court nominees to the extent that historically one in five is rejected.

THE JUDGES
District Court and Appeals Court Judges

> Supreme, district, and appeals court judges all have lifetime tenure.

Federal judges are predominantly middle-aged white men with substantial salaries and the exceptional job security of knowing that they can be removed only through impeachment.[6] This situation still did not satisfy at least a few federal judges, who

[6]In 1992, district court judges received $129,500 in annual compensation; court of appeals judges, $137,300; associate justices of the Supreme Court, $159,000; and Chief Justice Rehnquist, $166,200.

TABLE 3.2   Judicial Nominees (numbers are percentages)

	Women	*Blacks*	*Hispanics*
U.S. Courts of Appeals			
Johnson	3	5	0
Nixon	0	0	0
Ford	0	0	0
Carter	20	16	4
Reagan	5	1	1
Bush	15	4	7
U.S. District Courts			
Johnson	2	3	3
Nixon	1	3	1
Ford	2	6	2
Carter	14	14	7
Reagan	8	2	5
Bush	15	7	2

Source: Congressional Quarterly Weekly Report, January 18, 1992, p. 112.

resigned to resume private law practices promising earnings well over $300,000 annually. No justice ever resigned from the prestigious Supreme Court for financial reasons, although several stepped down in response to the pressures of the position.

Until the Carter administration, the federal judiciary was almost entirely white and male.

As Table 3.2 shows, the Carter administration nominated women, African-Americans, and Hispanics to the lower federal courts standing out in contrast to its predecessors and the Reagan years. Jimmy Carter's impact in diversifying the federal judiciary was aided by the Omnibus Judgeship Act of 1978, which created 152 new judgeships to handle the ever-increasing federal court caseload. Carter nominated, and the Senate confirmed, 56 appointments to courts of appeals and 206 to district courts. Reagan appointed 72 judges to courts of appeals and 292 district court judges.

District courts are concerned with the facts of cases; appeals courts are concerned with questions of judicial error and misinterpretation of law.

The ninety-four United States district courts are staffed by 575 judges, who annually decide over 200,000 civil cases and 40,000 criminal cases. At this level, the judges are concerned primarily with the facts of the case, not with the interpretation of law and constitutionality. In contrast, the 156 courts of appeals judges never hear new factual evidence; they depend on the records of the lower courts from which the appeals are made. Usually sitting in groups of three, appellate court judges rule on questions of judicial error and interpretation of law in cases appealed from the lower courts.

TABLE 3.3   Justices of the Supreme Court

1993 Judges	*Appointed by*	*Age**
William Rehnquist†	Nixon/Reagan	67
Byron White	Kennedy	75
Harry Blackmun	Nixon	83
John Paul Stevens	Ford	72
Sandra Day O'Connor	Reagan	62
Antonin Scalia	Reagan	56
Arthur Kennedy	Reagan	56
David Souter	Bush	52
Clarence Thomas	Bush	45

*Ages as of January 1, 1993
†Appointed associate justice by Nixon in 1971; appointed chief justice by Reagan in 1986.

Supreme Court Justices

The median age of Supreme Court justices in 1993 was sixty-two.

As Table 3.3 illustrates, turnover among Supreme Court justices is not rapid. Most justices remain in office until declining health forces a retirement decision. Each individual judge decides when it is an appropriate time to resign.

In the Supreme Court's history, only three justices have not been white males. The first African-American justice, Thurgood Marshall, was appointed in 1967 by Lyndon Johnson. When Marshall retired in 1991, President Bush selected Clarence Thomas, the second black justice in the history of the Court. The only female justice, Sandra Day O'Connor, was appointed in 1981 by Ronald Reagan.

The chief justice is nominated by the president for that specific office.

William Rehnquist   The chief justice in 1993 is sixty-seven-year-old William Rehnquist, who was appointed to his current position by President Reagan in 1986 and was first appointed to the Court by President Nixon in 1971. Rehnquist was one of the Burger Court's most conservative members and, as chief justice, he is increasingly activist in attempting to impose his conservative ideology. Before his appointment to the Court, Rehnquist served as an assistant attorney general in the Justice Department's Office of Legal Counsel. As chief justice, Rehnquist chairs the Friday conferences of the Court, at which (meeting with only the justices present) the Court discusses and decides cases. When Rehnquist decides with the majority, he must assign to a particular justice the writing of the majority opinion. When the chief justice is in the minority, the most senior justice in the majority assigns the writing of the majority opinion.

Although nominees often have experience as judges, judicial experience is not required for nominaiton to the Court.

Byron R. White   John F. Kennedy's only appointee was Byron R. White, who in 1993 was seventy-five years of age. White ran the Citizens for Kennedy organization in the 1960 presidential campaign. He was rewarded with an appointment as deputy attorney general and, in 1962, an appointment to the Supreme Court. In keeping with his emphasis on vigor, Kennedy appointed a lawyer who, as "Whizzer" White, led the National Football League in ground gaining in 1938 and whom Kennedy first met in the Navy during World War II. Over the years White has grown increasingly conservative in his decisions. He votes most of the time with the extreme conservative bloc of Rehnquist, Scalia, and Thomas.

Harry Blackmun Appointed by Eisenhower to the court of appeals and by Nixon to the Supreme Court in 1970, Blackmun has grown more liberal over the years. With the retirements of Brennan in 1990 and Marshall in 1991, Blackmun (eighty-three) is the Court's leading defender of individual rights.

John Paul Stevens John Paul Stevens, seventy-two years of age in 1993 and the only Ford appointee, joined Blackmun, Scalia, Kennedy, Souter, and Thomas as court of appeals judges on the Supreme Court. In 1975, Stevens replaced William O. Douglas, who had served on the Court for thirty-six years—longer than any justice in the nation's history. Douglas's record of unusually strong advocacy for civil liberties and environmentalism so angered his conservative detractors that at one time Ford, then Republican House minority leader, called for Douglas's impeachment. Stevens's moderate-to-liberal record has been by no means as controversial as that of Douglas.

Until President Reagan appointed Sandra Day O'Connor in 1981, the Court had been an all-male institution.

Sandra Day O'Connor A previous edition of this book predicted that Carter would nominate a woman to serve on the Supreme Court. Carter made no Supreme Court appointments, but the Court's days as an all-male institution were in fact numbered. In 1981, Reagan nominated, and the Senate confirmed, Sandra Day O'Connor as an associate justice of the Supreme Court. An Arizona appeals court judge at the time of her nomination, O'Connor was boosted for the nomination by influential Sen. Barry Goldwater (R.-Ariz.), as well as by Associate Justice Rehnquist, a Stanford Law School classmate. They convinced the Reagan administration that O'Connor would become the type of justice Reagan envisioned. Sixty-two years of age in 1993, she has voted most of the time with the conservatives forming, with Justices Kennedy and Souter, a moderate conservative bloc.

Antonin Scalia The first Italian-American on the Supreme Court, fifty-six-year-old Antonin Scalia was appointed by President Reagan in 1986, the same year Reagan appointed Rehnquist chief justice. Scalia served in the Nixon and Ford administrations and was a University of Chicago law professor before his appointment as associate justice. Along with Chief Justice Rehnquist, Scalia represents the most extreme conservative positions on most decisions.

Arthur M. Kennedy Following the rejection of Robert Bork and the withdrawal of Douglas Ginsberg, Reagan nominated Arthur M. Kennedy as associate justice. Kennedy, who taught law at McGeorge School of Law in Sacramento, was unanimously confirmed by a Senate anxious to avoid confrontation after the grueling Bork debates. Never as outspokenly conservative as Scalia, Kennedy (fifty-six) has moved toward the center to form a moderate conservative bloc with O'Connor and Souter.

David H. Souter   In 1990 George Bush appointed David H. Souter, then a fifty-year-old New Hampshire judge who only three months before had been appointed to the U.S. Court of Appeals. Little known outside New Hampshire, Souter's scholarly manner and knowledge of judicial precedent was impressive in his confirmation hearings. On the Court, Souter sides consistently with Chief Justice Rehnquist.

Clarence Thomas   Appointed to the U.S. Court of Appeals by George Bush in 1990 and to the Supreme Court one year later, Clarence Thomas is the youngest justice at forty-four years of age. He came to the Court when liberal activist Justice Thurgood Marshall retired. Thomas, a strident conservative, promised during the hearings that he would give the issues facing the Court a fresh view. Nevertheless, once confirmed, he has voted consistently with the most conservative judges.

How Judges Decide

Knowing who judges are and how they think is important, because judges do not objectively apply the law as a concrete entity that can be correctly ascertained through study. Instead, they make policy through their interpretations and decisions, which necessarily involve their own personal policy preferences. As Justice Felix Frankfurter wrote, "The meaning of 'due process' and the content of terms like 'liberty' are not revealed by the Constitution. It is the justices who make the meaning. They read into the neutral language of the Constitution their own economic and social views. . . . Let us face the fact that [the] justices of the Supreme Court are the molders of policy rather than the impersonal vehicles of revealed truth."[7]

Judges interpret laws on the basis of their own values.

Discretion in judicial behavior is found primarily at the Supreme Court level, for district court judges are usually more concerned with the facts of a case (and appellate court judges with judges' errors) than with the interpretation of law. Only after the facts of a case are clear (for example, that a police officer really did arrest and question a suspect without informing her of her constitutional rights) and a subsequent question of the interpretation of a law or the validity of a law arises does a case reach the Supreme Court. District courts and courts of appeals almost never decide a case by ruling a law unconstitutional.

Judicial decisions list relevant precedents, explaining why they are interpreting the law as they are.

The myth of "the law"   Although Supreme Court justices do indeed make decisions based on their own social views, legal tradition insists that justices in general not admit this. Instead, they give the impression that they make decisions by applying the "correct" statute or the "correct" constitutional provision with proper reasoning. They justify rulings on the basis of *stare decisis,* which means "to stand

[7]Felix Frankfurter, "The Supreme Court and the Public," *Forum* 83 (June 1930) pp. 332–334.

by what has been decided" (commonly called *precedent*); they search for a previous case involving similar principles. Because there are invariably several precedents supporting the plaintiff and the defendant, justices choose the precedent they wish to find applicable to the facts of the case.

With the availability of so many precedents in the Supreme Court's many years of cases, the Court rarely finds it necessary to overrule one of its own decisions. This gives constitutional law a logical continuity supportive of the myth that there is "the law," which has an existence independent of what the justices say it is. This myth, that the "law" exists before judicial decisions, which merely "speak the law," helps to legitimate judicial actions.

The Court tries to create an aura of solemn professionalism to enhance respect for the institution and its decisions.

If the judicial function is purely passive, simply telling us what "the law" is, judicial decisions become more than the opinions and values of common mortals. They become professional statements of reality, similar to a medical doctor's diagnosis. Likewise similar to the medical profession, the legal profession has its own jargon, which helps obscure its dealings. Any group of practitioners wishing to legitimate its actions can do so most effectively by claiming professional status. Because part of being professional involves possession of specialized expertise, the professional can argue that his or her actions or decisions may be properly evaluated only by other professionals having the same expertise. Thus, many judges claim their decisions are objective, value-free, professional determinations of reality ("the law") and, as such, are beyond criticism except by other professionals. Because many laypeople also accept this notion of professional objectivity, the decisions of judges, including Supreme Court justices, are usually respected— further legitimating Court decisions.

THE OPERATION OF THE COURT SYSTEM

This chapter focused on the Supreme Court, the ultimate arbiter of federal cases and controversies and the locus of important policy changes. Yet only a very small percentage of the thousands of federal cases involve questions of constitutional law sufficiently important to reach the Supreme Court. Each year the Court is asked to hear approximately 5,000 cases; it declines all but about 130 of the requests. The vast majority of cases are resolved without involving the Court— either in the lower judicial courts, which include the district courts, courts of appeals, and special judicial courts, or in the administrative courts.

Only a minute proportion of federal cases reaches the Supreme Court.

Lower Judicial Courts

Courts of appeals The courts of appeals, the tribunal immediately below the Supreme Court, are asked to hear over 40,000 cases annually. All of these come up on appeal from the district courts, territorial courts, Tax Court, or independent regulatory commissions. The courts of appeals have three options when handling cases brought before them. They may affirm a lower court or commission decision;

they may reverse such decisions, either deciding the issue or setting the stage for an appeal to the Supreme Court; or they may *remand* (send the case back) to the lower courts for further review. For example, in 1973 District Court Judge John Sirica ruled that President Nixon had to turn over nine "Watergate tapes" to the court for scrutiny (*United States* v. *Mitchell et al.*, 377 F. Supp 1326 [1974]). Nixon appealed with an argument based on the separation of powers between government branches. A court of appeals rejected this argument and affirmed the district court's original decision (*Nixon* v. *Sirica*, 487 F.2d 700 [1974]). Nixon chose not to appeal the decision to the Supreme Court and turned over the tapes to Sirica.

The appeals courts may affirm, reverse, or remand lower court decisions.

District courts   The bulk of the work of the federal judiciary is handled by the district courts, which have only original jurisdiction. The 575 full-time judges of these courts handle all violations of federal laws, as well as civil actions arising under the Constitution, laws, or U.S. treaties, and cases involving citizens of different states. The last category is handled by state courts unless at least $50,000 is claimed. However, in cases involving citizens of different states, even if over $50,000 is involved, the state courts may still handle the case if the litigants agree. The district courts also handle admiralty and maritime cases, as well as any other that Congress prescribes. Over 250,000 matters are filed with the district courts each year.

Most federal cases are civil in origin (based on diversity of state residence), not criminal.

Each case is handled by a single judge sitting with a jury unless the litigants agree to a nonjury trial. In the vast majority of cases, the final determination occurs at the district court level, because most losers find themselves without a sufficiently good case or the funds for an appeal.

In addition to judges, significant officers at the district level are United States marshals and United States attorneys. The former make arrests, guard prisoners, and serve court orders; the latter prosecute for the government in criminal cases. Both serve under the authority of the attorney general and are appointed by the president with Senate approval. Traditionally these appointments, one of each in the ninety-four district courts, have been patronage positions.

The offices of U.S. marshals and attorneys have traditionally been patronage positions.

Special courts   Special judicial courts differ from district courts in that special courts adjudicate cases in specified substantive areas. The Court of International Trade and the Court of Appeals for the Federal Circuit are judicial courts whose judges have lifetime appointments. The other special courts are administrative courts whose judges have fixed-term appointments.

Court of International Trade   The largest of the three most major special courts is the Court of International Trade, whose nine members (no more than five of whom may be members of the same political party) each receive $129,500 annually. This court hears civil cases arising from claims that rulings and appraisals by customs officials are in error. The judges sit in panels of three in various ports of entry.

Court of Appeals for the Federal Circuit   The Court of Appeals for the Federal Circuit has only appellate jurisdiction over decisions made in the Court of International Trade, the patent office, the tariff commission, the Claims Court, and the Court of Veterans Appeals. The court has twelve members, who each receive $137,300 annually. Like all judges in judicial (as distinct from administrative) courts, they face removal only by impeachment.

Individuals who believe the federal government wronged them can sue in the Claims Court.

Claims Court   The Claims Court is an administrative court that in 1982 replaced the court of claims, a judicial court founded in 1855. The court adjudicates citizens' suits for damages against the federal government. Individuals who believe the government has reneged on contract obligations, taken their property without just compensation, or caused personal injury (through the negligent behavior of a government employee) must sue in this court rather than in a general-purpose court. The court has sixteen members, each compensated at $129,500 annually, who serve terms of fifteen years.

Tax Court   The nineteen members of the Tax Court are appointed to twelve-year terms by the president with the consent of the Senate. Each compensated at $129,500 per year, the judges respond to taxpayer claims that the Internal Revenue Service misinterpreted the tax code in a specific application to the plaintiff. Thus, the Commissioner of Internal Revenue is always the defendant in these cases.

Territorial courts   The territorial courts differ widely in their authority, for each is tailored to local customs and needs. In Puerto Rico, for example, the court has jurisdiction only over questions of national law, because Puerto Rico has separate local courts. In Guam, the Virgin Islands, and the Northern Mariana Islands (administered by the United States under a United Nations trusteeship agreement) the courts handle local disputes as well. The judges of these courts, appointed by the president and confirmed by the Senate, serve ten-year terms except in Puerto Rico, where the judges enjoy lifetime tenure.

Military personnel accused of misbehavior while on duty are subject to court-martial procedures, not trial in the regular judicial courts.

Court of Military Appeals   The Court of Military Appeals has an unusual record in that in over half the cases it hears it overturns the verdict of the court-martial. The court, composed of three civilian judges, is the final appellate tribunal in court-martial cases. It was established in 1950 as part of the revision of the Uniform Code of Military Justice, the first major overhaul of the military justice system in 150 years. Its three judges are appointed for fifteen-year terms by the president with Senate confirmation. At its discretion, the Court of Military Appeals is authorized to review decisions of courts-martial involving prison sentences of more than one year and/or bad-conduct discharges. The court is required to review any decision considered suspect by the judge advocate general as well as all decisions involving generals or admirals or the imposition of the death sentence.

The role of this court is not inconsequential, since over two million Americans are subject to military justice. The court has in fact had a substantial impact, effecting the application of most of the Bill of Rights to courts-martial. In 1967, for example, it ruled that the "Miranda procedures," by which suspects are read their rights at the time of arrest, apply to military justice as well as civilian justice (*United States* v. *Tempia*, 16 USCMA 629). In 1969, the disparity in rights afforded

Over time, the Court of Military Appeals has applied the same standards of judicial process used in other federal courts to military hearings.

military personnel compared with civilian rights was further reduced by a Supreme Court ruling that, during peacetime, service personnel would be tried in civilian courts for offenses committed while off duty or on leave (*O'Callahan* v. *Parker,* 395 U.S. 258). Continuing the trend toward affording military defendants the same rights as civilian defendants, Carter in 1980 ordered courts-martial to use the same rules of evidence applied in federal criminal trials.

Bankruptcy courts When Congress tried to establish bankruptcy courts as judicial courts, but without the independence of other judicial courts, the Supreme Court ruled the effort unconstitutional. The Bankruptcy Reform Act, signed into law by President Carter in 1978, requires bankruptcies to be filed in bankruptcy courts rather than district courts. The new bankruptcy courts were to be under the jurisdiction of president-appointed bankruptcy judges with fourteen-year terms. In 1982, however, the Supreme Court ruled parts of the Bankruptcy Reform Act unconstitutional because the act authorized bankruptcy judges to exercise the duties of district judges, but without lifetime tenure. In 1984 Congress passed new legislation to address the problem of bankruptcy judges lacking adequate independence from the executive branch. One change is that bankruptcy judges now are appointed by courts of appeals to fourteen-year terms. The other is that, in more serious cases, such as those involving claims of personal injury, the bankruptcy judge merely makes findings of fact and recommendations to the district judge who enters final judgment. The Supreme Court has upheld this arrangement.

Court of Veterans Appeals In response to requests from veterans' organizations, in 1988 Congress created this court to review decisions of the Board of Veterans Appeals. Veterans dissatisfied with decisions of the Department of Veterans Affairs must appeal first to the Board of Veterans Appeals, but may then further appeal to the Court of Veterans Appeals.

Supreme Court Procedures

Jurisdiction The Supreme Court, as noted earlier in this chapter, has two types of jurisdiction: original and appellate. Most cases that the Court decides involve appellate jurisdiction; that is, they are appeals by the loser in a lower federal court or a state court of last resort. The lower federal court is usually an appeals court because cases may be appealed directly to the Supreme Court from a district court only in special, rare circumstances (for example, a decision holding an act of Congress unconstitutional) and because cases from the special-purpose courts are rarely reviewed by the Supreme Court. Cases from a state court of last resort (usually called the state supreme court) are appealed directly to the Supreme Court if the loser feels a substantial question of federal law or the Constitution is involved.

The Supreme Court rarely hears a case under its own original jurisdiction.

The writ of certiorari An appeal to the Supreme Court is no guarantee the Court will agree to take the case; four justices must vote to place the case on the docket before it can be heard. Only questions of substantial social and/or legal importance

The Court decides which cases it will hear on appeal, accepting only a small percentage of the cases appealed to it.

are granted writs of *certiorari* (a Latin term meaning "made more certain") and called up; 95 percent of petitions for *certiorari* are denied, usually without explanation. Besides rejecting cases too minor in subject matter for the Court's time, justices sometimes refuse cases because of the sensitive issues involved. Often this involves the "political-question" doctrine discussed earlier in this chapter.

The Supreme Court refused to rule on the Vietnam War's constitutionality, although it was presented with several cases challenging the war's legality. There is no way of knowing the reasoning of the nine justices, but several historians suggest that their refusal was based on political reality. Had the Court ruled the war unconstitutional and demanded the immediate withdrawal of all U.S. troops from Vietnam, the president might simply have refused to obey. Such an action by any president would throw the nation into a constitutional crisis, accompanied by massive chaos and bewilderment. The ultimate outcome would be uncertain, but Supreme Court justices are well aware that in any confrontation with the other government branches, all the money and all the guns are in other hands. The Court does not operate in a political vacuum.

Amicus curiae *briefs* Another indication of the Supreme Court's political nature is the use of *amicus curiae* briefs in a substantial number of cases. Such briefs are rarely used in lower courts. An *amicus curiae* brief ("friend of the court" in Latin) is a document presented to a court supporting the arguments of one of the parties in a case. An *amicus curiae* brief attempts to bolster the litigant's position by providing additional legal argumentation and demonstrating organizational or interest-group support. *Amicus curiae* briefs are a means by which interest groups and other political organizations communicate their views on issues to the Court. Those submitting such briefs are usually groups, either governmental (for example, the city of New York or the state of Mississippi) or organizational (for example, the American Civil Liberties Union, National Right to Life Committee, National Abortion Rights Action League, or Friends of Animals).

In most Supreme Court cases, several *amicus curiae* briefs are filed.

The Supreme Court in session The Supreme Court of the United States is in session from October through June in the District of Columbia's 1935 replica of the Greek Temple of Diana at Ephesus. Monday through Thursday the justices hear cases from 10 A.M. to 2:30 P.M.—one of Washington's fascinating free exhibitions. With rare exceptions, a lawyer is permitted one-half hour to state a client's case, although some of this time is used by the justices posing questions and asking for clarifications. On Fridays, the justices meet privately (the Friday conference), deciding on applications for *certiorari* and determining the results of cases already heard. At the Friday conference, the chief justice gives his position on each case first, followed by the other justices in order of seniority. The final vote is taken in the opposite order, from the newest justice through the chief justice. After that vote, the chief justice assigns the opinion's author if the chief justice is a member of the majority; otherwise, the most senior member of the majority decides who will write the majority opinion. Justices may, of course, submit concurring or dissenting opinions either individually or in combination.

Four days a week, the justices listen to oral arguments on cases; on Fridays the justices meet together privately to discuss their decisions

CONCLUSION

In comparison with most of the world, the U.S. court system is independent and powerful.

The American judicial system differs from those in most nations in that it functions with greater independence from the parties in power in the executive and congressional branches. Throughout most of the world, it is unlikely that a court would rule an act of the ruling party or coalition unconstitutional. It is even less likely that such a ruling would be respected and the orders of the court followed by the executive or legislative branch.

The Supreme Court exhibits immense potential for exercising political power, but the actualization of that potential is determined by the "climate" in which the Court operates. The justices are acutely aware that the area of jurisdiction open to them is determined by Congress. Neither can the Court ignore the persuasive powers inherent in the office of the president regarding presidential-congressional relations. If the Court digresses too far or too consistently from the interpretation of "reality" ("the law") as it is viewed by Congress and/or the president, legislative pressure to remove the relevant cases from the Court's jurisdiction inevitably results. Thus, the parameters within which the Court is free to act are set by the president and Congress, yet these parameters are wide enough that the Court may, if it is willing and politically astute, assume a role of effective leadership.

The Supreme Court operates in a political world, providing leadership in many ways, but it cannot stray too far from public opinion for too long.

Selected Additional Readings

Baum, Lawrence. *The Supreme Court.* 4th ed. Washington, D.C.: Congressional Quarterly, 1992.

Carp, Robert A., and Stidham, Ronald. *The Federal Courts,* 2nd ed. Washington, D.C.: Congressional Quarterly, 1991.

Cooper, Phillip J. *Hard Judicial Choices: Federal District Court Judges and State and Local Officials.* New York: Oxford University Press, 1988.

Stumpf, Harry P. *American Judicial Politics.* Chicago: Harcourt Brace Jovanovich, 1988.

C A S E   H I S T O R Y : S u p e r f u n d

The Courts

118–119   It was noted in the text that the U.S. court system is hierarchically arranged, consisting of multiple layers. Thus, despite the importance and complexity of the Comprehensive Environmental Response, Compensation and Liability Act of 1980 (CERCLA), only one case based on this statute reached the Supreme Court during the original act's existence. Despite the lack of significant involvement by the Supreme Court, the federal courts have played an important role by clarifying the legislation, legitimating it, and settling disputes between litigants with different views of how the law should be applied.

The first case brought to federal court under CERCLA was filed in the U.S. District Court of New Jersey (*Lesniak et al.* v. *United States et al.*) soon after President Jimmy

Carter signed the legislation. Section 114(c) of the law is commonly known as the "preemption" provision, because it preempts the states from establishing a tax, or fee, on any "person" (a legal term that includes corporations) for the same purposes (that is,

128 to cover the same cleanup operations) as those covered by the federal tax on petroleum and chemical companies. This is a complex way of saying that no one may be taxed twice for the same purpose.

Several states, however, had already passed fee-based hazardous-substance response programs similar to Superfund. It was unclear what parts of these programs would be illegal because they would fall under the preemption provision of the Superfund law. The plaintiffs in the Lesniak case sought a judgment from the court that Congress did not intend Section 114(c) of CERCLA to apply to a number of state hazardous waste activities, such as buying equipment to respond to hazardous waste releases. If Lesniak won the case, the states could continue taxing chemical companies, spending money for the specific state hazardous waste activities not covered by Superfund. The court set January 25, 1982, as the hearing date for the Lesniak case.

On January 23, just two days before the hearing date, EPA Administrator Anne Gorsuch approved an out-of-court settlement admitting the correctness of Lesniak's position. Thus,

129 even though the case never reached the hearing stage, the court served a valuable function in the policy-making process. Because the court accepted the Lesniak suit, it forced the executive branch to clarify CERCLA by having EPA admit that the functions listed in the suit were not at odds with the preemption provision of Section 114(c). As a result, more states passed hazardous-waste fee-based legislation modeled after the fee system represented in the Lesniak suit. This out-of-court settlement helped preserve, at the state level, a potentially powerful mechanism for funding state participation in the Superfund program and permitting state responses to those hazardous-substance releases into the environment that the federal government either could not or would not clean up.

The Lesniak agreement was not the last word on preemption. The one Supreme Court case involving Superfund was a 1986 decision (*Exxon Corp.* v. *Hunt, 475 U.S. 355*) invalidating parts of a New Jersey statute. The Court ruled CERCLA's preemption provision

127 meant New Jersey could not use tax money collected from petroleum and chemical facilities to fund hazardous-waste cleanups. The Exxon case decision was not significant, because the conference committee working on the Superfund reauthorization had reached agreement to remove the preemption provision from Superfund. Both the states and the petrochemical industry knew that as soon as the reauthorization passed, the states could freely spend funds collected by special fees for activities that might potentially also be funded by Superfund.

The second case brought to the federal court system is much more complex, because it deals with executive branch politics, rather than the law's structure itself. Section 105

129 of CERCLA holds:

> Within one hundred and eighty days after the enactment of this Act, the President shall, after notice and opportunity for public comments, revise and republish the national contingency plan for the removal of oil and hazardous substances, originally prepared and published pursuant to Section 311 of the Federal Water Pollution Control Act, to reflect and effectuate the responsibilities and powers created by this Act.

The National Contingency Plan (NCP) was the "blueprint" used by the federal government and the states in cleaning up oil spilled into the nation's surface waters. Congress required the executive branch ("the President") to revise the NCP so it would cover the release of virtually any toxic substance, pollutant, or contaminant into the environment. Further, the NCP was, according to Section 105 of CERCLA, to be revised and republished, providing national guidelines to the thirteen federal agencies and the states—all of which play a role in the cleanup of hazardous waste sites and chemical spills—by June 9, 1981 (180 days after Carter signed the bill into law).

Through the latter half of 1980 and the first several months of 1981, bureaucrats from EPA worked closely with the other federal agencies comprising the National Response Team (NRT) to draft a revision of the NCP so it would be acceptable to the entire federal establishment. This was, however, the period of transition from one administration to another and therefore a time of flux in the federal government. The inauguration of Ronald Reagan changed the philosophy of the top management of those federal agencies charged with protecting the environment. Industry would have a much greater influence over the Reagan administration's policies than it had exerted during the Carter years.

From Reagan's inauguration through May 20, 1981, EPA was without an administrator. When Anne Gorsuch took over as agency head, she distrusted the previous work accomplished on the NCP (and it was, at that point, virtually completed), and decided to begin with a fresh team. The new administration would not meet the congressionally mandated NCP deadline.

Environmental groups, concerned that the lack of an NCP would mean the lack of effective cleanup, pressured the new administration. Letters requesting information on new deadlines for NCP publication and personal visits to EPA officials followed, but by September 1981 the NCP was still not ready. In fact, Section 105 of CERCLA specifies that the NCP should be revised and republished only "after notice and opportunity for public comments." This terminology means the EPA could not simply "publish" the document in "final form." The agency was required to inform the public, beforehand, of what would be proposed as the final version. Thus, before a document like the NCP could be "binding"—i.e., have the force of law—it first must be printed in the Federal Register so that the public would have the opportunity to comment on the proposed provisions. By September 1981, the NCP had not even been proposed in the Federal Register—EPA was in violation of Section 105 of CERCLA.

On September 3, 1981, the Environmental Defense Fund (EDF), a Washington, D.C.-based environmental group, brought suit in the District Court for the District of Columbia for "injunctive relief," ordering EPA to revise and republish the NCP by February 1, 1982. The court ordered EPA to respond to the EDF suit within sixty days (by November 3, 1981). This schedule indicates the slow pace of court system operations. The sixty-day time frame was the period within which EPA was required by the court to respond to EDF's complaint. If there was no response, "judgment by default" would be taken against EPA, and the court would mandate publication of the NCP on February 1, 1982. As usually occurs in court cases, the defendant (EPA) took the full sixty days to respond to the EDF complaint. The agency's response was followed by an "amended complaint" filed by EDF on November 19; again, EPA had additional time to respond to the amended complaint. This process of

140–141

complaint, followed by response, followed by an amended complaint and subsequent response is yet another delaying tactic often used in the court system. So long as the court permits both plaintiffs and defendants to continue the argument, the court is unable to issue an opinion.

Finally, on February 12, 1982, eleven days after the date on which the EDF suit had requested final NCP publication, U.S. District Judge John H. Pratt found for the plaintiffs, EDF et al. In his opinion, the statutory timetable noted in CERCLA evidenced congressional concern that the NCP be issued expeditiously and the "defendants have ignored the intent expressed in the statute." As a result, the judge ordered EPA to propose the NCP in the Federal Register no later than 30 days after the date of his ruling—that is, by March 12, 1982. He further ordered a limit on the public comment period to thirty additional days and publication of the final NCP version within ninety days of his ruling. On Friday, March 12, 1982, EPA Administrator Gorsuch announced the proposed National Contingency Plan. It was published on that date, as required, in the Federal Register. Nine months later than the congressional deadline for finalization, the NCP was at last proposed for public comment. Yet, even as plans for proposal were under way, EPA was requesting that the Department of Justice file a motion for reconsideration with the district court. The agency was unable to meet the other two deadlines imposed by the court, but at least the plan was before the public. It would not have come out as quickly as it did were it not for the intervention of the federal courts.

143–144   A number of cases have involved challenges to the constitutionality of parts of the Superfund law. In these cases, the lower courts have consistently upheld the act, and the Supreme Court has not granted *certiorari*. For example, in *Missouri* v. *Independent Petrochemical Corp.* (610 F. Supp. 4 [E.D. Mo. 1985]), the District Court for the Eastern District of Missouri rejected the claim that the application of CERCLA to intrastate hazardous-waste disposal is unconstitutional. Lawyers for a chemical company argued that the commerce clause of the Constitution restricts Congress from regulating waste that does not cross state borders. The court ruled that, by the legislative history of CERCLA, Congress considered intrastate hazardous-waste disposal to affect interstate commerce, and that this had a rational basis.

128   More cases have involved questions of interpretation than challenges to the constitutionality of the law. For example, in *United States* v. *Northeastern Pharmaceutical and Chemical Co.* (810 F.2d 726 [1986]), the Court of Appeals for the Second Circuit rejected claims that CERCLA does not impose liability for acts committed before its enactment date (December 11, 1980). The court ruled that the use of verbs in the past tense in the Superfund law and its legislative history both demonstrate that Congress intended the act to impose retroactive liability on polluters. The firm that years earlier had generated the waste found at a Superfund site in Missouri was held liable for costs incurred in the site's cleanup.

125   Court cases often involve questions of whether the agency provided due process to individuals in its implementation of public policy. For example, in *SCA Services of Indiana, Inc.* v. *Thomas* (634 F. Supp. 1355 [N.D. Ind. 1986]), the district court rejected the claim that the EPA must hold a hearing before listing a site on the National Priorities List (NPL). The owner of a property argued that because even a proposed listing on the NPL was

bad publicity for his land, the EPA should have provided him an opportunity to present evidence at a hearing before the proposed listing was made public. The court ruled that the plaintiff had sufficient opportunity to present evidence during the sixty-day comment period subsequent to the publication of the proposed NPL listing in the Federal Register. In addition, the court ruled that because the owner had the opportunity to sue in the Court of Appeals for the District of Columbia to request removal of the site from the NPL, there was also sufficient opportunity for the owner to present his views after the site was formally listed. In summary, the court concluded that the EPA had not denied the owner due process either by including his land in the proposed NPL additions in the Federal Register or by formally adding the site to the NPL. There is no requirement for a hearing before listing a site.

122   We have noted in the text that Congress can determine what kinds of cases the courts can hear. With the exception of cases regarding narrow procedural questions, CERCLA does not allow district courts to hear claims from companies that sites should not be added to the NPL. In 1990, for example, a district court ruled it lacked jurisdiction to review a company's claim that two sites it owned should not be added to the NPL (*Barmet Aluminum Co.* v. *EPA*, U.S. DC WDistKy, 88-0173-0).

141   A large amount of the litigation involving CERCLA are civil cases in which corporations sue each other in the federal courts over questions of what share of the cleanup costs each should pay. The courts generally force former property owners to share cleanup costs, except when the owner is a government that invokes sovereign immunity. This is the principle that citizens of a state cannot sue the state itself—see *N L Industries* v. *Kaplan* (24 ERC 2127 [1987]) and *City of New York* v. *Exxon Corp.* (24 ERC 1361 [1986]). Depending on specific state laws, however, sovereign immunity does not always protect municipalities from liability. In *Transportation Leasing Co.* v. *CA* (DCC Calif, No. CV89-7368 [1991]), a district court ruled that twenty-nine California cities would have to pay a share of the cleanup costs for a contaminated landfill in Monterey. The decision was that municipalities that hauled waste, hired haulers, or licensed haulers are liable for Superfund costs.

126   We noted in the text that most laws overturned by federal courts have been state and local laws, not national legislation. Sometimes federal courts will interpret two federal laws that, in combination, overturn a state law. *In re Torwico Electronics Inc.* (U.S. Bankr Ct NJ, No. 87-06071, 1991), a bankruptcy court overturned part of New Jersey's Environmental Cleanup Responsibility Act. The New Jersey law gave cleanup obligations preferred treatment in bankruptcy proceedings. The court ruled that it could not find a basis for such preferences in either CERCLA or federal bankruptcy law. Therefore, the court voided that part of the New Jersey law assigning preferences to cleanup obligations as in conflict with federal bankruptcy law.

121   We noted earlier that SARA addressed preemption disputes arising from the original 1980 Superfund law by stating that states could enact whatever taxes they favored for their own hazardous waste cleanup programs. Sometimes, however, fresh legislation intended to address a problem in a law creates even more litigation. One area of dispute in the original law was the question of the responsibility for cleanup costs by owners not directly responsible for creating the contamination. In a 1986 case (*U.S.* v. *Maryland Bank and Trust,* 24 ERC 1193), the court ruled that an owner who acquired land through a foreclosure procedure was liable for cleanup costs. The banks lobbied Congress to revise CERCLA to absolve such ''innocent'' owners from Superfund liability. In SARA, Congress responded by protecting owners who acquire property without knowing about hazardous waste problems from liability. SARA does state, however, that new owners are protected only if they exercised ''reasonable due care'' when acquiring the property. The absence of any definition of ''reasonable due care'' has produced much litigation. If a bank is asked to lend money to a firm to buy property, what should the bank do to exercise ''reasonable due care'' that the land is not contaminated? If the firm were to go bankrupt, the bank would then own the land and, if the land became a Superfund site, have to demonstrate that it had exercised ''reasonable due care.'' In the early 1990s, the banks returned to Congress, lobbying for a more definitive protection from Superfund liability.

The SARA expansion of protection to ''innocent'' owners did have some impact. In *Snediker Developers Ltd. Partnership* v. *Evans* (DC EMich, No. 89-72979 [1991]) the court ruled that persons who inherited a Superfund site were not liable for cleanup costs. Because they inherited the land, nobody could charge that they had not exercised ''reasonable due care'' in acquiring it.

120   The federal judiciary includes administrative courts as well as judicial ones. In 1992 the EPA established an Environmental Appeals Board composed of three judges. The board is empowered to hear appeals of administrative penalty decisions, including those emanating from Superfund.

129   Just as the courts were involved in 1981 and 1982 with ordering the EPA to move ahead with implementing the original CERCLA, in 1990 and 1991 the courts again ordered the EPA to comply with legislated deadlines. A provision of SARA required the EPA to examine potential hazardous waste sites on land owned by the federal government for inclusion on the NPL. In July 1991, the U.S. District Court for the District of Massachusetts ruled (*Conservation Law Foundation of New England* v. *EPA,* 755 F Supp 475, 32 ERC 1641) that the EPA had failed to meet the eighteen-month deadline in SARA for assessing federal sites. The court gave the agency until July 1992 to assess potential federal sites and until July 1993 to determine if any belong on the NPL.

In the next end-of-chapter segment of the case study, we look more closely at the bureaucracy and the pressures brought to bear on it by the other branches of government as well as hazardous-waste generators and environmentalists.

4

THE FEDERAL BUREAUCRACY

No treatment of the federal government's established institutions would be complete without devoting considerable attention to the "fourth branch." Although not specifically established by the Constitution, the Founders assumed that some type of administrative structure would evolve and that it would be officially under the president's control. Such control is necessarily incomplete, in that the president must persuade bureaucrats to do what he wants just as he tries to persuade members of Congress. The bureaucracy is very much an important political force independent of the president.

The bureaucracy is the one political structure that exercises the most direct and pervasive influence over the life of the average American citizen. Yet it remains the least understood and most maligned arm of the national government. Its development and proliferation not only exemplify the interrelated nature of governmental institutions but also account for the continued interdependence among the three constitutionally established branches of government. To speak of the impact of the president, Congress, or the courts without reference to the bureaucracy is an exercise in futility.

CHARACTERISTICS OF BUREAUCRATIZATION

Organizations are bureaucracies to the extent that they have a division of labor, hierarchical structure, and a fixed framework of rules.

In the late nineteenth century, the German sociologist Max Weber analyzed the elements identifying bureaucracies. Although we use the popular term "bureaucracy" to refer to the executive branch of the federal government, it is important to remember that any organization, from General Motors to a small business, can be a bureaucracy. According to the Weberian model, organizations are judged "bureaucratic" to the degree that they exhibit the fundamental characteristics of (1) a division of labor, (2) a hierarchical structure, and (3) a fixed framework of rules. A division of labor means the bureaucracy is organized with different employees performing different functions according to areas of specialization. In the State Department, for example, some employees work at the East Asian desk, while others work at the Latin American desk; the employees are specialists, not generalists.

A hierarchical structure means that authority flows from the top down, with inferiors reporting to and receiving instructions from superiors. A bureaucracy has clearly defined levels, with employees at lower levels responsible to employees at higher levels. Because there are almost invariably more lower level employees, a bureaucracy's organization chart resembles the familiar pyramid. On top is one individual; in the case of the State Department, the secretary of state.

A fixed framework of rules means employee activities are governed by preestablished formal rules and regulations. Decisions in a Weberian bureaucracy are made by applying the appropriate rule to any given situation. Every employee must apply the same rule in the same way to every situation in which the rule is deemed applicable. Discretion in rule application must therefore be studiously avoided. Advancement or promotion in such hierarchical structures is determined by the employee's competence in memorizing and applying the formal rules.

Of course, no organization perfectly embodies these three characteristics (division of labor, hierarchy, and fixed rules). In fact, organizational tensions exist between the specializations produced by the division of labor and the formal authority inherent in hierarchy. Specialists often resent having to follow directives from a superior who is less well informed about a particular subject than they. Moreover, it is nearly impossible (and perhaps undesirable) to remove all discretion (choice) from bureaucratic decision making. Overemphasis on procedures can result in organizational rigidity, so that internal rules supersede policy goals.

It is also important to remember that these three characteristics of bureaucracy are based on an "ideal type"—they are only more or less descriptively accurate. Theoretically, in the public sector, the end result of this combination of specialization, hierarchy, and formal rules is the efficient implementation of government policies. In practice, internal bureaucratic struggles combine with a changeable and often hostile environment to produce delay, confusion, waste, and rigidity.

THE ORGANIZATION OF THE FEDERAL BUREAUCRACY

The federal bureaucracy has a variety of organization types.

The federal bureaucracy comprises almost three million civilian employees working for hundreds of departments, agencies, bureaus, commissions, interagency committees, citizen advisory groups, and presidential committees, commissions, and task forces. This chapter's aim is not to provide an encyclopedic listing of federal agencies; the *United States Government Manual* does that, in more than 900 pages. Instead, this chapter describes the four main elements of the bureaucracy (cabinet departments, independent regulatory commissions, independent executive agencies, and government corporations), explains their similarities and their differences, and shows how these elements of the bureaucracy interact with and are affected by the other three branches of government.

The Cabinet Departments

Department heads form the president's cabinet.

The fourteen cabinet-level departments are the largest bureaucratic structures within the federal government. Each department is headed by a secretary (the attorney general in the case of the Justice Department) who holds cabinet rank and presidential appointment with senatorial consent. Immediately below the secretary begins each department's unique proliferation of under secretaries, deputy under secretaries, assistant secretaries, executive secretaries, and bureau chiefs, ad infinitum. Figure 4.1 shows the organization of the Department of the Treasury, which, although unique (in that no other department is organized in exactly the same way), is representative of the type of organizational structure in all the departments.

The early departments dealt mostly with foreign affairs.

Cabinet development Cabinet-level, or executive, departments date from 1789, when George Washington appointed secretaries of war, state, and treasury. An attorney general also has held cabinet rank from that time but did not receive a department until 1870. The Department of the Navy was added in 1798, precipitating a series of conflicts with the War Department that continued until the two were merged (together with the Air Force) to create the Department of Defense in 1949. Subsequent conflicts between the services have been viewed as "intradepartmental" and are therefore, theoretically more easily resolved.

The postmaster general was admitted to the cabinet in 1829, although his department (established as an independent agency of the national government in 1792) did not receive cabinet-level recognition until 1872—a status that they both lost in 1971 when the post office was reorganized as a governmental corporation. By the middle of the nineteenth century, one other department (Interior) had been added, resulting in a cabinet of five departments (War, State, Treasury, Navy, and Interior) and seven officers (secretaries of each department plus the attorney general and postmaster general).

By World War I, departments responsive to farm, business, and labor interests had been added to the cabinet.

Drastic alterations in the American economy toward the end of the nineteenth century produced a broader and more direct government role in economic matters, which in turn prompted congressional response in the form of new cabinet posts. Thus, in 1889, the Department of Agriculture (under a commissioner since 1862) was elevated to cabinet rank as Congress responded to the demands of the nation's farmers. Pressures emanating from business and industry prompted the inclusion of a Department of Commerce and Labor in 1903, which was quickly split into two departments ten years later in recognition of the different needs being served. President Lyndon Johnson proposed that, for efficiency's sake, the Departments of Labor and Commerce be recombined into one department, as they had been during Theodore Roosevelt's presidency. This proposal quickly died in Congress because business interests feared that labor would control the combined department, and labor interests feared the opposite.

As governmental concerns and involvements broadened since World War II, Congress responded by creating new cabinet positions. The Department of Health, Education and Welfare (established in 1953) combined a number of formerly independent agencies in order to coordinate their operations better and to indicate

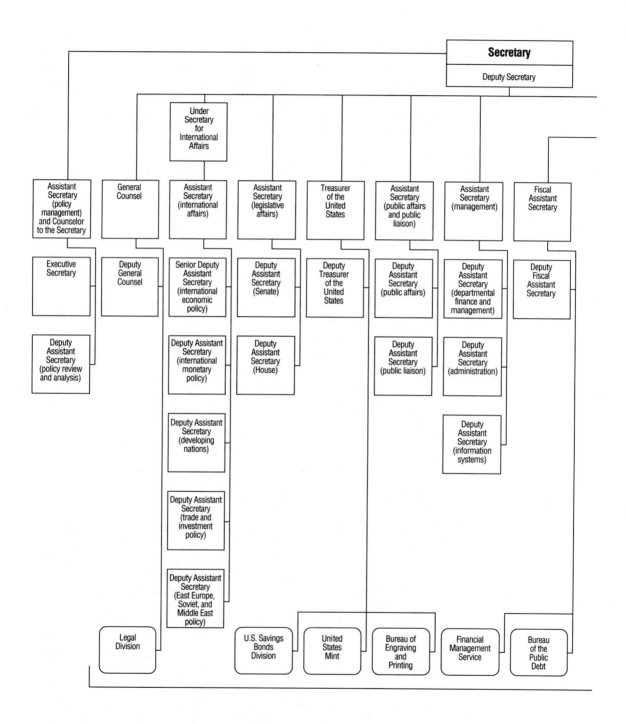

FIGURE 4.1   Organization Chart of the Department of the Treasury

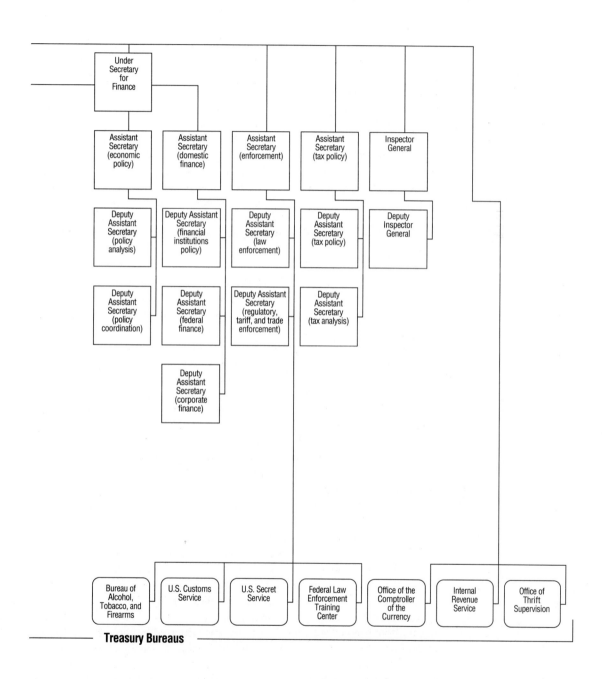

a national commitment to help provide all Americans with adequate human services. In 1979, this department was split into two departments: Health and Human Services, and Education. Interests favoring increased federal support for education were successful in their push for a new department focused solely on education, believing that having "their own department" would aid their efforts. In contrast, President Ronald Reagan campaigned to abolish the new Department of Education as part of his efforts to reduce federal involvement in education. Supporters of the department, however, were able to thwart Reagan's attempt.

In the post-World War II era, agencies demonstrating the nation's commitment to health, education, energy, transportation, housing, and urban needs were elevated to department status.

In the 1960s, urban problems came to the forefront, resulting in the creation of a Department of Housing and Urban Development (1965) and a Department of Transportation (1966). By the mid-1970s, Americans were justifiably concerned with problems of energy and the allocation of increasingly scarce natural resources. Congress again responded to both public and presidential pressure creating the Department of Energy in 1977. This department's creation is an excellent illustration of congressional response to extracongressional pressures. It also demonstrates how previously existing federal agencies can become established as cabinet-level departments.

On March 1, 1977, President Jimmy Carter proposed the creation of a new energy cabinet department to Congress. For the next three months, Congress held hearings on and debated the wisdom of such a department. In the end, the president received the authorization to proceed, but with some modification of his original proposal. The newly created Department of Energy consolidated all powers previously wielded by the Federal Power Commission (FPC), the Federal Energy Administration (FEA), and the Energy Research and Development Administration (ERDA), as well as the powers of various energy programs scattered throughout the bureaucracy. The most important alteration from the original proposal was Congress's refusal to accede to the president's wish that the secretary of the new department be granted the power, previously held by the FPC, to set the price of natural gas. Congress, responding to lobbying pressures from American companies, vested that and similar economic powers not in the new secretary but in an independent regulatory commission within the new department. This important alteration of the president's proposal demonstrates that the process by which departments are created, merged, split, and disbanded involves congressional response to pressures. Congress, not the president, has the final word on establishing cabinet-level departments.

In October 1988, Congress passed, and the president signed, a bill transforming the Veterans' Administration from an independent executive agency into the fourteenth cabinet department. The Secretary of Veterans' Affairs heads one of the largest departments in the cabinet. In 1988, the Veterans Administration had a $28 billion budget, employed over 250,000 people, and paid benefits to nearly five million disabled veterans. The move was criticized by conservatives, anxious to cut back the size of government by decreasing the number of cabinet posts, and by representatives of the National Academy of Public Administration, who doubted it would improve the management of veterans' affairs. However, the measure's political popularity was clear: it passed the House with only seventeen negative votes and was unanimously approved by the Senate. Reagan's endorsement of the new cabinet department represented a dramatic departure from his 1980 goal of cutting back the size of the cabinet. By 1992, the budget of the Department of Veterans Affairs had grown to over $32 billion, and it still employed more than 250,000 people.

Characteristics of cabinet members   In selecting cabinet members, presidents generally proceed quite cautiously, realizing that cabinet officers are key actors in implementing the administration's policies. Cabinet members differ from the leaders of Congress in both age and background. While the seniority system ensures that many leaders of Congress will serve well beyond the standard retirement age of sixty-five, the cabinet member over sixty-five is a rarity. In 1990, the average age of the Bush cabinet was fifty-seven.

In background, cabinet members tend to be of urban origin, with careers in business or law, a combination that makes them more likely to reside in large metropolises. Cabinet officials sometimes interrupt lucrative business or legal careers to serve in Washington. In assembling his cabinet, however, George Bush placed a greater emphasis on governmental experience. Of his initial fourteen cabinet appointments, only two came directly from the private sector—Secretary Louis Sullivan, Dean of the Morehouse School of Medicine in Atlanta, and Secretary Robert Mosbacher, an executive in the oil business in Texas. In fact, eleven of Bush's cabinet officers lived within the Washington metropolitan area at the time of their initial appointments.

Women and minority group members did not hold cabinet positions until the 1970s.

Cabinet members, like congressional leaders, are almost certain to be white males. The first successful attempt to open the cabinet to blacks and women was that of the Carter administration, which included a black Secretary of Housing and Urban Development (HUD), Patricia Harris, and the first female Secretary of Commerce, Juanita Kreps. The Bush administration included three minority-group cabinet officers—Secretary of Health and Human Services Louis W. Sullivan (the sole black cabinet officer), Secretary of the Interior Manuel Lujan, Jr., and Education Secretary Lauro Cavazos. By the end of his term, the three women serving on the Bush cabinet were Carla A. Hills, the United States Trade Representative (a post with cabinet rank), Secretary of Commerce Barbara Franklin, and Labor Secretary Lynn Martin.

The large number of cabinet appointments by any president does not necessarily mean that different individuals are brought into the upper echelons of the federal bureaucracy. Often, the same individuals served in previous administrations in varying capacities. In the Bush cabinet, for example, Treasury Secretary Nicholas Brady, Attorney General Richard Thornburgh, and Secretary of Education Lauro Cavazos were all originally appointed to those posts by Ronald Reagan. Secretary of State James Baker served as both White House Chief of Staff and Treasury Secretary in the Reagan administration; Labor Secretary Elizabeth Dole served as Transportation Secretary during the Reagan years; and Secretary of Agriculture Clayton K. Yeutter was United States Trade Representative under Reagan. Cabinet members sometimes even move from position to position under the same president.

At the end of his administration, for example, Bush moved Robert A. Mosbacher from his position as Secretary of Commerce to a new position as general chairman of the Bush reelection campaign and Transportation Secretary Samuel K. Skinner replaced the discredited John Sununu as White House Chief of Staff, only to be replaced in turn by Secretary of State Baker.

Although the FBI is formally under the attorney general, the agency has used its sensitive function to operate independently within the Department of Justice.

Autonomy of units within departments   Each cabinet department's organization reflects its particular historical development in response to governmental and nongovernmental pressures. Thus, the Federal Bureau of Investigation, while a Justice Department agency under the titular authority of the attorney general, is actually controlled by the director of the FBI and operates with a degree of autonomy that certainly violates the Weberian characteristics of bureaucratic organization.

Under its founder and first director, J. Edgar Hoover, the FBI developed such a positive image among most Americans that Hoover could operate independently of the wishes of the attorney general (Hoover's superior in the Justice Department). Although the attorney general possessed the formal authority to fire the director of the FBI, Hoover's popularity made such a firing politically impractical. Presidents John Kennedy and Lyndon Johnson clearly would have preferred a director who would have enforced civil rights laws more vigorously than did Hoover, but they both believed the political costs of removing Hoover were too great.

Several factors combined to reduce the power of the FBI director after Hoover's death in 1972. His successors have lacked the personal prestige and national image that Hoover enjoyed, and the bureau was tainted by improprieties connected both with Hoover's autocratic rule and with the Watergate affair. As a result, Congress moved to insulate the director from political pressures that might emanate from the White House, while simultaneously minimizing the possibility that the director would wield concentrated, autocratic control within the bureau. The Crime Control Act of 1976 prescribed a single, ten-year term of office for the director. William Webster, appointed by Carter and confirmed by the Senate in 1978, served as FBI director through 1987. William S. Sessions, appointed by Reagan and confirmed by the Senate in 1987, will serve as FBI director through 1996. So, although Sessions is formally under the attorney general, the FBI director cannot be replaced except "for cause." Because what constitutes adequate "cause" for removal is unclear, Sessions has great autonomy to run his bureau as he sees fit. Such a situation is at variance with the standards of a true Weberian bureaucracy.

The proximity of the Secret Service to the president promotes its independence within the Treasury Department.

Another agency within a cabinet-level department with a great deal of independence from the department secretary is the Secret Service. Established in 1865 to combat the counterfeiting of U.S. currency, the Secret Service was given the added responsibility of protecting the president's life after the 1901 assassination of William McKinley. From then on, the relationship between the Secret Service and the hierarchical organization of the Treasury Department gradually changed. Because of their close association with the White House staff, Secret Service agents have engaged in matters of little or no concern to the Treasury, without the knowledge of the assistant secretary to whom they are supposedly responsible. Thus, during the Nixon presidency, agents of the Secret Service tapped the phones of the president's brother, operated an elaborate secret taping system in the White House, and opened the White House safe of E. Howard Hunt after the Watergate burglary. These acts were committed without the knowledge or approval of the secretary of the treasury.

Independent Regulatory Commissions

Independent regulatory commissions set rules in areas of business and commerce. The president appoints commission members with the approval of the Senate but, once they are appointed, cannot remove them.

Organization of regulatory commissions Independent regulatory commissions differ from cabinet departments in very fundamental aspects of operation and function (Table 4.1). The commissions are headed by five or seven members (with the exception of the Interstate Commerce Commission, which has eleven) appointed on a bipartisan basis by the president, with the approval of the Senate, for a specified number of years. Appointments are staggered to reduce the possibility of any presidential attempt to "stack" commissions. Each commission was created by act of Congress for the express purpose of regulating a specific economic interest.

Development of the ICC: The regulatory commission prototype The Interstate Commerce Commission (ICC) was Congress's first attempt to establish a regulatory commission (Figure 4.2). Such a commission would have to combine the necessary

---

TABLE 4.1   Comparative Characteristics of the Federal Bureaucracy

	Cabinet Departments	Independent Executive Agencies	Independent Regulatory Commissions	Government Corporations
Head	Cabinet secretary	Administrator or commisison	Multimember board or commission	Boards or commmisions
Appointment	Presidential, with Senate approval	Presidential (some with Senate approval)	Presidential, bipartisan with Senate approval	Presidential (some with Senate approval)
Term of Office	President's discretion	Presidential discretion (or specified[a])	Specific, staggered	President's discretion
Removal	President	President (or for cause only[a])	For cause only	President[b]
Role	General administration	Specialized programs	Economic regulation	Business enterprises
Functions	Administrative Quasi-judicial Quasi-legislative	Administrative—all Quasi-judicial—some Quasi-legislative—some	Administrative Quasi-judicial Quasi-legislative	Administrative

[a]Only those independent executive agencies to which quasi-judicial and/or quasi-legislative authority has been specifically granted by Congress have members who can be removed only for cause and who have specified terms of office.

[b]Some corporations have boards whose members serve a fixed term. They can be removed only for cause.

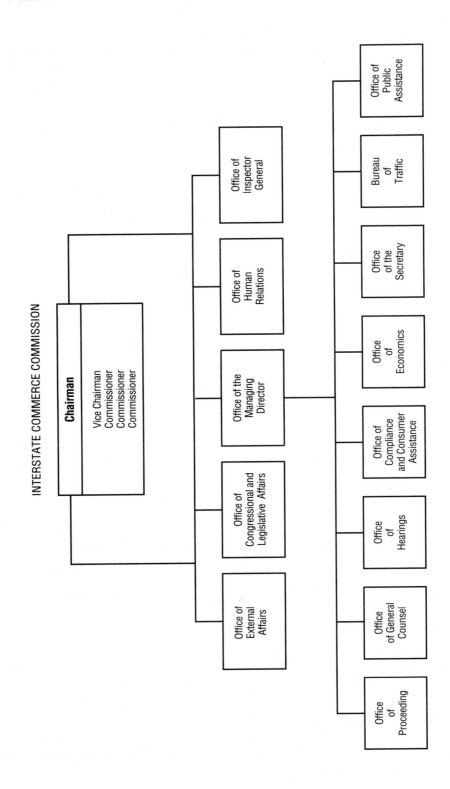

INTERSTATE COMMERCE COMMISSION

degree of expertise, continuity, quasi-legislative and quasi-judicial powers, and immunity from governmental and nongovernmental interests in order to function effectively in the economic sphere. Quasi-legislative and quasi-judicial authority are best understood as authority granted by Congress to an agency to advance specific regulations under the terms of the broad powers conferred on the agency and to adjudicate disputes arising out of the enforcement of those regulations. The "broad power" conferred on the ICC was the authority to regulate all interstate surface transportation and was eventually expanded to include trains, buses, interstate waterway and coastal shipping, freight forwarders, oil pipelines, and express companies. The ICC's quasi-legislative authority permits it to design regulations for these industries that have the effect of law, while its quasi-judicial authority permits it to adjudicate disputes arising from its own regulations.

> Independent regulatory commissions both set rules and adjudicate disputes arising from those rules.

Created by the 1887 Act to Regulate Commerce, the ICC was the response of Congress to a Supreme Court ruling the previous year (*Wabash, St. Louis, and Pacific Railroad* v. *Illinois,* U.S. 557 [1886]) that prohibited state regulation of interstate commerce. Agrarian interests, especially in the Midwest, were being openly exploited by railroad magnates who charged exorbitant and discriminatory rates for the shipment of farm products.

Originally under the Secretary of the Interior's jurisdiction, the ICC gained administrative independence within two years of its creation—a process mirrored in the development of subsequent commissions. It was not until 1920 that the ICC fully realized its regulatory powers. Several acts of Congress (most notably the Hepburn Act of 1906) removed judicial interference as an effective tool of the railroads in blocking ICC regulatory decisions. The railroads were finally, it seemed, subject to government regulation, but the meaning of *regulation* was about to undergo significant changes—changes predicted in 1892 by Attorney General Richard S. Olney:

> The [ICC] as its functions have now been limited by the Courts, is, or can be made of great use to the railroads. It satisfies the popular clamor for a government supervision of railroads, at the same time that the supervision is almost entirely nominal. Further, the older such a Commission gets to be, the more inclined it will be found to be to take the business and railroad view of things. It thus becomes a sort of barrier between the railroad corporations and the people and a sort of protection against hasty and crude legislation hostile to railroad interests.[1]

> Independent regulatory commissions are sometimes "captured" by the industries they are supposed to be regulating.

Regulation as protection from competition A number of regulatory commissions have followed the pattern predicted by Attorney General Olney, each eventually coming under the control of the very interests it had been designed to regulate. Commission members are frequently drawn from the regulated interests, because that is where the experts are found. If these connections between regulator and regulated are not mitigated sufficiently by congressional oversight, court decisions, and agency staff personnel (who can develop substantial influence over policy), commissions may take regulated interests under their wing to "protect" them from

[1]James M. Smith and Paul L. Murphy, eds. *Liberty and Justice* (New York: Knopf, 1958), pp. 292–293.

the development of economic environments hostile to their profits. In that case, regulation becomes protection.

Industries that have control over an independent regulatory commission oppose deregulation because they would then have to compete with new businesses and with one another.

This tendency was evident in the battle between the Ford administration and the trucking industry. In announcing his proposed deregulation legislation, Gerald Ford said, "It is now clear that this patchwork regulatory structure has not kept pace with changes in the industry and the economy. We have permitted regulation designed in theory to protect the public interest to become in practice the protection of special industry interests." At issue was whether the ICC should continue to issue "certificates of convenience and necessity" granting individual carriers exclusive operating rights for specified interstate trucking routes. These certificates, issued by the ICC at no cost to the truckers, became so valuable that one bankrupt New York City trucking firm netted almost $21 million in July 1976 by selling its certificates to other companies at public auction. The trucking industry lobbied so heavily against the proposed deregulation that the legislation remained bottled up in congressional committees until Ford was out of office. Carter, who had campaigned with promises to eliminate regulations restricting competition detrimental to the public, proposed legislation similar to Ford's to deregulate the trucking industry. Congress did pass the Motor Carrier Act of 1980, facilitating the entrance of new companies into the industry, promoting competition, and reducing ICC's power in the trucking area. However, critics charged that industry lobbyists had watered down the bill, successfully retaining many regulations inimical to the public interest. Reagan, campaigning against government regulations in general, proclaimed in 1980 that he would not support any further deregulation of the trucking industry. Pleased with his position, the Teamsters Union was one of only two national unions to endorse Reagan for the presidency.[2]

Throughout all the controversy over efforts to deregulate the trucking industry, one constant element has been the preference of the large trucking firms and their union *for* regulation. What this means is that even though a president might wish to deregulate a particular industry, such action may be extremely difficult because, among other reasons, the "regulated" interests enjoy their "regulations."

Regulatory commissions as decision makers Encouraged by its early experience with the ICC, Congress responded to subsequent political pressures from various economic segments by establishing additional independent commissions (Table 4.2). These commissions exert tremendous power over the U.S. economy's operation, most notably in their ability not only to administer but to legislate and adjudicate as well. The courts are constitutionally limited (Article III) from initiating actions against the bureaucracy, including the regulatory commissions, and can intervene only after suit has been filed by a third party. Thus, the regulatory commissions administer broad congressional legislation in specific areas (thereby themselves making policy) and subsequently adjudicate disputes arising from their own decisions.

Decisions made by independent regulatory commissions can rarely be challenged in the courts.

[2]The other union to endorse Reagan was the Professional Air Traffic Controllers Organization. This union died after Reagan fired all of its members who engaged in an illegal strike.

TABLE 4.2 Principal Independent Regulatory Commissions

Commission	Date of Creation	Number of Members	Term (in Years)	Principal Tasks
Interstate Commerce Commission (ICC)	1887	11	7	To regulate railroads and carriers
Federal Reserve Board	1913	7	14	To regulate banking practices
Federal Trade Commission (FTC)	1914	5	7	To regulate industry by protecting consumers from unfair business practices
Federal Communications Commission (FCC)	1934	7	7	To license and regulate all radio and TV frequencies and establish telephone and telegraph rates
Securities and Exchange Commission (SEC)	1934	5	5	To supervise all security and financial markets, including brokerages and stock market
National Labor Relations Board (NLRB)	1935	5	5	To rectify unfair labor practices and designate appropriate bargaining units
Nuclear Regulatory Commission (NRC)	1974	5	5	To license and regulate the uses of nuclear energy, protecting the public health and safety and the environment

One example of the breadth of power exerted by regulatory commissions is the Federal Communications Commission. The FCC determines what proportion of prime-time television must be of local origin as opposed to network programs, what proportion of air time must be "public-interest" broadcasting, and even how strong a station's transmitter is permitted to be. A station that is out of favor with the FCC may find its license renewal request rejected. Thus, it is not surprising that in 1973, after FCC Chairperson Dean Burch, responding to White House pressures, spoke out against radio talk shows with sexual topics, several of these shows shifted overnight from discussing sex to debating football. These stations became "wholesome," fearing that the FCC would otherwise find a reason to reject their license renewal request.

Regulation as harassment Thus, *regulation* can come to mean political harassment rather than protection. In the FCC case, the regulatory commission, in effect, lost some of its independence to the White House, thereby opening up the possibility of harassment of regulated interests. As Clay Whitehead, head of the Nixon White

House Office of Telecommunications Policy, proclaimed, "Station managers and network officials who fail to correct imbalance or consistent bias from the networks—or who acquiesce by silence—can only be considered willing participants, to be held fully accountable . . . at license-renewal time."[3] Because the FCC, not the White House Office of Telecommunications Policy, rules on license renewals, Whitehead could not have made this statement if the FCC were truly independent.

Regulations are sometimes used to harass businesses well beyond the intentions of a commission's enabling legislation.

Regulation as consumer protection   Thus far this chapter has considered regulations as industry efforts to control competition or as harassment by ideologically motivated bureaucrats. This is an incomplete characterization of the independent regulatory commissions. Although critics complain that the Nuclear Regulatory Commission (NRC) is too dependent on nuclear industry sources for its information, on more than a few occasions the NRC has refused to grant licenses to nuclear power-generating plants because NRC inspectors found evidence that safety precautions at these plants were insufficient. What plant owners then called "harassment" and "overregulation," environmental groups termed "good decisions in the public interest." One can cite similar examples for each of the independent regulatory commissions, from citizens saved from stock swindlers by the Securities and Exchange Commission to consumers protected from unscrupulous sales techniques by the Federal Trade Commission. It is all too easy to dwell on the mistakes and problems of these commissions and other bureaucracies while neglecting their contributions to quality of life.

When independent regulatory commissions actively protect consumer interests, the commissions may come under harsh attack by industries accustomed to regulation as protection from competition.

Nevertheless, to a number of people, government regulation means government interference in the private sector. The argument is made that regulations generate unnecessary costs for businesses, causing inflationary pressures at home and a lack of competitiveness abroad. The Reagan administration came to Washington in 1981 proclaiming it would deregulate the American economy. Reagan was particularly concerned with environmental and workplace safety regulations, which he saw as especially heavy burdens on American industry. The president appointed then Vice President George Bush to head the administration's task force on deregulation. When Bush was elected President in 1988, he in turn appointed Vice President Quayle as the head of the newly formed Council on Competitiveness to continue the work of the task force that Bush had chaired under Reagan.

It is important to remember, however, that despite rhetorical support for "regulatory relief," it is often the regulated industries themselves that favor federal standards. Federal regulation serves three purposes for the industries regulated. First, regulation stabilizes organizational environments, making business decisions more routine and market risks less severe. Second, federal regulations often include government certification of product fitness; for example, the Department of Agriculture's "U.S.D.A. Approved" stamps for beef. Such certification acts as a form of third-party guarantee, making consumer purchase more likely. Third, federal regulation acts to preempt state and local regulations, which in some areas may be more stringent and detailed than those the federal government imposes. In addition, industry usually prefers dealing with one set of overall regulatory guidelines rather than a variety of state and local rules.

On January 1, 1985, the Civil Aeronautics Board (CAB), ceased to exist, becoming the only independent regulatory commission ever to "go out of business." The CAB was established in 1938 to supervise and license all airline routes and rates. In 1978, responding to air-carrier pressures for deregulation, Congress passed a law setting the schedule for eventual deregulation. The act contained a provision by which the CAB would cease to exist in 1985. It is significant, however, that Congress dealt with the question again in 1984—not in terms of deregulation or for the purpose of retaining the CAB but because Congress, in 1978, had failed to provide for the preservation of the consumer-protection function of the board. As a result, on September 20, 1984, Congress transferred the CAB's consumer-protection function to the Department of Transportation, thereby preserving that function while still disbanding the board.

The Board of Governors of the Federal Reserve System sets monetary policy; members are appointed by the president with Senate confirmation but cannot be removed during their fourteen-year terms.

The Federal Reserve Board   One independent regulatory commission targeted by much congressional criticism is the Federal Reserve Board. When Congress set up "the Fed" in 1913, the legislative intent was to provide a body with sufficient independence that it could pursue its functions free of short-range political pressures. The seven members of the Board of Governors are appointed by the president with Senate confirmation for fourteen-year terms, staggered so that one term expires every two years. The chair is appointed from among the seven governors for a four-year term.

The Federal Reserve Board sets policy for the twelve regional federal reserve banks and the 6,000 member banks of the Federal Reserve System. The board determines the buying and selling of government securities, the amount of money each member bank must keep on hand as reserves, and the interest charged to banks borrowing from the Federal Reserve System to cover short-term needs. These policies greatly impact the economy's money supply. An increased money supply lowers interest rates, makes borrowing easier, and spurs the economy, but may have inflationary consequences. A decreased money supply has the opposite effects of tougher borrowing, higher interest rates, economic slowdowns, but reduced inflation. By functioning as a national bank, the Federal Reserve System controls monetary policy. Although every president tries to promote economic health, the Fed's independence limits presidential attempts to persuasion. He cannot order the board to do anything, nor can he fire recalcitrant members. The power to set economic policy is dispersed in our national government and requires cooperation for coherence to emerge.

Independent Executive Agencies

Organization of independent executive agencies   Independent executive agencies form a third and no less important element of the federal bureaucracy. Table 4.3 illus-

TABLE 4.3   **Selected Major Independent Executive Agencies**

Agency	Employees (in 1992)	Principal Tasks
ACTION	413	To mobilize volunteers for service in VISTA (in the U.S.) and in the Peace Corps (in developing countries)
Environmental Protection Agency	18,339	To protect and enhance the environment
General Services Administration	21,085	To manage government property and records
National Aeronautics and Space Administration	24,566	To conduct research on flight within and outside the earth's atmosphere
National Endowment for the Arts	272	To support progress in the arts and humanities
National Science Foundation	1,435	To support scientific research, including social science efforts, that can lead to improvements in the quality of life
Panama Canal Commission	8,659	To coordinate operation of the Panama Canal with the Republic of Panama
Small Business Administration	6,700	To aid the interests of small business
Smithsonian Institution	4,317	To preserve for study and reference items of scientific, cultural, or historical interest

Independent executive agencies perform services for specific groups or have special areas of responsibility (such as the Environmental Protection Agency).

trates the size and diversity of some of the major independent executive agencies. The heads of these agencies (some of which are directed by multimember boards) are presidential appointees whose appointments may require Senate approval. Each independent executive agency is responsible for a specialized area of jurisdiction, and within that area it may exercise quasi-legislative and/or quasi-judicial functions. The agencies are independent of cabinet departments and report directly to the president. They were set up outside the departments, either because their subject matter did not fit well within any of the departments (for example, the case of the National Aeronautics and Space Administration), or because Congress and the president thought that independence from established departments would engender fresh approaches to policy problems.

The larger independent executive agencies have regional offices similar to those of departments.

Diversified functions of independent executive agencies Unlike regulatory commissions, independent executive agencies are not designed to deal primarily with economic regulations but rather to perform some specific service or administrative function. These functions are diverse in purpose and range from assisting small groups (as does the Farm Credit Administration) to performing special functions for large government departments (as does the General Services Administration). To fulfill these functions, it is often necessary for the agencies to have regional offices scattered throughout the country (Figure 4.3). For administrative purposes, the United States is divided into ten regions, with the principal city in each region serving as the headquarters for the entire area. Most government bureaucracies offering wide-ranging services dispensed outside Washington, D.C., operate on the same ten-region plan. Thus, the organization charts of both the Environmental Protection Agency and a cabinet department such as the Department of Health and Human Services indicate regional offices in the same ten cities.

As with regulatory commissions, the actual degree of agency independence is a result of historical development as well as the conditions under which Congress established the agency. All independent agencies develop a degree of independence from congressional and presidential control, consistent with the influence of the organizations they serve. The National Science Foundation (NSF), for example, often works with professional associations representing academic disciplines by publicizing the programs that the NSF offers the academic community. The National Aeronautics and Space Administration (NASA), in unison with the aerospace industry, emphasizes the benefits and—in the wake of the Challenger tragedy—the safety of space exploration. Such agency self-promotion attempts to establish an independent support base, giving the agency more political leverage than it otherwise would have when dealing with members of Congress.

Of course, the independence of these agencies does not negate the oversight function of Congress. During the first Reagan administration, congressional investigators became convinced that the administrator of the Environmental Protection Agency, Anne M. Gorsuch, was failing to perform her mandated functions of enforcing the nation's environmental laws. In fact, one of her assistant administrators, Rita Lavelle, ultimately served time in prison for perjury connected with the case. By the time it was over, after almost two years of often acrimonious struggle between Congress and the executive, at least twenty-five high-level Reagan appointees resigned or were dismissed from the EPA. William Ruckelshaus, the agency's first administrator under Nixon in 1970, returned to Washington to accept Gorsuch's post.

Government Corporations

Government corporations are the newest addition to the bureaucratic maze, dating from the early 1930s. These corporations are actually quasi-business enterprises established by acts of Congress to accomplish specific, primarily economic tasks either in specified localities or across the nation. The Federal Deposit Insurance

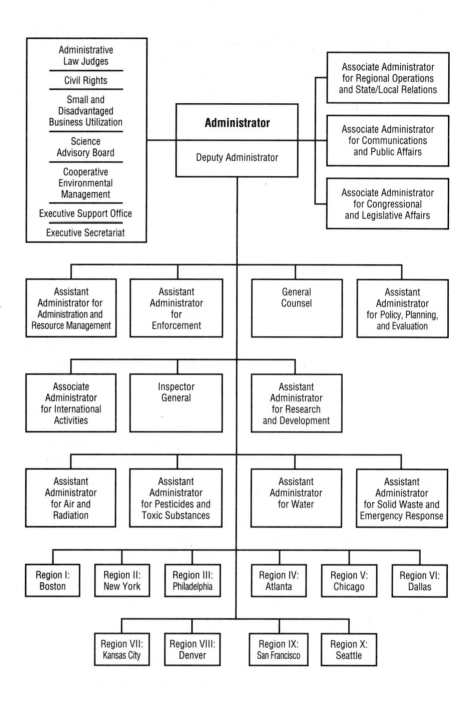

FIGURE 4.3 Organization Chart of the Environmental Protection Agency

Corporation, for example, monitors funds and protects deposits in banks across the country, while the Tennessee Valley Authority operates in one specified area, providing electrical power and other services for economic development and recreation. Another government corporation with responsibilities for economic development in a specified area is the Saint Lawrence Seaway Development Corporation. Such corporations were originally semiautonomous, but the Government Corporation Control Act of 1945 placed them more directly under the control of Congress and the president.

Government corporations generally are headed by boards or commissions appointed by the president. In some instances, to isolate the boards from political pressure, Congress has mandated bipartisan membership, removal by the president only for cause, and long terms of service. Similar to private businesses, government corporations can borrow money and undertake specific projects without congressional approval.

Government corporations are nonprofit entities that perform infrastructural tasks such as postal services.

One of the newest government corporations is the United States Postal Service, a cabinet department until 1971. The Postal Service, employing more than 650,000 people, performs a communication function absolutely vital to the nation's economy. The controversy engulfing the Postal Service in recent years is at least partly a result of its government corporation status. On the one hand, private business has actually entered into competition with the Postal Service and taken over many of its money-making operations. (United Parcel Service, for example, has taken over much of the Postal Service's package-delivery business. Yet, while private enterprise would be more than happy to assume the lucrative New York-Chicago-Los Angeles type of mail run, no private business has offered to deliver mail to rural Alaska at any price; this remains the responsibility of the Postal Service.) On the other hand, Congress continues to keep a wary eye on this government corporation because many rural congressional constituencies feel threatened by the Postal Service's moves to decrease the number of rural post offices, employees, and delivery days in order to increase cost effectiveness. As a quasi-business enterprise, then, the Postal Service can neither compete effectively with private enterprise nor depend entirely on government subsidy.

THE BUREAUCRATS

Developing a Civil Service

Until 1883, all federal jobs were filled under the patronage system.

The spoils system Responding to an ambassadorial appointment by President Andrew Jackson in 1832, Senator William Learned Marcy of New York admitted, "To the victor belong the spoils." This was the federal government's tendency from its inception. George Washington was convinced that the best and most influential men in the colonies should and would be drafted for service in the new national structure, a process he ensured by naming former colleagues of the Constitutional Convention to his cabinet.

When Thomas Jefferson, who resigned from Washington's cabinet in protest over Alexander Hamilton's economic policies, succeeded to the presidency, cabinet posts were given to Democratic Republicans rather than to Federalists. It is interesting to note that Albert Gallatin, whom Jefferson chose as Hamilton's successor as secretary of the treasury, continued the policies of his predecessor virtually unchanged. This lack of policy change was understandably facilitated by the presence, barely a decade old, of a bureaucratic structure (the Treasury Department), accustomed to implementing certain policies and therefore reluctant to enforce new policies.

Creation and expansion of the civil service   Bureaucratic structures became increasingly important as the patronage originally governing the entire system gave way to the civil service. The first commission to investigate possibly establishing such a service was formed in 1871 by Grant, who, ironically, had one of the most corrupt administrations in history. Congress's reluctance to appropriate the needed funds for such a project aborted it in 1875. Six years later the assassination of a president highlighted the need for a civil service: on July 2, 1881, Charles J. Guiteau, after a vain attempt to procure the post of ambassador to Austria or consul to Paris, shot and killed President James Garfield.

The Garfield and Chester Arthur ticket of 1880 had united a reform president and an anti-reform (or "Stalwart") vice-presidential candidate in order to balance the Republican platform. But Guiteau's cry as he assassinated Garfield ("I am a Stalwart and now Arthur is president") spelled the end of his own life and that of the spoils system itself. Arthur, dismaying his Stalwart friends and in light of aroused public opinion in the assassination's aftermath, endorsed and signed into law the Civil Service Reform Act of 1883 (known as the Pendleton Act). This first congressional attempt to replace the spoils system provided for 10 percent of the federal bureaucracy to be chosen on the basis of merit, as determined by competitive examination. Since then the figures have been reversed: Civil service positions now account for over 90 percent of the bureaucracy's personnel. At the lower levels of the civil service, hiring is still conducted by competitive examination, and usually involves a written test, even though similar positions in industry would not. Examiners must sometimes strain to create an appropriate examination for a particular position, as demonstrated by the following questions designed for elevator operator applicants:

> Now the vast majority of federal jobs fall under civil service regulations.

1. A sign inside your car states that no smoking is allowed. A passenger carrying a lighted cigarette enters your car. You should say (A) "Read that sign and then put your cigarette out." (B) "Peruse the announcement, sir, and then extinguish your cigarette." (C) "Smoking not permitted." (D) "No smoking, please."

2. A sudden stop in an elevator is undesirable mainly because it (A) wrecks the mechanism (B) is not allowed (C) may lead to the loss of his job by the operator (D) discommodes and may injure passengers.[4]

[4]Sample questions taken from David R. Turner, *Civil Service Handbook: How to Get a Civil Service Job* (New York: Arco, 1972), pp. 30–31. The correct answer to each question is *D*.

The mid-level to the upper ranges of the civil service replace competitive examinations with primary reliance on an extensive federal "resume" known as the Standard Form (SF) 171. The SF 171 requires the applicant to list all previous positions and salaries, along with the requirements and duties of each job held. In addition, especially at the higher levels of the civil service, an applicant may be required to complete a "Supplementary Statement" (which may run ten to twenty pages) detailing his or her suitability for the advertised position, and may include writing samples, previous employer's assessment of job performance, and other factors. The Personnel Department then reviews these documents and ranks candidates according to how well they fit the job's criteria. Only the names of those ranked "qualified" for the position are sent from the Personnel Department to the official filling the position. That official, in turn, may convene a panel of experts to further winnow down the number of applicants before interviewing the finalists. It is not unusual for this process to take six to nine months before a position is finally filled.

Personnel

The president is entitled to appoint primarily administrators at the highest levels of the bureaucracy.

Remaining appointive positions As previously mentioned, fewer than 10 percent of all federal jobs are currently outside the civil service system. The appointive positions remaining can be roughly divided into three categories:

1. *Appointive policy-making positions*: These account for approximately 600 direct presidential appointments. These officials often are granted considerable latitude by the White House when they, in turn, appoint several hundred additional subordinates. All these positions, theoretically superior to the career civil servant positions, form the main component at the top of the bureaucratic hierarchy.

2. *Independent regulatory commissioners*: These number several dozen members appointed by the president, but their set terms of office and concomitant independence effectively remove them, once in office, from presidential control.

3. *Lower-level nonpolicy patronage positions*: These are similar to the appointive positions mentioned in (1) except that they are nonpolicy-making positions, such as secretarial assistants to the policymakers. The logic behind this type of appointment is that the policymaker should be free to appoint people who can be trusted to handle sensitive matters. In practice, many of the people who hold these nonpolicy-making positions exert considerable influence on policy. Similar nonpolicy-making positions are available for patronage appointments by senators and local party leaders. The number of positions in this category was drastically reduced in 1971 with the reorganization of the Post Office Department by the United States Postal Service Act. In accord with the provisions of the act, most of these positions became career-merit, rather than senatorial-patronage, in nature.

TABLE 4.4   Salaries, United States Government, Effective January 1992

Grade	Sample Occupation	Starting Salary— Top Salary
GS–18	(Top career official)[a]	
GS–17	(Supervisory professional)[a]	
GS–16	(Supervisory professional)[a]	
GS–15	(Senior analyst)	64,233–83,502
GS–14	(Chief accountant)	54,607–70,987
GS–13	(Personnel director)	46,210–60,070
GS–12	(Accountant, experienced)	38,861–50,516
GS 11	(Buyer)	32,423–42,152
GS–10	(Engineering technician)	29,511–38,367
GS–9	(Secretary, experienced)	26,798–34,835
GS–8	(Accountant, beginning)	24,262–31,543
GS–7	(Engineer, beginning)	21,906–28,476
GS–6	(Secretary, beginning)	19,713–25,626
GS–5	(Junior draftsman)	17,686–22,996
GS–4	(General stenographer)	15,808–20,551
GS–3	(Typist, experienced)	14,082–18,303
GS–2	(Keypunch operator, beginning)	12,905–16,237
GS–1	(File clerk, beginning)	11,478–14,356

[a]These so-called "supergrades" have been replaced by the Senior Executive Service, with a salary range of $87,000–$143,000.

Distribution of personnel   The distribution of civil service personnel across the bureaucracy demonstrates the relative size of the various elements in the federal structure. Over 32 percent of all civil service personnel are employed by the Department of Defense (counting civilian employees only), with the Postal Service following with 25 percent of the total, and the Department of Veterans' Affairs employing about 8 percent. The remaining third of civil service personnel are distributed throughout the rest of the bureaucracy. Most of these employees are paid on what is known as the "General Schedule" (see Table 4.4), and spend their professional careers advancing from one GS level to another.

> The Defense Department employs by far the largest number of civilian government employees.

The federal bureaucracy, with almost 3.2 million civilian workers, is undoubtedly large. We must note, however, that only 19 percent of government employees work for the national government; the other 81 percent work in state or local government bureaucracies. Similarly, most money is spent at the state and local levels rather than by the federal government. Although some political candidates may rail at "big government in Washington," the vast preponderance of the government we experience is at the state or local level, delivered by state or local bureaucrats.

> Most government employees work for state or local governments, not the national government.

For that matter, most of the people employed by "the government in Washington" do their work outside the nation's capital and the metropolitan Washington

T A B L E   4 . 5   **Percentage of Women and Minorities in the Federal General Schedule (GS/GM) and Executive Schedule (ES)**

	GS/GM	ES
Women	49.0	10.27 %
Blacks	16.13	4.74
Hispanics	4.75	1.39
Asians	3.15	.82
Native Americans	1.42	.60

Source: U.S. Equal Employment Opportunity Commission, FY 1989 Data

Only 12 percent of federal employees work in the Washington area.

area. Only 12 percent of federal employees work in the Washington area; the rest work in the ten regional headquarters of federal activities and thousands of district offices.

Representative bureaucracy?   Federal bureaucrats are similar to the American population as a whole, although more differences appear among high-ranking civil servants. As Table 4.5 demonstrates, women and minorities are more highly represented in the General Schedule (GS/GM) than in the Executive Schedule (SES). Thus, at the lower pay scales of the federal government women were slightly underrepresented (approximately 52 percent of the general population is female), blacks well represented (12 percent of the general population is black), and Hispanics underrepresented (roughly 7 percent of the general population is Hispanic). When we look at the Senior Executive levels, however, the bureaucracy appears to suffer from the same "glass ceiling" effect documented in private industry, with fewer women and minorities on the upper rungs of the corporate ladder. In general, women and minorities in federal jobs earn significantly less than the average white male, because they are commonly found in the lowest-paying jobs and rarely attain supergrade positions.

Actually, the federal government's record in nondiscriminatory hiring and promotion policies is better than that of the private sector. Furthermore, trends in the past twenty years are toward a lessening of racial and gender-based discrimination. Yet, while the number of women and minorities in higher level civil service positions has increased steadily over the past decade, similar growth in the number of white males can be demonstrated.

Higher-level civil servants, those with the most policy-making discretion, do not differ greatly from other Americans with similar educations. Their parents are likely to be richer than the parents of a general sample of Americans, but in this relatively upper-status background the higher civil service does not differ from similarly trained administrators and professionals employed in the private sector. There is no evidence, for example, that scientists working for the Environmental Protection Agency have social backgrounds different from scientists employed by private sector industries or universities.

The distribution of at-
titudes of higher-level
bureaucrats is similar to
that of other Americans.

Politicians sometimes depict the federal bureaucracy as composed of ideo-logues out of step in their thinking with the American people. This is simply wrong, for surveys show federal bureaucrats to be diverse in their thinking, just as are the American people. There is a slight tendency for bureaucrats to be more liberal than the American populace as a whole, but the differences are minor. The key factor in predicting bureaucrats' attitudes is to examine the mission of their agency. Civil servants rarely disapprove of their agencies' missions. For example, an employee of the Department of Education is likely to favor more federal aid to education programs, and a Defense Department employee is likely to want in-creased defense spending. Where a bureaucrat's office is located is a good predictor of where that bureaucrat stands on issues, at least those relevant to his or her agency.

Finally, how do bureaucrats leave office? Because civil service rules restrict firings for political reasons, the bureaucracy has developed the reputation of be-ing a large, stagnant mass whose members leave only to retire. Although civil servants during the 1980s left their jobs at only half the rate of private sector employees, the recession of the early 1990s caused a sharp decrease in these numbers. In 1991, for example, white-collar workers who quit their government jobs fell by 30 percent over comparable 1989 figures, and the turnover rate among SES level employees dropped to 3 percent from 8.5 percent in 1990. This change can be attributed to the recession (a lack of comparable jobs in the private sector) and the significant pay raises achieved in 1990 by federal employees. During the 1980s, on the other hand, there were 700,000 or so annual departures, only 20 percent of which were retirements. One-third were employees who simply quit, presumably to seek employment elsewhere. Another third, over 200,000 annually,

There is substantial turnover among bureaucrats,
including 200,000 people
annually fired.

were fired. Twelve percent were "riffed": a "reduction in force" in their agency eliminated their positions. The remaining departures were suspensions without pay. During both the Reagan and Bush administrations, RIFs increased as the ad-ministration sought to reduce federal involvement in domestic policy areas.

BUREAUCRATIC LEADERSHIP

To understand bureaucratic leadership, we must distinguish between bureaucracies in theory and bureaucracies in fact. In theory, bureaucracies implement public policies and are merely the tools of elected officials. Federal bureaucracies, for example, owe their existence to Congress and to the president. Their jurisdictions are limited by the enabling legislation that created them. However, in spite of these formal restrictions, bureaucracies can and do exercise independent leadership.

Bureaucratic leadership is defined by discretion or choice among alternative courses of action. Bureaucrats often have wide discretion when implementing public policy. Moreover, bureaucrats frequently influence the nature and extent of the available options for implementing policy. Such leadership capability is based on three distinct sources of influence—specialization and expertise, the civil service system, and agency alliances within and outside of government.

Sources of Bureaucratic Leadership

Politicians are generalists; bureaucrats are specialists.

Specialization and expertise Politicians are generalists, whereas bureaucrats are specialists. This explains a great deal about leadership potential in this century, in which increased specialization, ranging from Henry Ford's assembly line to the world of modern medicine, has been the rule. The specialization of the private sector is paralleled by an increasingly complex and compartmentalized federal government. Americans expect the government to handle issues as diverse as economics, defense strategy, nuclear energy, space exploration, earth transportation, and agriculture. Neither the president nor Congress can possibly possess all the information required to administer a government with such varied responsibilities. However, with the assistance available in the bureaucracies, elected officials can at least begin to address this myriad of policy concerns.

Expertise gives bureaucrats influence over policy formulation.

Because bureaucrats have expertise, they are important information sources for politicians formulating policy. When legislation is being considered, bureaucrats from the affected agencies often testify at committee hearings, thereby influencing the development of policies they may later implement. Moreover, their expertise may afford bureaucrats substantial influence over the implementation of public policies. In the area of government regulation, for example, Congress often delegates broad powers to regulatory agencies, allowing them wide discretion to design the administrative rules that put legislation (and presumably congressional intent) into practice.

Specialization and expertise also make it difficult for the president to control bureaucratic behavior. In fact, the idea that bureaucracies can be viewed as merely mechanical administrative bodies under the control of elected or appointed officials is illusory. Inherent specialization at each level of the bureaucratic structure results in each level establishing its own specific goals. These goals are established over the years in response to the particular political and administrative environment (congressional liaison, pressure group influence, and so forth) in which the specialization occurs. As a result, even lower-level career administrators have far more familiarity with the programs and policies of the department or agency in question than transient political appointees of the president could ever hope to gain. The "inferiors" in the hierarchical structure are therefore relatively free from interference by the appointed officials, and unless controversies develop or the situation is publicly aired, the president may neither know nor act on the continued noncooperation and intransigence of a career administrator.

Civil service gives bureaucrats independence from political control.

Civil service as a source of influence Civil service reforms were intended to protect government employees from partisan politics. The modern civil service system has succeeded admirably in doing just that. By controlling the initial recruitment of new employees and the promotion of existing personnel through merit-based systems, civil service affords bureaucrats substantial independence from direct political control. Longevity in office permits bureaucrats to outlast the political appointees who are ostensibly in charge of policy. Consequently, bureaucrats can channel new policy initiatives through organizationally comfortable standard operating procedures, which may effectively modify policy goals. Civil service protection even makes it possible for bureaucrats to sabotage an occasional policy initiative with which they disagree. At the very least, astute political appointees will soon realize that if they hope to achieve even part of their political agenda, they must negotiate policy changes with the personnel in their agencies. This process allows bureaucrats to modify or even redirect policy initiatives; it is one of the important bases for leadership potential in the bureaucracy.

Bureaucrats can make it extremely difficult for a new administration even to acquaint itself with the workings of the bureaucratic maze. In fact, it is never easy, even with the support of the bureaucrats, for a new president to discover exactly how the bureaucracy operates; without their support, it is virtually impossible. As one White House aide during Nixon's years expressed it, "President Nixon doesn't run the bureaucracy; the civil service and the unions do. It took him three years to find out what was going on in the bureaucracy. And God forbid if any President is defeated after the first term, because then the bureaucracy has another three years to play games with the next President."[5]

Bureaucracies may use one branch of the government as an ally against another branch.

Alliances within and outside of government Separation of powers makes it possible for bureaucracies to use one branch of government as leverage against another. For example, federal agencies often use congressional contacts to fend off budget cuts proposed by the president. Thus, Reagan's attempts to destroy the Legal Services Corporation were blocked several times when the agency rallied its supporters in the Congress. In the Reagan administration's early years, the Department of Defense could resist congressional attempts to limit military spending because the president, committed to the defense buildup, was a powerful ally. But, even the president as an ally is no guarantee of success, as illustrated by Bush's inability to prevent a similar military downsizing after the collapse of the Soviet Union and the Eastern bloc.

One of the more interesting techniques used by bureaucrats to defend their budgets from potential cuts by an administration is the time-honored process of leaking information to the press. While the budget process is lengthy and complex (as discussed in Chapter 2), it is also, in its early stages, quite secretive. Departments and agencies propose their budgets more than a year in advance to the Office of Management and Budget, which often pares down their requests— frequently eliminating programs that are out of favor with the president. When the department or agency finds out about a program's elimination by OMB, they will often leak this information to the press, galvanizing their supporters in various interest groups and Congress to pressure the administration to reverse its decision. Such was the case, for example, in the mid-1980s when, one afternoon, OMB sent a discussion paper to the White House that included eliminating a program assisting the poor to buy heating oil. That evening the television news reported that the president wanted to kill the program, and even interviewed several aid

[5]Quoted in Richard P. Nathan, "The Administrative Presidency," *The Public Interest,* no. 44 (Summer 1976), p. 44.

recipients. Terminating the aid program was rejected by the White House by 8:00 A.M. the next day!

Almost every federal agency has a clientele relationship with some interest group whose members are provided a service or "regulated" by the agency. Examples are obvious and numerous. There are extensive ties between unions and the Department of Labor, defense contractors and the Department of Defense, environmentalists and the Environmental Protection Agency, veterans and the Department of Veterans' Affairs, and other agencies and interest groups. Such relationships are examples of mutual self-interest. The interest groups hope to maintain access to the agencies directly involved in programs crucial to their members; the agencies seek to develop external alliances that will serve as political leverage in their dealings with political leaders. For example, both the interest groups and the agencies favor increased funding for their programs. Such increases please the bureaucrats because the agency expands (thereby increasing its workforce, power, and prestige). Increased funding pleases interest groups because their leaders can point with pride to their success in helping their members.

Subgovernments develop around federal subsidy programs and contracts.

Some policy areas encourage three-way relationships among agencies, interest groups, and congressional committees or subcommittees. These subgovernments, or "iron triangles," are particularly evident when federal subsidies or federal contracts are involved. Under this arrangement, the bureaucracies use both the interest groups and the congressional committees as political resources to maintain and, if possible, increase the size of their programs—with the support of both the interest group and the members of Congress involved. Federal policies supporting dairy prices, for example, are effectively maintained by iron triangles connecting powerful dairy-farm lobbyists, the agriculture committees and relevant subcommittees composed of members from dairy-producing states, and the United States Department of Agriculture, which implements dairy price supports.

In recent years, the increased number and diversity of interest groups in Washington has broadened the base of many of these subgovernments. This has led observers to characterize some of the relationships among interest groups, congressional committees or subcommittees, and executive agencies as "policy networks," with a membership more fluid and internally conflictive than iron triangles.[6] For example, the distribution of federal highway funds is now a more open and controversial issue as groups supporting greater federal assistance to urban mass transit vie with traditional automobile interests for federal support. Such internal conflicts have mitigated the influence of what was once an iron triangle. As the pressures in Congress for Highway Trust Fund money became more diverse, the way funds are allocated by the Federal Highway Administration became increasingly public. Thus, internal group conflict made it more difficult for that agency to rely on any one external support network and opened up a former iron triangle to a variety of inputs. In summary, subgovernments create a political support system

[6]Hugh Heclo, "Issue Networks and the Executive Establishment," in Anthony King, ed., *The New American Political System* (Washington, D.C.: American Enterprise Institute, 1978), pp. 88–124.

around government agencies, representing a source of bureaucratic influence and leadership, although less so with policy networks than with iron triangles.

LIMITATIONS ON BUREAUCRATIC LEADERSHIP

Political limitations have three components. The first concerns the influence of the executive, legislative, and judicial branches on bureaucratic discretion and hence leadership. The second involves the limiting effects of external relationships on bureaucracy, and the third component concerns the bureaucracy's own internal limitations.

Governmental Limitations

Relations with the president   Several of the president's powers mentioned in the first chapter directly affect his relations with the bureaucracy. Those powers that were considered under the heading "Presidential Leadership" are particularly important—using persuasion to threaten, cajole, plead, and bargain can be aimed as much at bureaucrats as elected officials. Presidential favors are prestigious regardless of the object of the president's attention. Presidential pressure is, of course, particularly effective when applied to presidential appointees (as seen in Table 4.1), many of whom are subject to dismissal at the president's discretion. However, every president must attempt to influence bureaucrats over whom he does not have dismissal authority. As already noted, these bureaucrats can make it extremely difficult for a new administration to acquaint itself with the workings of the bureaucratic maze.

> The president's task in persuading bureaucrats is similar to his task in persuading Congress.

This is not to suggest, however, that the president is impotent in dealing with the bureaucracy. Both directly and indirectly, through congressional allies, the president exerts great influence over the bureaucracy. This influence is greater when he wishes to stop bureaucrats from doing what he does not want than when he wants reluctant bureaucrats to follow his lead.

First, the president, together with Congress, dictates the annual budget. An agency in the president's favor is likely to receive increased funding, while an agency that has incurred the president's wrath can expect a sharp cut or even elimination. For example, the Legal Services Corporation (LSC) provides assistance to poor citizens in civil disputes, a federal activity President Reagan disliked. Every year Reagan proposed cutting off all funding to the LSC, thereby eliminating the agency and effectively firing all of its employees. Although congressional allies saved the LSC from extinction, it survived with sharply reduced funding.

> White House involvement in budgeting, reorganizing the bureaucracy, promotions, and modifying regulations may also be used to persuade agencies to implement programs as the president desires.

Second, under his executive or administrative authority, the president can reorganize departments. If he believes that a particular policy is not being effectively administered by a certain bureau in a department, he can shift the responsibility for administering that policy to a different bureau. The use (or threat of use) of such reorganizations helps the president persuade the bureaucracy to do what he wants.

Third, the president and his high-level political appointees have more control over civil servant personnel policies than one would expect in a strict Weberian bureaucracy. Promotions are supposedly awarded entirely by merit, but especially at the highest grades, civil servants who enthusiastically endorse the president's policies may be found to have more "merit" than employees who have reservations about the wisdom of the president's ideas. Civil servants at the lower grade levels cannot be fired, except for cause, but they may be harassed at times into choosing other employment. A GS-12, for example, who takes a public position against the administration might be given few or no responsibilities and denied any real promotion potential. Rather than "stagnate" at that level, doing nothing, the dissatisfied employee may choose to resign.

For members of the civil service at the supergrade level (GS-16 and above) who have elected to enter the Senior Executive Service (SES), the control exercised over their positions by the political level is even more extensive. Any career civil servant who wishes to advance to the highest government managerial levels must enter the SES, but in doing so may lose a good deal of security. An SES civil servant with close family ties in Virginia and a new home there may be given a transfer to the bureau's office in Seattle. The SES career bureaucrat has only two choices: accept the transfer or resign from the government. Not every president or cabinet secretary has made frequent use of such distasteful methods, but bureaucrats know that if they become too obnoxious to their political bosses, the probability increases that such methods will be applied.

Fourth, the president can change regulations to clarify how legislation is to be implemented. For example, if the president believes that the bureaucracy has been too quick to provide black-lung benefits to former miners with respiratory problems, he can require additional authentication of each applicant's case, usually by issuing orders through OMB. This would reduce the bureaucracy's efficiency in processing claims but realize the president's purpose.

Relations with Congress   Congress, like the president, relies most heavily on the appropriation process to limit the power of the bureaucracy. Congressional "power of the purse" is a formidable weapon, rendered even more imposing by the long tenure of powerful appropriations subcommittee chairpersons. In that their tenure often outlasts that of any president, these members of Congress can exercise an elephantine memory for the activities of executive departments and agencies. Agency representatives must appear annually before Congress to justify their budget requests, at which time they are often questioned on the entire range of the agency's activities.

Congress's involvement in the budgetary process is its key resource in attempting to influence behavior in the bureaucracy.

The mere fact that a program's budget request has cleared the OMB and is included in the president's budget proposal to Congress is no guarantee the program will receive the requested amount or, for that matter, any money at all. President Carter's amnesty program for draft resisters serves as an illustration. The administration had lobbied against and defeated a congressional move to reject the amnesty program, but many of its provisions were inoperable without federal funds. Despite the president's victory, Congress, when it passed the 1978 budget, refused to appropriate any funds for the program's operation.

Monetary considerations also play a part in the congressionally controlled General Accounting Office (GAO) and the Office of the Comptroller General. The GAO acts as the congressional "watchdog" of the Treasury. The head of GAO, the comptroller general, is appointed with the consent of the Senate and may be removed only with the consent of both houses of Congress. All government expenditures must be authorized by the GAO and bear the signature of the comptroller general. For the bureaucrat, it can be a long, arduous road from the OMB, through Congress, to the GAO—a road on which more than one program has been robbed of every cent.

The GAO also uses this "watchdog" authority over the manner in which the Treasury's dollars are spent to evaluate entire federal programs for Congress. At the request of a member of Congress, the GAO may enter virtually *any* area of operation of a federal department or agency and conduct an investigation. This investigative function is often augmented by the physical presence, in the same building that houses the department or agency, of full-time GAO investigators. Wily federal bureaucrats, however, can still thwart the investigators. While executive branch employees are required, by law, to turn over to GAO investigators any and all information that they request, GAO has to know what to ask for. If the GAO investigator doesn't know of the existence of a specific document, for example, the bureaucrat is not obliged to volunteer the information that the document exists and, therefore, GAO may never gain access to it.

Aside from strictly monetary and investigative considerations, Congress also retains the option of program authorization and amendment. Consequently, bureaucrats seek to appease powerful congressional leaders and actively court their favor. Congress has increasingly granted broad authorization to the bureaucracy to pursue its programs, but such programs can be changed or even eliminated through a "reduction in force—called a "RIF"—(the wholesale elimination of job positions), by Congress at any time. The wise bureaucrat must balance this against both the desires of the agency or department he or she represents and those of the president—a feat of no mean proportion.

In performing oversight activities, Congress may elicit public pressure on an agency.

Members of Congress, on an individual basis, also seek to influence bureaucratic activities through public exposure. Efforts by members of Congress to influence the implementation of the Superfund legislation by the Environmental Protection Agency, discussed in the case study in this book, often involved public prodding. Failing to persuade EPA officials in private communications, members tried to build public political pressure to force EPA to act.

The bureaucracy employs lobbyists to advance its positions on Capitol Hill.

Congressional-bureaucratic relations are not a one-way street with Congress trying to get bureaucrats to do what it wants. The bureaucracy employs hundreds of lobbyists (although they cannot legally be called lobbyists) who provide "informational assistance" to Congress. Lobbyists for the bureaucracy, regardless of what they are called, behave like private interest-group lobbyists in working to persuade Congress to pass legislation favorable to their interests. The Department of Defense, for example, has one of the largest lobbying staffs in Washington. Daily it sends dozens of officers from the Pentagon to the Capitol to advance military interests. Members in key positions with records of enthusiastic support for Pentagon spending proposals are likely to be rewarded by the placement of military installations in their districts. Other agencies, with fewer resources to reward their congressional supporters, have greater difficulty maintaining congressional support for their programs.

Relations between bureaucracies and the courts   The courts also retain some degree of control over the activities of the bureaucracy. As previously noted, Congress has the constitutional prerogative to establish judicial authority in the lower courts, and the Supreme Court has ruled that this same congressional authorization of the right to adjudicate can be extended to independent regulatory commissions and other agencies established by congressional mandate. Thus, the courts may not intervene or accept appeals from the quasi-judicial proceedings of the bureaucracy.

If a suit disputing the authority of a bureaucracy is filed by a third party, the court must first determine the "delegation of congressional intent" (whether Congress had the power to delegate this authority to the department or agency). Once the delegation of congressional intent is granted, the court is limited to a determination of the question of *ultra vires* (beyond legal power)—that is, whether the agency is operating within the confines of the legislation in question. To rule *ultra vires*, however, the court must point to congressionally enumerated limitations of power in the statute, which the agency has violated. Given the broad delegation of authority that Congress usually imparts to the bureaucracy, such rulings are rare. Thus, except in questions of constitutionality, the bureaucracy is relatively free from external judicial review.

The courts rarely accept challenges of administrative decisions.

Although the courts rarely question actions by the bureaucracy, judges have been more willing to hear suits claiming that the bureaucracy has failed to act as mandated by law. An example of this type of involvement appeared in the case study at the end of Chapter 3. In that case, an environmental group, joined by the states of New Jersey and Connecticut, sued the Environmental Protection Agency because EPA had failed to promulgate regulations within the time frame specified by Congress. This type of suit is often brought against bureaucracies to prod an administration into acting in an area in which it has a mandate to act but is reluctant to do so for policy reasons.

Extragovernmental Limitations

The second major limitation on bureaucratic leadership arises from the interest-group structure around which bureaucracy is organized. As previously mentioned, the personnel who serve in the federal government's "four branches," are drawn disproportionately from the upper socioeconomic strata of the society. Further, because society's resources are not randomly distributed throughout the population, but rather concentrated in the same strata from which these personnel are recruited, the influences brought to bear on the bureaucracy reflect "the business or upper-class bias of the pressure system."[7] Admittedly, some exceptions to this general rule do exist, but the interests of consumers and of the disadvantaged in American society (for example, the poor, migrants, women, and blacks) generally find weak representation in the pressure system.

Upper-class and upper-middle-class interests are more effective than those groups working for the needs of disadvantaged people.

Because of such unevenness in outside pressures, it is very difficult for the bureaucracies representing the interests of the disadvantaged to exercise leadership on these issues. The allocation of government resources is a highly competitive process even during the best of times. During periods of high deficits and policy retrenchment, the competition for scarce resources is even more fierce. Bureaucracies serving the disadvantaged segments of society find themselves in a weak bargaining position vis-a-vis those agencies concerned with economic development, military matters, or middle-class entitlement programs, which are protected by powerful constituency groups who can exert considerable pressure.

However, not all limitations in this area arise because of resource differences. Exerting effective pressure at any point in the political process requires an interest group to use organization, concentration, and the necessary financial or political resources to make its voice heard. Without money or votes, an interest group is unlikely to be effective. In general, the more diversified interest groups are less effective than the more specialized ones that are able to focus their energies. Thus, the Chamber of Commerce of the United States exerts less influence than the American Medical Association (AMA), given the latter's ability to concentrate its considerable resources on specific legislation.

Interest groups that focus their energies on particular subject areas are generally more effective than larger, more heterogeneous interest groups.

However, the effectiveness of specialized interest groups is usually limited to the group's area of specialization. The American Legion, for example, is a very influential interest organization when lobbying for veterans' benefits. Leaders of the Department of Veterans' Affairs and of the veterans' affairs committees of Congress pay careful attention to Legion statements on the needs of veterans and often modify policies based on Legion lobbying efforts. However, when the Legion moves outside its area of specialization to urge that certain policies be adopted in the realm of foreign relations or internal security, its recommendations receive little serious attention.

Internal Limitations

Specialization and inefficiency   Finally, the bureaucracy itself contains its own limitations. Within the hierarchical structure, specialization is the order of the day. Such a division of labor ensures incomplete control of superiors over inferiors, because bureaucratic "inferiors" are likely to possess a degree of expertise in a given area

[7]E. E. Schattschneider, *The Semi-Sovereign People* (New York: Holt, Rinehart and Winston, 1960), p. 31.

of specialization not equaled by their superiors. This tension between formal authority and expertise can make it extremely difficult for a bureau to operate efficiently. More to the point, it often makes it difficult for a bureau to present a united front in its relations with other branches of government or with outside interest groups. Thus, the very setup that helps generate bureaucratic strength by allowing agency personnel to resist the wishes of political appointees also weakens overall bureau influence by producing tensions among personnel at different levels of the bureaucracy.

Agencies fight among themselves, as do offices within agencies, for power, prestige, and money.

Institutional loyalty   Harold Seidman characterized bureaucracies as affected by "deeply ingrained cultures and subcultures reflecting institutional history, ideology, values, symbols, folklore, professional biases, behavior patterns, heroes and enemies."[8] Strong institutional loyalty can produce not only the refusal to submit to hierarchical authority but also fierce disputes over jurisdictional questions with parallel bureaucratic structures in other agencies. Entire bureaucratic structures may be so affected, resulting, for example, in little or no communication between the Department of Labor and the National Labor Relations Board or between the Department of Commerce and the Federal Trade Commission. Such lack of cooperation and reciprocity only increases the confusing nature of the bureaucratic maze and weakens the ability of the competing agencies to function effectively. Indeed, as one agency's ambition counteracts another's, there develops an informal system of checks and balances among parts of the bureaucracy—a counterpart to the constitutional system of checks and balances among the president, Congress, and the federal courts.

CONCLUSION

Instances of poor service to individuals are inherent in bureaucratic organizations.

It is easy, perhaps too easy, to write cynically of the bureaucracy. Everyone has personal horror stories about misfortunes dealing with public and private bureaucracies, including those at American universities and colleges. Sometimes a person's particular need does not match up well with relevant rules and regulations, so that what seems to be a simple problem with an obvious solution gets bogged down in red tape, generates exchanges with rude officials who seem insulted that the problem does not fit one of the ready categories, and never does result in the adoption of the obvious solution. Although well-managed and well-funded bureaucracies can reduce such problems, they can never be entirely eliminated, for the complexity of the human experience defies the creation of an appropriate rule for every circumstance.

One reason the federal bureaucracy is an easier target for criticism than private bureaucracies is that individuals can avoid many private bureaucracies that have angered them. If employees of a restaurant treat a person rudely, he or she can

[8]Harold Seidman, *Politics, Position, and Power,* 2nd ed. (New York: Oxford University Press, 1975), pp. 98–99.

avoid that restaurant; if the bad experiences are with the Internal Revenue Service or the Postal Service, what is a person to do? A citizen can (and should) complain to appropriate officials to obtain fair treatment, but does not have the simple solution of going to a different Internal Revenue Service.

Much presidential and congressional time and effort are spent attempting to control the bureaucracy.

The bureaucracy frustrates elected officials as well as individual citizens. This book has tried to show that much of the political dynamics in Washington involves White House and congressional efforts to persuade entrenched bureaucrats to administer programs the way the president and Congress want them administered. The other side of the coin is that much politics involves the bureaucrats and their interest-group allies attempting to persuade the president and Congress to adopt policies favorable to the individual agencies. More than one president has concluded that dealing with *his* bureaucracy is similar to punching out a pillow: You get exhausted after exerting much energy, but after the struggle ends, the pillow returns to its original shape.

If there are such significant problems with the federal bureaucracy, why not try to get rid of it? At rallies in the 1960s and 1970s, presidential candidate George Wallace suggested just such a dismantling (except for the Defense Department), to the wild cheers of his followers. With similar appeals in 1980, Ronald Reagan was elected to the presidency.

The bureaucracy survives and prospers because it alone is capable of accomplishing certain of our national goals.

The essential reason the bureaucracy exists is the American people want certain tasks accomplished, tasks that only the federal government can perform. This is not to say that the bureaucracy is not in need of reform, or that none of its activities is wasteful, or that some its functions could not beneficially decentralized to states and localities. The point is that the American people want certain things done, things only large-scale public bureaucracies can accomplish. Two examples of successful bureaucratic responses to public demands are the space program and Social Security.

The bureaucracy has at times performed impressively in accomplishing difficult tasks.

Americans want to be able to retire from their jobs before they die and to be free of devastating medical expenses in their senior years. The states and private pension arrangements cannot provide such security in an equitable manner to all Americans who have worked throughout their lives. The Social Security Administration, through the system of employer and worker contributions to old-age insurance and Medicare funds, has been able to send monthly checks to millions of senior citizens and to provide medical insurance. Although no one is saying the system is perfect, it does provide a means of living in dignity and security for millions of retired people. This is no small accomplishment.

Another example of successful bureaucratic behavior is the placement of a man on the moon only ten years after America's space effort began on a serious level. Starting far behind the Soviets, the American space program surpassed the Soviet effort in only a decade. This trip to the moon was celebrated, as it should have been, as a remarkable scientific and technological accomplishment. It was just as much a bureaucratic accomplishment, for the National Aeronautics and Space Administration amassed and organized the talent and material necessary to get the job done. With Congress, the president, and the bureaucracy in agreement on what was to be done, the policy was effectively implemented.

Selected Additional Readings

Bryner, Gary C. *Bureaucratic Discretion: Law and Policy in Federal Regulatory Agencies.*
Elmsford, N.Y.: Pergamon Press, 1987.

Kozak, David C., and Keagle, James M. (eds.) *Bureaucratic Politics and National Security.* Boulder, Colo.: Lynne Rienner, 1988.

Riley, Dennis D. *Controlling the Federal Bureaucracy.* Philadelphia: Temple University Press, 1987.

Rourke, Francis E. (ed). *Bureaucratic Power in National Policymaking,* 4th ed. Boston: Little, Brown, 1986.

CASE HISTORY : S u p e r f u n d

THE BUREAUCRACY

By the time President Jimmy Carter signed the Comprehensive Environmental Response, Compensation and Liability Act of 1980 (CERCLA) on December 11, the U.S. Environmental Protection Agency was already prepared to implement the legislation. By February 1980, EPA had formed a new office to plan for the implementation of Superfund. That office forced EPA to concentrate on issues likely to confront the agency when the bill passed.

175 By the end of 1980, the Superfund organization in EPA, named the Office of Hazardous Emergency Response (OHER), virtually monopolized the competence required to manage the huge hazardous-waste cleanup program. For the first five months of the Reagan administration, EPA had no administrator. Anne M. Gorsuch was not named to the post until May 20, 1981. During that interim period, OHER continued its activities, but now, with CERCLA a reality, the office focused its attentions on the specifics of implementing the law.

The National Contingency Plan (NCP), one such specific, had originally been written to provide for a federal response capability to spills of oil or certain hazardous materials into the navigable waters of the United States. With the passage of CERCLA came the responsibility of revising and republishing the NCP to include multimedia responses involving any hazardous substance. However, with the passage of CERCLA, something else came to EPA—the lobbyists who had been working Congress trying to influence the legislation.

Now that the legislation had passed, environmental groups and industry representatives shifted their focus and tried to influence the specific regulations and policies by which the law would be implemented. The chemical industry had, in effect, "lost" the congressional battle. CERCLA had passed through Congress in the eleventh hour, but Con-

176–177 gress does not implement the laws it passes; only the bureaucracy has that authority. The battle lines were drawn anew.

When Gorsuch took office on May 20, she began the process of appointing her subordinates, the new upper-level managers in EPA. Barely a month later, she announced her choices for several key positions, and environmental groups were outraged. The agency, previously viewed as the protector of the environment, was now looked on by many as a polluters' stronghold. Several iterations of drafts of the NCP circulated through EPA during this period. In June, and again in October, the Chemical Manufacturers' Association (CMA) sent lengthy position papers to EPA outlining what it wanted to see in the upcoming NCP proposal. CMA's position on policies was often incorporated in subsequent NCP drafts.

The influence of CMA and other industry-based groups became so blatant that Rep. Toby Moffett (D.-Conn.), chairperson of the House Government Operations subcommittee, summoned Administrator Gorsuch and Deputy Administrator John Hernandez to answer allegations that the latter's meetings with industry representatives were policy-making sessions. In six meetings held between June 19 and September 29, chemical industry representatives, but no environmental or public-interest groups, met with Hernandez to discuss issues that were then before the agency. Clearly, Moffett argued, the industry "perceives this as unusual and delightful."

179–180

Against this backdrop of perceived industry influence on the agency, the Environmental Defense Fund (EDF) filed suit to compel EPA to propose the NCP in the Federal Register. EDF staffers reasoned that the longer the agency delayed, the more pervasive industry's influence would be.

181

OHER, which was now renamed the Office of Emergency and Remedial Response (OERR), operated during this period on the basis of "interim guidance," that is, policy decisions that were promulgated by OERR to implement the cleanup program in the absence of an NCP. Using a complex ranking system identifying the more dangerous hazardous-waste sites around the country, OERR generated a list of 115 "interim priority sites" for Superfund to move against. "Movement" at these sites, however, did not necessarily mean "cleanup." Often the agency's attorneys, using a variety of legal mechanisms (notice letters, administrative orders, and so on), sought to compel private-party cleanup rather than Superfund-financed cleanup. It was not until mid-1982 that the program office (OERR) and the legal (enforcement) offices were able to move concurrently at many of the sites on the interim priority list.

The law required that the state in which the site was located contribute to the cost of cleanup. In the early 1980s, with the cutbacks in federal support to state governments, many states could not afford their share (10 percent of the cost if the site were privately owned, and 50 percent or more if the site had been owned or operated by the state or a municipality). Before EPA could undertake a remedial action, the state was required to sign either a cooperative agreement (if the state was going to do most of the work) or a contract (if the agency had the lead at the site) and provide required assurances that it would be able to come up with its share of the cleanup cost. This cost-sharing requirement meant that no action was taken at many sites, because a state was unable or unwilling to provide the necessary assurances.

Administrator Gorsuch consciously followed procedures designed to "conserve" the money in the fund. She announced at a mid-1982 press conference at which the National Priorities List (NPL) was updated (adding more sites) that it would not be necessary to reauthorize the Superfund tax when it expired in 1985. Career bureaucrats at EPA were appalled at this notion and at the obvious maneuvering of Gorsuch and other senior Reagan appointees to delay cleaning up sites. Partially in response to this, William N. Hedeman, Jr., whom Gorsuch had named director of OERR, initiated the methodological development and data collection required to complete the studies called for by Congress under Section 301 of CERCLA. This is a good example of the "incomplete control" of superiors over

152

inferiors in a bureaucracy (mentioned in the text of this chapter). The studies, demonstrating the need to reauthorize CERCLA, were initiated by a career bureaucrat without the knowledge of the administrator, who publicly claimed no such need existed. Work continued on the studies for the entire eight-month period after their initiation, completely unbeknownst to political appointees in EPA. When Gorsuch was forced to resign on March 9, 1983, she was still unaware that they had been started.

182–183

Gorsuch's Superfund management resulted in her resignation. Since Superfund's passage, Congress had been performing its oversight function, and its studies of the mismanagement and antienvironmental bias developing within the agency were constantly in the nation's press. When Anne M. Burford (she married in 1983, and took her new husband's name) resigned, her action precipitated a wave of resignations among other high-level political appointees in EPA.

179–180

Reagan's choice to succeed Burford was viewed as beyond reproach by almost everyone. William D. Ruckelshaus was President Nixon's first EPA administrator when it was founded in 1970. Reagan brought him back to head the now-embattled agency again. Ruckelshaus at that time had the confidence of environmentalists, the business community, and Congress, as well as the support of the president. With Ruckelshaus came a team of senior-level managers that set about returning the agency to its traditional standards of professional administration of environmental laws.

165–166

Lee M. Thomas was named Assistant Administrator for Solid Waste and Emergency Response, taking the place of Rita Lavelle, who was later convicted of perjury for her role in the failure to enforce the Superfund law. Thomas not only "got Superfund moving" but, also, with the concurrence of the new administrator, ordered the Section 301 studies to be completed, thereby positioning the agency to be an active player in Superfund's reauthorization. When Ruckelshaus resigned as EPA administrator in December 1984, Thomas was named to replace him.

Most observers applauded Lee Thomas for his administration of Superfund during Reagan's second term. The severe shortages of money during 1985 and 1986 stopped almost all long-term remedial cleanup activities as the agency struggled to find the funds to perform emergency response actions at dangerous sites and to keep the program intact. When the SARA money became available, EPA moved quickly to comply with most provisions of the act. Whereas the initial Superfund act focused almost entirely on cleaning up uncontrolled hazardous-waste sites, SARA includes other substantial activities:

1. "Right to know" provisions requiring firms to provide communities with information on what chemicals are used at their plants;

2. Radon sections charging EPA with tasks leading to reduced quantities of radon, a carcinogenic gas produced by natural uranium deterioration in the earth, in private homes; and

3. Provisions charging the agency to develop a new program, complete with its own trust fund, to clean up hazardous chemical leaks from underground storage tanks.

Although the present discussion is limited to cleanup of hazardous-waste sites (the original legislative charge), the new mandates of SARA placed substantial new administrative responsibilities on the agency. Nevertheless, a substantial number of long-term cleanup efforts moved into the construction stage during 1987 and 1988, Thomas's last two years as head of EPA.

However, since 1988, EPA administrators Lee M. Thomas (under Reagan) and William K. Reilly (under Bush) faced charges that Superfund implementation is poorly managed. The GAO reported in 1988, 1989, and 1991 that the agency did not effectively manage the private contractors who do most of the on-site cleanup work. Specific criticisms included charges that the agency delegated contract management authority to the regional offices without providing sufficient headquarters oversight, allowed contractors to make their own cost estimates without EPA checks, and spent too much money on administration rather than direct cleanup activities. Administrator Thomas's response included, in 1988, setting up a new program designed to facilitate long-term planning for the most difficult sites. The Alternative Remedial Contract Strategy (ARCS) included 45 sites by late 1991. Administrator Reilly's response also included the appointment of twenty "trouble-shooters" with authority to deal with specific Superfund site problems, the creation of a new position of Superfund Director, and the development of a plan to limit management costs.

One reason for discouragement is the slow pace of cleaning up hazardous waste sites. A site with contaminated groundwater, for example, may require pumping the water to the surface and treating it over a period of thirty years. Of the 34,600 sites in the EPA information system at the end of 1991, most had been evaluated and almost twelve hundred were on the NPL, but only 63 sites were completely cleaned up and delisted from the NPL. EPA projections are that 200 sites will be delisted by January 1, 1994, and 650 by the year 2000. These numbers include sites on federal lands where other federal agencies are responsible for commencing cleanup actions. Although the agency has performed hundreds of emergency actions to protect citizens at risk from hazardous wastes about to escape from sites, Congress still returns to the question of the number of sites at which EPA has finished its work.

Some frustrations with Superfund administration are inherent in the situation. Citizens living near a site often expect the removal of all contaminated earth and water within a few months of identification of the problem. They are not pleased to learn that cleanup procedures in SARA, including those requiring a public hearing to discuss the proposed remedy, ensure that the cleanup must take years to complete. Of course, the more complex and dangerous the site, the more the process is lengthened by phased cleanups and necessary studies. In addition, most cleanups leave some contaminated materials at the site in sealed landfills or other containment facilities. This solution is necessitated by engineering considerations, the danger involved in moving certain volatile compounds, and cost factors; it rarely pleases local homeowners.

Other frustrations with Superfund administration emerge from differing interests and perspectives. Environmentalists generally want a more aggressive administration that will clean up more sites, more quickly, with less concern for cost, and to the highest standards. Citizens near a site often want their site cleaned up, now, regardless of the wisdom of further studies or greater potential dangers from sites elsewhere. Manufacturers, especially the petroleum and chemical industries, generally favor greater attention to cost factors, argue that EPA often employs unnecessarily stringent cleanup standards, and point to

181–182

recent research suggesting cheaper cleanup methods that the manufacturers want quickly brought on line in Superfund cleanups.

It should be clear from this part of the case history that the bureaucracy does not exist in a vacuum. Its actions face checks from the president and his appointed senior management, oversight by Congress, squabbles within the bureaucracy, interest-group pressures, and the requirements of the law. The one constant throughout this case history

178–183 is broad popular support for a national program to clean up abandoned hazardous-waste sites; without that popular support no legislation would have passed, and no dangerous sites would have been cleaned up. Just as the bureaucracy does not exist in a vacuum, apart from other political institutions, the other institutions do not exist in a vacuum either— they are accountable to public opinion and expectations.

POLITICS AND ECONOMICS

Government's ability to allocate resources, many of which are material in nature, depends to a large extent on society's economic organization. Conversely, a complex society's economic production is unavoidably influenced by government policies. Thus, the political and economic worlds are highly interdependent. This addendum addresses the relationship between politics and economics in the United States. It has two purposes. First, it illustrates how economics acts as a constraint on government policymakers on the one hand and is affected by those policymakers on the other. Second, it provides an overview case study of how the political actors and institutions analyzed in Chapters 1 through 4 handle one of society's most fundamental issues—economic organization

In the United States, the government distributes wealth but generally does not produce it. Therefore, political leaders must be sensitive to the needs of business interests, whose economic activities provide the foundation for government allocation programs. On the other hand, the business sector relies on government to maintain the stable economic and political climates at home and abroad essential for commercial transactions. Thus, the relationship between economic and political sectors is fundamentally important to each, because neither can fulfill its basic function without the other. To explore the relationship further, this addendum is divided into four sections. The first analyzes the effects of ideals like "rugged individualism" and laissez faire on United States public policy. The second section examines government regulation of the free market. The third analyzes the modern welfare state, which, in many ways, contradicts the individualistic ideal. The final section looks at different views of government macromanagement of the economy.

INDIVIDUALISM, LAISSEZ FAIRE, AND THE AMERICAN IDEAL

To understand how economics and politics affect each other, it is useful to examine the evolution of the American mixed economy. The United States has a capitalist economy, meaning most goods and services are produced in the private sector. Over the years, economic, technological, and political forces have brought some segments of the private sector into closer and more direct relationships with government. Indeed, many of these relationships have been institutionalized in independent executive and regulatory agencies (see Chapter 4). Nevertheless, few societies have a greater philosophical commitment to laissez faire (minimum government involvement in the economy) than the United States. Laissez faire complements the American notion of constitutionally limited government and readily fits a social order that places strong emphasis on individualism. In fact, the notions of laissez faire and rugged individualism form the cultural core of the American economic order.

The American concept of individualism is founded on the work ethic: Individuals who are ambitious and energetic will enjoy material success, and those with little ambition and energy will fail. The work ethic interprets success as a manifestation of individual worth and failure as a consequence of individual shortcomings. In popular American culture, the Horatio Alger stories celebrated the links between hard work and material success. The intellectual roots of these attitudes are found in the writings of the social Darwinists, who took the biological theories of Charles Darwin and applied them to an analysis of social systems. Darwin's ideas of "natural selection" and "survival of the fittest" were found useful not only to explain the evolution of life forms but also to analyze material success and failure in a social setting. To the social Darwinists, material success was simply evidence that stronger individuals thrive in a competitive environment.

The emphasis on individualism formed the basis for Adam Smith's classic work, *The Wealth of Nations*. Smith contends that an utterly self-interested individual pursuing his or her own selfish ends benefits the larger society in ways he or she neither controls nor intends. This occurs because a self-correcting marketplace—an "invisible hand"—promotes social progress without the need for government involvement. Competition in a free market means that successful entrepreneurs produce goods or services consumers want at prices they are willing to pay. Such entrepreneurial success, a product of the match between individual initiative on the one hand and consumer desires on the other, provides social benefits in the form of the desired goods and services, general economic growth, and an increased number of available jobs. A laissez faire approach to the economy, in Smith's view, is a prerequisite for long-term economic stability. American capitalism has been based philosophically on this laissez faire approach, permitting, indeed encouraging, each individual to pursue his or her own material ends without regard for a broader social good. Guided by the natural laws of supply and demand and restrained only by the minimal legal limits needed to prevent commercial anarchy, this pursuit supposedly results naturally in a greater social good.

Today, the emphasis on individual incentive and minimal government involvement is less pronounced than in the past, but it nevertheless remains a potent influence on American politics. In the discussion of constitutionally limited government, this book's introduction showed that Americans take the idea of individual political rights quite seriously; judging from public policy, it appears they feel the same way about economic individualism. In the early 1980s, for example, the federal government lowered its maximum income-tax rates twice, to a fifty-year low of 28 percent (33 percent for some taxpayers) and deregulated a number of basic industries. The arguments supporting these policies emphasized the importance of individual incentives and economic competition to a healthy overall economy. Indeed, Ronald Reagan's 1980 campaign was based on the notion that government is not the solution to but rather the cause of many social problems. Such Republican policies on the national level were also implemented by a number of state governments, such as New York and Massachusetts, which were under the control of Democrats.

Laissez faire philosophy notwithstanding, the U.S. government involved itself in economic matters from the very beginning. In many cases, government involvement resulted from the needs of commercial interests for stable economic environments. The Constitution provided a legal framework for commercial transactions, allowing federal regulation of interstate commerce and upholding the obligation of contracts. In 1791, Congress, acting (according to Treasury Secretary Alexander Hamilton) under the "implied powers" clause discussed in Chapter 2, created a national bank to coordinate the nation's economic affairs. The federal government also implemented a variety of economic development projects that provided direct benefits to producers in order to generate long-term benefits to the country as a whole; examples include import tariffs that supported domestic producers and land-grant subsidies to the railroads. In a society theoretically committed to laissez faire, such programs represent the considerable disparity that can arise between ideology and reality.

GOVERNMENT REGULATION OF THE ECONOMY

The Industrial Revolution greatly changed methods of production and substantially increased federal responsibilities. Increased government involvement in the economy followed the late-nineteenth-century development of the modern corporation in the private sector, which was the result of four factors. First, when the original entrepreneurs who started businesses passed from the scene, the companies they created still required management. Second, as greater amounts of capital became necessary for expansion, companies needed an external source of funds. Third, as job-related tasks and resources became increasingly specialized, a formal method of internal organizational integration was required. And fourth, as specialized business enterprises serving production grew in number, it became necessary to coordinate their various activities. The corporate model addressed all these needs by providing professional management and increased capital from the sale of company stock to outside investors. By 1900, the corporation was the dominant form of business organization in the United States.

As mentioned earlier, proponents of the "invisible hand" theory argued that self-interested people competing in the free market unwittingly produce a general public good by single-mindedly pursuing their individual interests. However, because of the increasing complexity and consequent interdependence of all parts of American society, the actions of any one part might affect society as a whole. A social agent was needed that would reflect and protect society's broader interests; this became the domain of independent regulatory commissions, established by an increasingly activist federal government. (For an analysis of independent regulatory commissions, see Chapter 4.) The Interstate Commerce Commission was created in 1887 to regulate the railroads and protect farmers from rate gouging (charging unfair prices to transport produce).

In the decades that followed, social complexity and interdependence increased, the American economy became less local and more national in scope, and large corporations sought stable economic environments. As a result, the federal regulatory role grew. In 1890, responding to the development of economic monopolies threatening to overwhelm market competition, Congress passed the Sherman Anti-Trust Act that prohibited conspiracies "in restraint of trade." This act was bolstered twenty-four years later by the passage of the Clayton Anti-Trust Act. In 1914, the federal government began regulating general business practices through the newly created Federal Trade Commission.

Since that early period, the extent of government regulation has changed dramatically. Unlike other industrial democracies, the United States avoids public ownership of critical industries, but it tempers the free market with an extensive system of federal regulatory agencies. As a result of the Great Depression in the 1930s, the Securities and Exchange Commission was established to regulate the securities industry, and the National Labor Relations Board was created to monitor management-worker interactions. In 1954, the Atomic Energy Commission (later reorganized as the Nuclear Regulatory Commission) was created, regulating and promoting the peaceful uses of nuclear power. In the 1960s, demands for increased auto safety, spurred by the investigations of consumer advocate Ralph Nader, led to the National Highway Traffic Safety Administration's establishment to enforce safety standards for American automobiles. In the 1970s, the realization that the environment was threatened caused the creation of the Environmental Protection Agency; problems with workplace safety resulted in the creation of the Occupational Health and Safety Administration; and concerns about product safety generated the Consumer Product Safety Commission.

The rationale for government regulation changed as social attitudes toward the free market evolved. Government actions prohibiting restraint of trade affirm the American belief in competitive markets. However, government regulations in recent decades reflect mistrust of the market rather than faith in it. Regulation of the securities industry reflects the view that government has a responsibility to minimize the risks of social dislocation and financial injury that can result from unregulated markets. Environmental regulations cast government in the role of protector of common resources against private disregard (see the case studies at the end of each chapter). Health and safety regulations find government playing the role of industry's adversary regarding the production process itself.

Given the history of increased regulation, it is not surprising that a reaction set in. The years since 1977 have seen a movement for deregulation. The airline industry was largely deregulated, and regulation on the railroad and trucking industries has eased. The deregulation movement reached its peak with Ronald Reagan's election. Reagan campaigned on the theme that many federal regulations promoted inefficiency by adding unnecessary burdens to businesses. In 1982, the Interstate Commerce Commission's jurisdiction over interstate bus companies narrowed considerably. Environmental regulation was deemphasized, and the administration sought to ease the licensing process for nuclear power plants. In November 1988, Reagan issued an executive order allowing the federal government to override state and local governments' refusal to ratify emergency evacuation plans for nuclear facilities.

In the early 1990s, Congress rejected proposals to ease banking industry regulations based partly on the argument that the savings and loan crisis, which cost taxpayers billions of dollars, had been brought on by deregulation in the early 1980s. The Bush administration, however, continued deregulation efforts by creating the White House Council on Competitiveness under the direction of Vice President Dan Quayle. The Council was intended as a behind-the-scenes effort to moderate regulatory activity. However, Quayle's refusal to provide information about the Council's operations to Congress caused a public confrontation which threatened the administration's program.

In regulating a modern corporate economy, political leaders must balance the twin values of efficiency and safety. A totally unregulated economy may be efficient, but at the cost of high individual risk and social instability. Conversely, extensive regulation may minimize risk and produce stability, but only at the price of inefficiency and a noncompetitive economy. It is quite difficult to achieve a state of balanced regulation. Since the Industrial Revolution, policymakers have generally increased the scope and specificity of government regulation. Besides the support of political reformers, increased regulation is often favored by the regulated interests, who see government intervention as a way to stabilize their business environments. Pressure to deregulate some parts of the economy seems to be diminishing; deregulation is not as high a priority for President Bush as it was for President Reagan. The most intense deregulation efforts may be over.

THE MODERN WELFARE STATE

Since 1933, government support of the economy has dramatically increased. Subsidy programs have grown in number and value. Some of these programs, such as the Export-Import Bank, function by providing subsidies directly to producers. Others make consumers out of individuals and groups who could not otherwise afford to consume. For example, the tax deduction for mortgage interest, coupled with federal insurance for the thrift industry, makes it possible for many middle-income families to afford a home, and (not coincidentally) helps support the construction and real-estate industries. Medicare, which subsidizes the elderly, and Medicaid, which subsidizes the poor, allow these groups to consume medical services they might otherwise have to forego and in the process pour billions of federal dollars into the medical industry. Because these subsidy programs are structured to channel federal money through the clients into the pockets of providers, they develop strong political support both among groups receiving direct benefits and those who provide the subsidized goods and services.

Since Franklin Roosevelt's New Deal, the federal government has assumed partial responsibility for addressing the economic and social problems of lower-income Americans. Spurred by the economic dislocations brought on by the Great Depression, the early welfare programs were structured to provide temporary relief to the "deserving poor" whose plight was created by the national economy's collapse. Immediate efforts focused on federal assistance to hard-pressed state and local relief programs. In 1935, the Roosevelt administration institutionalized the federal responsibility for welfare in the Social Security Act. The two components of this legislation were an insurance program for the elderly and the unemployed, to be paid for out of earmarked payroll taxes, and a welfare program for the blind, for children, and for the aged. These groups were considered exceptions to the more general rule that those left behind by free market forces should be assisted either by private charities or local governments. In spite of the breadth of the economic problem, federal benefits were limited in scope, and the insurance component of the program was financed with a highly *regressive* tax (a tax taking proportionately more from lower-income than from upper-income groups).

By the 1960s, the federal government began to deal with the *structural* problems of poverty. Members of the Kennedy and Johnson administrations were convinced that government programs could not only assist low-income groups with subsidies but also help them overcome the socioeconomic and political sources of their problems. To that end, President Johnson pushed through Congress the Economic Opportunity Act of 1965, known popularly as the "war on poverty." The act replaced simple cash subsidies with benefit-in-kind subsidies, such as education and job training programs, and attempted to empower the poor with the Community Action Program so that they might make their demands known through the political process. These efforts at community action were soon discontinued after protests by local officials, who argued that the program encouraged militancy among some segments of the poor. Because the "war on poverty" generally lacked a strong political support base—its clients were not a potent political force—Richard Nixon's election in 1968 signaled the effective end of the effort. (See the analysis of "iron triangles" and "issue networks" in Chapter 4.)

Welfare-state programs in the United States have operated within the overall constraints of a modern corporate economy and have contributed to a change in the nature of that economy. The welfare state was a radical concept when Franklin Roosevelt took the first steps to render federal assistance to the poor. Although Ronald Reagan and George Bush both attacked many of the basic notions of the welfare state, their actions were generally aimed at the margins of social spending. In fact, Reagan specifically endorsed social security and unemployment insurance as part of a social "safety net." It is worthy of note that the most conservative president in half a century endorsed welfare-state programs once condemned as radical and socialist. This indicates the extent of social changes since the

Depression, as well as the power of the political support groups that have grown up around these programs. (See the analysis of the American consensus in the introduction to this book.)

In summary, the growth of government regulation and the welfare state indicates clearly the interrelatedness of economic and political realities. The professionalization and growth of the business sector produced a need for similar adaptations in government; the evolution of corporate enterprises demanded new statutes and regulations standardizing commercial and financial interactions. When monopolies developed, distorting the workings of a free market and the invisible hand by neutralizing competition, government action was necessary. With the growth of large industrial cities to house factories and great numbers of workers, government assumed a greater role in infrastructure development and the maintenance of social order. The economic collapse of the 1930s resulted in political demands that were addressed by developing the American welfare state. Also, the increasing use of hazardous materials in production required extended government monitoring of business activities. In short, the Industrial Revolution of the nineteenth and early twentieth centuries generated pressure for a more activist government than the one provided for in laissez-faire philosophy; subsequent events reinforced that trend.

Government Macromanagement of the Economy

As the size and scope of the public sector increased, it became clear that government actions, while constrained by economic realities, could in turn directly influence those realities. Government attempts to influence the general economy's direction are known as *macromanagement* The primary strategies for economic macromanagement are fiscal policy and monetary policy. *Fiscal policy* refers to government taxing and spending decisions; *monetary policy* refers to government manipulation of the basic money supply. Both of these strategies are employed to cope with the business cycle, that is, the tendency of free-market economies periodically to stall, generating recession (or worse, depression), or to overheat, producing inflation.

Some observers, most notably the British economist John Maynard Keynes, believed that government actions could mitigate the worst aspects of the business cycle. Rather than waiting for the "invisible hand" of the market to correct economic problems, the Keynesians suggested government policies designed to control the volatility of such problems. Keynesian economists addressed the demand side of the supply and demand equation. According to the Keynesians, during times of recession (declining sales and rising unemployment), the federal government should fuel economic growth with deficit spending (disbursing more than it collected in revenues). Such spending (in the form of public works programs, for example) puts people back to work and thereby increases the demand for goods and services. This increased demand translates into an economic upswing, preventing any further downward slide. As economic times improve, government can use surplus tax collections to retire past debt.

Keynesian economics was adopted implicitly by Franklin Roosevelt and explicitly by Presidents Kennedy, Johnson, and Nixon. (Nixon announced in 1970 that "we are all Keynesians.") In 1980, however, Ronald Reagan attacked Keynesian assumptions and argued for a fiscal policy called *supply-side economics*. From this perspective, economic growth is best promoted by increasing the amount of the nation's savings. This is achieved by enacting large tax cuts, particularly directed at those income groups expected to save and invest their windfall. This new supply of capital, which would be increasing relative to demand and therefore available at lower interest rates, could then be used for expansion by American corporations. The expansion would fuel economic growth, job creation, and increased government revenues. Indeed, supply-siders contend that the increased revenues brought about by economic expansion would more than make up for the tax cuts government implemented to generate the capital for investment.

Neither Keynesian nor supply-side economics has proven infallible. In the 1970s, following thirty years of sustained growth marred by periodic recessions, the combination of high inflation, high interest rates, and increasing unemployment (a condition termed *stagflation* by the economists) helped usher Keynes out and supply-side in. Supply-side policies resulted in over seventy months of economic growth, the longest uninterrupted period since World War II. Yet supply-side also resulted in huge budget deficits, which more than tripled the national debt in ten years. In fact, since 1980 the United States has gone from being the world's biggest creditor to the world's biggest debtor nation. Ironically, supply-side policies have not increased savings rates; the percentage of savings in the United States in 1990 was lower than it was before the supply-side experiment began.

Monetarists such as Milton Friedman argue that fiscal policy represents an unwise attempt to fine-tune the economy; they recommend monetary policy as a more suitable alternative. Even nonmonetarists understand that monetary policy can be a useful complement to fiscal policy. Monetary policy is directed by the Federal Reserve Board ("the Fed"), created by act of Congress in 1914. The Fed influences the economy through a system of twelve regional Federal Reserve banks. All nationally chartered banks must join the Federal Reserve Bank (see Chapter 4). Through its influence over interest rates, the Fed directly influences the amount of credit available at any point in time. It does this by manipulating the *discount rate* (the rate of interest the Fed charges its member banks), by changing reserve fund requirements (the amount of funds banks must keep in reserve to support loans), and by buying and selling federal securities to member banks. For example, if the Federal Reserve Board want lower interest rates in order to assist a stagnant economy (one threatened by increasing unemployment), it lowers the discount rate, decreases reserve fund requirements (making more dollars available for loans), and/or buys securities from member banks (thereby increasing the banks' supply of lendable capital). In 1991, the Federal Reserve Board, seeking lower interest rates to combat a lingering recession, decreased the discount rate substantially.

Because members of the Federal Reserve Board serve for specified terms and are therefore protected from removal except for cause, the Fed is relatively insulated from political control. In the past, presidents seeking reelection appear to have succeeded in persuading the Fed to "loosen" money so that economic growth coincided with the election season. In the late 1970s, however, the Fed, under Chair Paul Volcker, tightened the money supply so dramatically that a major recession developed, with unemployment rates at the highest levels since World War II. This was meant to wring inflation out of the economy. The policy was "successful" in the broadest sense—inflation dropped steadily—but only at the price of personal pain and economic dislocation for millions of Americans.

S U M M A R Y

There are two striking characteristics of the relationship between politics and economics in the United States. The first is the inherent tension between political equality and economic inequality: The political system guarantees equality before the law, but the economic system guarantees at best only equality of opportunity. The second characteristic concerns the ever-widening gap between social theory and social practice.

American society faces the difficulty of balancing democracy and a modern corporate economy, each exerting pressure on the other. Maintaining this balance between two potent social values presents two related dilemmas. On the one hand, the right of private property (the modern corporate component) must be protected, while popular sovereignty (the democratic component) is affirmed. On the other hand, the unequal distribution of property must not "contaminate" the political system so that only the wealthy have meaningful influence on policymakers. It is clear that the American political system limits government power and protects property rights, thereby addressing the first dilemma. However, the second dilemma is more of a problem. Debates concerning public financing of election campaigns and limitations on the power of political action committees (PACs) often revolve around this very issue.

In general, the United States handles the pressures produced by this dilemma through the mixed-economy approach. The mixed economy satisfies many of the political demands for public services, while not ceding to government the right to socialize (control) the means of production. Under a mixed-economy approach, the private sector remains the "engine" that produces wealth for a society, while government assumes a distributive (and mildly redistributive) role. This process is stable as long as the total economic pie (the value of private production) increases fast enough to keep up with the demand for government programs. However, during periods when growth is smaller than necessary, the nation may face economic and political crises arising from the mismatch of available resources and demand for government services. (See the analysis of congressional budgeting in Chapter 2.)

The second characteristic of the relationship between politics and economics concerns the gap between economic theory and reality. Although the country developed a large welfare state with a wide scope of regulatory powers, the ideals of rugged individualism and laissez faire remain symbolically potent in the United States. Government is expected to deliver and pay for services within the framework of a philosophy that decries big government and "burdensome taxes." As expectations of citizens at all income levels for government services and/or subsidies increase, so does the problem. In 1992, the federal government spent approximately $290 billion on defense, over $375 billion on Social Security and Medicare (most of which went to the politically powerful middle class), and over $150 billion on social welfare expenditures (much of it in the form of entitlement programs guaranteeing assistance to eligible recipients). In the 1992 budget, the federal government continued to subsidize areas such as agriculture, education, and urban mass transit and continued offering popular tax deductions such as the one for interest on home mortgages.

The national debt may be seen as a measure of mismatch between the commitment to a strong national defense and the welfare state on the one hand and philosophical notions of limited government on the other. In 1981, the national debt was roughly $1 trillion, and debt amortization costs (payments on the interest on the debt) were $69 billion, or 10 percent of the total budget. In 1992, the national debt was almost $4 trillion, and debt amortization was $206.3 billion, or 14 percent of the budget. Much of this debt payment increase reflects the public's desire for substantial government services and programs and the equally strong desire that Washington's tax demands be as small as possible.

Thus, the political and economic sectors, while separate and independent, are closely tied together in the United States. Some argue that the close ties produce economic dislocations and inefficiency as government interferes in free market processes; others contend that business-government connections provide business with undue influence over public policy-making; and still others believe the connections generate continually changing balances of social costs and benefits. Different perspectives on the effects aside, the economic and political worlds will, and probably must, continue their symbiotic relationship.

THE CONSTITUTION OF THE UNITED STATES

We the people of the United States, in Order to form a more perfect Union, establish Justice, insure domestic Tranquility, provide for the common defense, promote the general Welfare, and secure the Blessings of Liberty to ourselves and our Posterity, do ordain and establish this Constitution for the United States of America.

Article I

Section 1. All legislative Powers herein granted shall be vested in a Congress of the United States, which shall consist of a Senate and House of Representatives.

Section 2. The House of Representatives shall be composed of Members chosen every second Year by the People of the several States, and Electors in each State shall have the Qualifications requisite for Electors of the most numerous Branch of the State Legislature.

No Person shall be a Representative who shall not have attained to the age of twenty five Years, and been seven Years a Citizen of the United States, and who shall not, when elected, be an Inhabitant of that State in which he shall be chosen.

Representatives and direct Taxes shall be apportioned among the several States which may be included within this Union, according to their respective Numbers, *which shall be determined by adding to the whole Number of free Persons, including those bound to Service for a Term of Years, and excluding Indians not taxed, three fifths of all other persons.*[1] The actual Enumeration shall be made within three years after the first Meeting of the Congress of the United States, and within every subsequent Term of ten Years, in such Manner as they shall by Law direct. The Number of Representatives shall not exceed one for every thirty Thousand, but each State shall have at Least one Representative; and until such enumeration shall be made, the State of New Hampshire shall be entitled to choose three, Massachusetts eight, Rhode-Island and Providence Plantations one, Connecticut five, New-York six, New Jersey four, Pennsylvania eight, Delaware one, Maryland six, Virginia ten, North Carolina five, South Carolina five, and Georgia three.

When vacancies happen in the Representation from any State, the Executive Authority thereof shall issue Writ of Election to fill such Vacancies.

The House of Representatives shall choose their Speaker and other Officers; and shall have the sole Power of Impeachment.

Section 3. The Senate of the United States shall be composed of two Senators from each State, *chosen by the legislature thereof*[2] for six Years; and each Senator shall have one Vote.

Immediately after they shall be assembled in Consequence of the first Election, they shall be divided as equally as may be into three Classes. The Seats of the Senators of the first Class shall be

---

[1]See Fourteenth Amendment. Throughout, italics are used to indicate passages altered by subsequent amendments.
[2]See Seventeenth Amendment.

vacated at the Expiration of the second Year, of the second Class at the Expiration of the fourth Year, and of the third Class at the Expiration of the sixth Year, so that one third may be chosen every Second Year; *and if Vacancies happen by Resignation, or otherwise, during the Recess of the Legislature of any State, the Executive thereof may make temporary Appointments until the next Meeting of the Legislature, which shall then fill such Vacancies.*[3]

No person shall be a Senator who shall not have attained to the Age of thirty Years, and been nine Years a Citizen of the United States, and who shall not, when elected, be an Inhabitant of the State for which he shall be chosen.

The Vice President of the United States shall be President of the Senate, but shall have no Vote, unless they be equally divided.

The Senate shall choose their other Officers, and also a President pro tempore, in the Absence of the Vice President, or when he shall exercise the Office of President of the United States.

The Senate shall have the sole Power to try all Impeachments. When sitting for that Purpose, they shall be on Oath or Affirmation. When the President of the United States is tried, the Chief Justice shall preside: And no Person shall be convicted without the Concurrence of two thirds of the Members present.

Judgment in Cases of Impeachment shall not extend further than to removal from Office, and disqualification to hold and enjoy any Office of honor, Trust or Profit under the United States: but the Party convicted shall nevertheless be liable and subject to Indictment, Trial, Judgment and Punishment, according to Law.

Section 4. The Times, Places and Manner of holding Elections for Senators and Representatives, shall be prescribed in each State by the Legislature thereof; but the Congress may at any time by Law make or alter such Regulations, except as to the Places of choosing Senators.

The Congress shall assemble at least once in every Year, and such Meeting shall be on the first Monday in December, unless they shall by Law appoint a different Day.[4]

Section 5. Each House shall be the Judge of the Elections, Returns and Qualifications of its own Members, and a Majority of each shall constitute a Quorum to do Business; but a smaller Number may adjourn from day to day, and may be authorized to compel the Attendance of absent Members, in such Manner, and under such Penalties as each House may provide.

Each House may determine the Rules of its Proceedings, punish its Members for disorderly Behavior; and, with the Concurrence of two thirds, expel a Member.

Each House shall keep a Journal of its Proceedings, and from time to time publish the same, excepting such parts as may in their Judgment require Secrecy; and the Yeas and Nays of the Members of either House on any question shall, at the Desire of one fifth of those Present, be entered on the Journal.

Neither House, during the Session of Congress, shall, without the Consent of the other, adjourn for more than three days, nor to any other Place than that in which the two Houses shall be sitting.

Section 6. The Senators and Representatives shall receive a Compensation for their Services, to be ascertained by Law, and paid out of the Treasury of the United States. They shall in all Cases, except Treason, Felony and Breach of the Peace, be privileged from Arrest during their Attendance at the Session of their respective Houses, and in going to and returning from the same; and for any Speech or Debate in either House, they shall not be questioned in any other Place.

No Senator or Representative shall, during the Time for which he was elected, be appointed to any civil Office under the Authority of the United States, which shall have been created, or the Emoluments

[3]See Seventeenth Amendment.
[4]See Twentieth Amendment.

whereof shall have been encreased during such time; and no Person holding any Office under the United States, shall be a Member of either House during his Continuance in Office.

Section 7. All bills for raising Revenue shall originate in the House of Representatives; but the Senate may propose or concur with Amendments as on other Bills.

Every Bill which shall have passed the House of Representatives and the Senate, shall, before it become a Law, be presented to the President of the United States; if he approve he shall sign it, but if not he shall return it, with his Objections to that House in which it shall have originated, who shall enter the Objections at large on their Journal, and proceed to reconsider it. If after such Reconsideration two thirds of that House shall agree to pass the Bill, it shall be sent, together with the Objections, to the other House, by which it shall likewise be reconsidered, and if approved by two thirds of that House, it shall become a Law. But in all such Cases the Votes of both Houses shall be determined by Yeas and Nays, and the Names of the Persons voting for and against the Bill shall be entered on the Journal of each House respectively. If any Bill shall not be returned by the President within ten Days (Sundays excepted) after it shall have been presented to him, the Same shall be a Law, in like Manner as if he had signed it, unless the Congress by their Adjournment prevent its Return, in which Case it shall not be a Law.

Every Order, Resolution, or Vote to which the Concurrence of the Senate and House of Representatives may be necessary (except on a question of Adjournment) shall be presented to the President of the United States; and before the Same shall take Effect, shall be approved by him, or, being disapproved by him, shall be repassed by two thirds of the Senate and House of Representatives, according to the Rules and Limitations prescribed in the Case of a Bill.

Section 8. The Congress shall have Power To lay and collect Taxes, Duties, Imposts and Excises, to pay the Debts and provide for the common Defence and general Welfare of the United States; but all Duties, Imposts and Excises shall be uniform throughout the United States;

To borrow Money on the credit of the United States;

To regulate Commerce with foreign Nations, and among the several States, and with the Indian Tribes;

To establish an uniform rule of Naturalization, and uniform Laws on the subject of Bankruptcies throughout the United States;

To coin Money, regulate the Value thereof, and of foreign Coin, and fix the Standard of Weights and Measures;

To provide for the Punishment of counterfeiting the Securities and current Coin of the United States;

To establish Post Offices and Post Roads;

To promote the Progress of Science and useful Arts, by securing for limited Times to Authors and Inventors the exclusive Right to their respective Writings and Discoveries;

To constitute Tribunals inferior to the Supreme Court;

To define and punish Piracies and Felonies committed on the high Seas, and Offences against the Law of Nations;

To declare War, grant Letters of Marque and Reprisal, and make Rules concerning Captures on Land and Water;

To raise and support Armies, but no Appropriation of Money to that Use shall be for a longer Term than two Years;

To provide and maintain a Navy;

To make Rules for the Government and Regulation of the land and naval Forces;

To provide for calling forth the Militia to execute the Laws of the Union, suppress Insurrections and repel Invasions;

To provide for organizing, arming, and disciplining the Militia, and for governing such Part of them as may be employed in the Service of the United States, reserving to the States respectively, the Appointment of the Officers, and the Authority of training the Militia according to the discipline prescribed by Congress;

To exercise exclusive Legislation in all Cases whatsoever, over such District (not exceeding ten Miles square) as may, by Cession of particular States, and the Acceptance of Congress, become the Seat of the Government of the United States, and to exercise like Authority over all Places purchased by the Consent of the Legislature of the State in which the Same shall be, for the Erection of Forts, Magazines, Arsenals, dock-Yards, and other needful Buildings;—And

To make all Laws which shall be necessary and proper for carrying into Execution the foregoing Powers, and all other Powers vested by this Constitution in the Government of the United States, or in any Department or Officer thereof.

Section 9. The Migration or Importation of such Persons as any of the States now existing shall think proper to admit, shall not be prohibited by the Congress prior to the Year one thousand eight hundred and eight, but a Tax or duty may be imposed on such Importation, not exceeding ten dollars for each Person.

The Privilege of the Writ of Habeas Corpus shall not be suspended, unless when in Cases of Rebellion or Invasion the public Safety may require it.

No Bill of Attainder or ex post facto Law shall be passed.

No Capitation, or other direct, Tax shall be laid, unless in Proportion to the Census or Enumeration herein before directed to be taken.

No Tax or Duty shall be laid on Articles exported from any State.

No Preference shall be given by any Regulation of Commerce or Revenue to the Ports of one State over those of another: nor shall Vessels bound to, or from, one State, be obliged to enter, clear, or pay Duties in another.

No Money shall be drawn from the Treasury, but in Consequence of Appropriations made by Law; and a regular Statement and Account of the Receipts and Expenditures of all public Money shall be published from time to time.

No title of Nobility shall be granted by the United States: And no Person holding any Office of Profit or Trust under them, shall, without the Consent of Congress, accept of any present, Emolument, Office, or Title, of any kind whatever, from any King, Prince, or foreign State.

Section 10. No State shall enter into any Treaty, Alliance, or Confederation; grant Letters of Marque and Reprisal; coin Money; emit bills of Credit; make any Thing but gold and silver coin a Tender in Payment of Debts; pass any Bill of Attainder, ex post facto Law, or Law impairing the Obligation of Contracts, or Grant any Title of Nobility.

No State shall, without the Consent of the Congress, lay any Imposts or Duties on Imports or Exports, except what may be absolutely necessary for executing its inspection Laws: and the net Produce of all Duties and Imposts, laid by any State on Imports or Exports, shall be for the Use of the Treasury of the United States; and all such Laws shall be subject to the Revision and Control of the Congress.

No State shall, without the Consent of Congress, lay any Duty of Tonnage, keep Troops, or Ships of War in time of Peace, enter into any Agreement or Compact with another State, or with a foreign Power, or engage in War, unless actually invaded, or in such imminent Danger as will not admit of delay.

Article II

Section 1. The executive Power shall be vested in a President of the United States of America. He shall hold his Office during the Term of four Years, and, together with the Vice President, chosen for the same Term be elected as follows:

Each State shall appoint, in such Manner as the Legislature thereof may direct, a Number of Electors, equal to the whole Number of Senators and Representatives to which the State may be entitled in the Congress but no Senator or Representative, or Person holding an Office of Trust or Profit under the United States, shall be appointed an Elector.

The Electors shall meet in their respective States, and vote by Ballot for two Persons, of whom one at least shall not be an Inhabitant of the same State with themselves. And they shall make a List of all the persons voted for, and of the Number of Votes for each; which List they shall sign and certify, and transmit sealed to the Seat of the Government of the United States, directed to the President of the Senate. The President of the Senate shall, in the Presence of the Senate and House of Representatives, open all the Certificates, and the Votes shall then be counted. The Person having the greatest Number of Votes shall be the President, if such Number be a Majority of the whole Number of Electors appointed; and if there be more than one who have such Majority, and have an equal Number of Votes, then the House of Representatives shall immediately choose by Ballot one of them for President; and if no Person have a Majority, then from the five highest on the List the said House shall in like Manner choose the President. But in choosing the President, the Votes shall be taken by States, the Representation from each State having one Vote; a quorum for this purpose shall consist of a Member or Members from two thirds of the States, and a Majority of all the States shall be necessary to a Choice. In every Case, after the Choice of the President, the Person having the greatest Number of Votes of the Electors shall be the Vice President. But if there should remain two or more who have equal Votes, the Senate shall choose from them by Ballot the Vice President.[5]

The Congress may determine the Time of choosing the Electors, and the Day on which they shall give their Votes; which Day shall be the same throughout the United States.

No person except a natural born Citizen, or a Citizen of the United States, at the time of the Adoption of this Constitution, shall be eligible to the Office of President; neither shall any Person be eligible to that Office who shall not have attained to the Age of thirty five Years, and been fourteen Years a Resident within the United States.

In Case of the Removal of the President from Office, or of his Death, Resignation, or Inability to discharge the Powers and Duties of the said Office, the Same shall devolve on the Vice President, and the Congress may by Law provide for the Case of Removal, Death, Resignation or Inability, both of the President and Vice President, declaring what Officer shall then act as President, and such Officer shall act accordingly, until the Disability be removed, or a President shall be elected.[6]

The President shall, at stated Times, receive for his Services, a Compensation which shall neither be encreased nor diminished during the Period for which he shall have been elected, and he shall not receive within that period any other Emolument from the United States, or any of them.

Before he enter on the Execution of his Office, he shall take the following Oath or Affirmation:— "I do solemnly swear (or affirm) that I will faithfully execute the Office of President of the United States, and will to the best of my Ability, preserve, protect and defend the Constitution of the United States."

Section 2. The President shall be Commander in Chief of the Army and Navy of the United States, and of the Militia of the several States, when called into the actual service of the United States; he may require the Opinion, in writing, of the principal Officer in each of the executive Departments, upon any Subject relating to the Duties of their respective Offices, and he shall have Power to grant Reprieves and Pardons for Offences against the United States, except in Cases of Impeachment.

He shall have Power, by and with the Advice and Consent of the Senate, to make Treaties, provided two thirds of the Senators present concur; and he shall nominate, and by and with the Advice and Consent of the Senate, shall appoint Ambassadors, other public Ministers and Consuls, Judges of the Supreme Court, and all other Officers of the United States, whose Appointments are not herein otherwise

[5]Superseded by the Twelfth Amendment.
[6]See Twenty-fifth Amendment.

provided for, and which shall be established by Law: but the Congress may by Law vest the Appointment of such inferior officers, as they think proper, in the President alone, in the Courts of Law, or in the Heads of Departments.

The President shall have Power to fill up all Vacancies that may happen during the Recess of the Senate, by granting Commissions which shall expire at the End of their next Session.

Section 3. He shall from time to time give to the Congress Information of the State of the Union, and recommend to their Consideration such Measures as he shall judge necessary and expedient; he may, on extraordinary Occasions, convene both Houses, or either of them, and in Case of Disagreement between them, with Respect to the Time of Adjournment, he may adjourn them to such Time as he shall think proper; he shall receive Ambassadors and other public Ministers, he shall take Care that the Laws be faithfully executed, and shall Commission all the Officers of the United States.

Section 4. The President, Vice President, and all civil Officers of the United States, shall be removed from Office on Impeachment for, and Conviction of Treason, Bribery, or other high Crimes and Misdemeanors.

Article III

Section 1. The judicial Power of the United States, shall be vested in one Supreme Court and in such inferior Courts as the Congress may from time to time ordain and establish. The Judges, both of the Supreme and inferior Courts, shall hold their Offices during good Behaviour, and shall, at stated Times, receive for their Services, a Compensation, which shall not be diminished during their Continuance in Office.

Section 2. The judicial Power shall extend to all Cases, in Law and Equity, arising under this Constitution, the Laws of the United States, and Treaties made, or which shall be made, under their Authority;—to all Cases affecting Ambassadors, other public Ministers and Consuls;—to all Cases of admiralty and maritime Jurisdiction;—to Controversies to which the United States shall be a Party;—to Controversies between two or more States;—*between a State and Citizens of another State*[7];—between Citizens of different States;—between Citizens of the same State claiming Lands under Grants of different States, *and between a State or the Citizens thereof, and foreign States, Citizens, or Subjects.*[8]

In all cases affecting Ambassadors, other public Ministers and Consuls, and those in which a State shall be Party, the Supreme Court shall have original Jurisdiction. In all the other Cases before mentioned, the Supreme Court shall have appellate Jurisdiction, both as to Law and Fact, with such Exceptions, and under such Regulations as the Congress shall make.

The Trial of all Crimes, except in Cases of Impeachment, shall be by Jury; and such Trial shall be held in the State where the said Crimes shall have been committed; but when not committed within any State, the Trial shall be at such Place or Places as the Congress may by Law have directed.

Section 3. Treason against the United States, shall consist only in levying War against them, or in adhering to their Enemies, giving them Aid and Comfort. No person shall be convicted of treason unless on the Testimony of two Witnesses to the same overt Act, or on Confession in open Court.

The Congress shall have Power to declare the Punishment of Treason, but no Attainder of Treason shall work Corruption of Blood, or Forfeiture except during the Life of the Person attainted.

Article IV

Section 1. Full Faith and Credit shall be given in each State to the public Acts, Records, and judicial Proceedings of every other State. And the Congress

[7]See Eleventh Amendment.
[8]See Eleventh Amendment.

may by general laws prescribe the Manner in which such Acts, Records and Proceedings shall be proved, and the Effect thereof.

Section 2. The Citizens of each State shall be entitled to all Privileges and Immunities of Citizens in the several States.

A Person charged in any State with Treason, Felony, or other Crime, who shall flee from Justice, and be found in another State, shall on Demand of the executive Authority of the State from which he fled, be delivered up, to be removed to the State having Jurisdiction of the Crime.

No person held to Service or Labour in one State, under the Laws thereof, escaping into another, shall in Consequence of any Law or Regulation therein, be discharged from such Service or Labour, but shall be delivered up on Claim of the Party to whom such Service or Labour may be due.[9]

Section 3. New States may be admitted by the Congress into this Union; but no new State shall be formed or erected within the Jurisdiction of any other State; nor any State be formed by the Jurisdiction of two or more States, or Parts of States, without the Consent of the Legislature of the States concerned as well as of the Congress. The Congress shall have Power to dispose of and make all needful Rules and Regulations respecting the Territory or other Property belonging to the United States; and nothing in this Constitution shall be so construed as to Prejudice any claims of the United States, or of any particular State.

Section 4. The United States shall guarantee to every State in this Union a Republican Form of Government, and shall protect each of them against Invasion; and on Application of the Legislature, or of the Executive (when the Legislature cannot be convened) against domestic Violence.

Article V

The Congress, whenever two thirds of both Houses shall deem it necessary, shall propose Amendments

[9]See Thirteenth Amendment.

to this Constitution, or, on the Application of the Legislatures of two thirds of the several States, shall call a Convention for proposing Amendments, which, in either Case, shall be valid to all Intents and Purposes, as Part of this Constitution, when ratified by the Legislatures of three fourths of the several States, or by Conventions in three fourths thereof, as the one or the other Mode of Ratification may be proposed by the Congress; Provided that no Amendment which may be made prior to the Year one thousand eight hundred and eight shall in any Manner affect the first and fourth Clauses in the Ninth Section of the first Article; and that no State, without its Consent, shall be deprived of its equal Suffrage in the Senate.

Article VI

All Debts contracted and Engagements entered into, before the Adoption of this Constitution, shall be as valid against the United States under this Constitution, as under the Confederation.

This Constitution, and the laws of the United States which shall be made in Pursuance thereof; and all Treaties made, or which shall be made, under the Authority of the United States, shall be the supreme Law of the Land; and the Judges in every State shall be bound thereby, any Thing in the Constitution or Laws of any State to the Contrary notwithstanding.

The Senators and Representatives before mentioned, and the Members of the several State Legislatures, and all executive and judicial Officers, both of the United States and of the several States, shall be bound by Oath or Affirmation, to support this Constitution; but no religious Test shall ever be required as a Qualification to any Office or public Trust under the United States.

Article VII

The Ratification of the Conventions of nine States, shall be sufficient for the Establishment of this Constitution between the States so ratifying the Same.

Done in Convention by the Unanimous Consent of the States present the Seventeenth Day of September in the Year of our Lord one thousand seven hundred and eighty seven and of the Independence of the United States of America the twelfth. In witness whereof We have hereunto subscribed our Names.

ARTICLES IN ADDITION TO, AND AMENDMENT OF, THE CONSTITUTION OF THE UNITED STATES OF AMERICA, PROPOSED BY CONGRESS, AND RATIFIED BY THE SEVERAL STATES, PURSUANT TO THE FIFTH ARTICLE OF THE ORIGINAL CONSTITUTION.

Amendment I

[Ratification of the first ten amendments was completed December 15, 1791.]

Congress shall make no law respecting an establishment of religion, or prohibiting the free exercise thereof; or abridging the freedom of speech, or of the press; or the right of the people peaceably to assemble, and to petition the Government for a redress of grievances.

Amendment II

A well regulated Militia, being necessary to the security of a free State, the right of the people to keep and bear Arms, shall not be infringed.

Amendment III

No Soldier shall, in time of peace be quartered in any house, without the consent of the Owner, nor in time of war, but in a manner to be prescribed by law.

Amendment IV

The right of the people to be secure in their persons, houses, papers, and effects, against unreasonable searches and seizures, shall not be violated, and no Warrants shall issue, but upon probable cause, supported by Oath or affirmation, and particularly describing the place to be searched, and the persons or things to be seized.

Amendment V

No person shall be held to answer for capital, or otherwise infamous crime, unless on a presentment or indictment of a Grand Jury, except in cases arising in the land or naval forces, or in the Militia, when in actual service in time of War or public danger; nor shall any person be subject for the same offence to be twice put in jeopardy of life or limb; nor shall be compelled in any criminal case to be a witness against himself, nor be deprived of life, liberty, or property, without due process of law; nor shall private property be taken for public use, without just compensation.

Amendment VI

In all criminal prosecutions, the accused shall enjoy the right to a speedy and public trial, by an impartial jury of the State and district wherein the crime shall have been committed, which district shall have been previously ascertained by law, and to be informed of the nature and cause of the accusation; to be confronted with the witnesses against him; to have compulsory process for obtaining witnesses in his favor, and to have the Assistance of Counsel for his defence.

Amendment VII

In Suits at common law, where the value in controversy shall exceed twenty dollars, the right of trial by jury shall be preserved, and no fact tried by jury, shall be otherwise reexamined in any Court of the United States, than according to the rules of the common law.

Amendment VIII

Excessive bail shall not be required, nor excessive fines imposed, nor cruel and unusual punishments inflicted.

Amendment IX

The enumeration in the Constitution, of certain rights, shall not be construed to deny or disparage others retained by the people.

Amendment X

The powers not delegated to the United States by the Constitution, nor prohibited by it to the States, are reserved to the States respectively, or to the people.

Amendment XI (1798)

The judicial power of the United States shall not be construed to extend to any suit in law or equity, commenced or prosecuted against one of the United States by Citizens of another State, or by Citizens or Subjects of any Foreign States.

Amendment XII (1804)

The Electors shall meet in their respective states and vote by ballot for President and Vice President, one of whom, at least, shall not be an inhabitant of the same state with themselves; they shall name in their ballots the person voted for as President, and in distinct ballots the person voted for as Vice President, and they shall make distinct lists of all persons voted for as President, and of all persons voted for as Vice President, and of the number of votes

for each, which lists they shall sign and certify, and transmit sealed to the seat of the government of the United States, directed to the President of the Senate;—The President of the Senate shall, in the presence of Senate and House of Representatives, open all the certificates and the votes shall then be counted;—The person having the greatest number of votes for President, shall be the President, if such number be a majority of the whole number of Electors appointed; and if no person have such majority, then from the persons having the highest numbers not exceeding three on the list of those voted for as President, the House of Representatives shall choose immediately, by ballot, the President. But in choosing the President, the votes shall be taken by states, the representation from each state having one vote; a quorum for this purpose shall consist of a member or members from two thirds of the states, and a majority of all the states shall be necessary to a choice. And if the House of Representatives shall not choose a President whenever the right of choice shall devolve upon them, *before the fourth day of March next following,*[10] then the Vice President shall act as President, as in the case of the death or other constitutional disability of the President.—The persons having the greatest number of votes as Vice President shall be the Vice President, if such number be a majority of the whole number of Electors appointed, and if no person have a majority, then from the two highest numbers on the list, the Senate shall choose the Vice President; a quorum for the purpose shall consist of two-thirds of the whole number of Senators, and a majority of the whole number shall be necessary to a choice. But no person constitutionally ineligible to the office of President shall be eligible to that of Vice President of the United States.

Amendment XIII (1865)

Section 1.   Neither slavery nor involuntary servitude, except as a punishment for crime whereof the party

[10]Altered by the Twentieth Amendment.

shall have been duly convicted, shall exist within the United States, or any place subject to their jurisdiction.

Section 2. Congress shall have the power to enforce this article by appropriate legislation.

Amendment XIV (1869)

Section 1. All persons born or naturalized in the United States, and subject to the jurisdiction thereof, are citizens of the United States and of the State wherein they reside. No State shall make or enforce any law which shall abridge the privileges or immunities of citizens of the United States; nor shall any State deprive any person of life, liberty, or property, without due process of law; nor deny to any person within its jurisdiction the equal protection of the laws.

Section 2. Representatives shall be apportioned among the several States according to their respective numbers, counting the whole number of persons in each State, excluding Indians not taxed. But when the right to vote at any election for the choice of electors for President and Vice President of the United States, Representatives in Congress, the Executive and Judicial officers of a State, or the members of the Legislature thereof, is denied to any of the male inhabitants of such State, being twenty-one years of age, and citizens of the United States, or in any way abridged, except for participation in rebellion, or other crime, the basis of representation therein shall be reduced in the proportion which the number of such male citizens shall bear to the whole number of male citizens twenty-one years of age in such State.

Section 3. No person shall be a Senator or Representative in Congress, or elector of President or Vice President, or hold any office, civil or military, under the United States, or under any State, who, having previously taken an oath, as a member of Congress, or as an officer of the United States, or as a member of any State legislature, or as an executive or judicial

officer of any State, to support the Constitution of the United States, shall have engaged in insurrection or rebellion against the same, or given aid or comfort to the enemies thereof. But Congress may by a vote of two thirds of each House, remove such disability.

Section 4. The validity of the public debt of the United States, authorized by law, including debts incurred for payment of pensions and bounties for services in suppressing insurrection or rebellion, shall not be questioned. But neither the United States nor any State shall assume or pay any debt or obligation incurred in aid of insurrection or rebellion against the United States, or any claim for the loss or emancipation of any slave; but all such debts, obligations, and claims shall be held illegal and void.

Section 5. The Congress shall have power to enforce, by appropriate legislation, the provisions of this article.

Amendment XV (1870)

Section 1. The right of citizens of the United States to vote shall not be denied or abridged by the United States or by any State on account of race, color, or previous condition of servitude.

Section 2. The Congress shall have power to enforce this article by appropriate legislation.

Amendment XVI (1913)

The Congress shall have power to lay and collect taxes on incomes, from whatever source derived, without apportionment among the several States, and without regard to any census or enumeration.

Amendment XVII (1913)

The Senate of the United States shall be composed of two Senators from each State, elected by the People thereof for six years; and each Senator shall have one vote. The electors in each State shall have the qualifications requisite for electors of the most numerous branch of the State legislatures.

When vacancies happen in the representation of any State in the Senate, the executive authority of such State shall issue writs of election to fill such vacancies; *Provided,* That the legislature of any State may empower the executive thereof to make temporary appointments until the people fill the vacancies by election as the legislature may direct.

This amendment shall not be so construed as to affect the election or term of any Senator chosen before it becomes valid as part of the Constitution.

Amendment XVIII (1919)

Section 1. *After one year from the ratification of this article the manufacture, sale, or transportation of intoxicating liquors within, the importation thereof into, or the exportation thereof from the United States and all territory subject to the jurisdiction thereof for beverage purposes is hereby prohibited.*

Section 2. *The Congress and the several States shall have concurrent power to enforce this article by appropriate legislation.*

Section 3. *This article shall be inoperative unless it shall have been ratified as an amendment to the Constitution by the legislatures of the several States, as provided in the Constitution, within seven years from the date of the submission hereof to the States by the Congress.*[11]

Amendment XIX (1920)

The right of citizens of the United States to vote shall not be denied or abridged by the United States or by any state on account of sex.

Congress shall have power to enforce this article by appropriate legislation.

[11]Repealed by the Twenty-first Amendment.

Amendment XX (1933)

Section 1. The terms of the President and Vice President shall end at noon on the 20th day of January, and the terms of Senators and Representatives at noon on the 3rd day of January, of the years in which such terms would have ended if this article had not been ratified; and the terms of their successors shall then begin.

Section 2. The Congress shall assemble at least once in every year, and such meeting shall begin at noon on the 3rd day of January, unless they shall by law appoint a different day.

Section 3. If, at the time fixed for the beginning of the term of the President, the President elect shall have died, the Vice President elect shall become President. If a President shall not have been chosen before the time fixed for the beginning of his term, or if the President elect shall have failed to qualify, then the Vice President elect shall act as President until a President shall have qualified; and the Congress may by law provide for the case wherein neither President elect nor a Vice President elect shall have qualified, declaring who shall then act as President, or the manner in which one who is to act shall be selected, and such person shall act accordingly until a President or Vice President shall have qualified.

Section 4. The Congress may by law provide for the case of the death of any of the persons from whom the House of Representatives may choose a President whenever the right of choice shall have devolved upon them, and for the case of the death of any of the persons from whom the Senate may choose a Vice President whenever the right of choice shall have devolved upon them.

Section 5. Section 1 and 2 shall take effect on the 15th day of October following the ratification of this article.

Amendment XXI (1933)

Section 1. The eighteenth article of amendment to the Constitution of the United States is hereby repealed.

Section 2. The transportation or importation into any State, Territory, or possession of the United States for delivery or use therein of intoxicating liquors, in violation of the laws thereof, is hereby prohibited.

Section 3. This article shall be inoperative unless it shall have been ratified as an amendment to the Constitution by conventions in the several States, as provided in the Constitution, within seven years from the date of the submission hereof to the States by the Congress.

Amendment XXII (1951)

Section 1. No person shall be elected to the office of the President more than twice, and no person who has held the office of President, or acted as President, for more than two years of a term to which some other person was elected President shall be elected to the office of President more than once. But this Article shall not apply to any person holding the office of President when this Article was proposed by Congress, and shall not prevent any person who may be holding the office of President, or acting as President, during the term within which this Article becomes operative from holding the office of President or acting as President during the remainder of such term.

Section 2. This article shall be inoperative unless it shall have been ratified as an amendment to the Constitution by the legislatures of three fourths of the several States within seven years from the date of its submission to the States by Congress.

Amendment XXIII (1961)

Section 1. The District constituting the seat of Government of the United States shall appoint in such manner as the Congress may direct:

A number of electors of President and Vice President equal to the whole number of Senators and Representatives in Congress to which the District would be entitled if it were a State, but in no event more than the least populous State; they shall be in addition to those appointed by the States, but they shall be considered, for the purposes of the election of President and Vice President, to be electors appointed by a State; and they shall meet in the District and perform such duties as provided by the twelfth article of amendment.

Section 2. The Congress shall have power to enforce this article by appropriate legislation.

Amendment XXIV (1964)

Section 1. The right of citizens of the United States to vote in any primary or other election for President or Vice President, for electors for President or Vice President, or for Senator or Representative in Congress, shall not be denied or abridged by the United States or any state by reason of failure to pay any poll tax or other tax.

Section 2. The Congress shall have power to enforce this article by appropriate legislation.

Amendment XXV (1967)

Section 1. In case of the removal of the President from office or of his death or resignation, the Vice President shall become President.

Section 2. Whenever there is a vacancy in the office of the Vice President, the President shall nominate a Vice President who shall take office upon confirmation by a majority vote of both Houses of Congress.

Section 3. Whenever the President transmits to the President pro tempore of the Senate and the Speaker of the House of Representatives his written declaration that he is unable to discharge the powers and duties of his office, and until he transmits to them a written declaration to the contrary, such powers and duties shall be discharged by the Vice President as Acting President.

Section 4. Whenever the Vice President and a majority of either the principal officers of the executive departments or of such other body as Congress may by law provide, transmit to the President pro tempore of the Senate and the Speaker of the House of Representatives their written declaration that the President is unable to discharge the powers and duties of his office, the Vice President shall immediately assume the powers and duties of the office as Acting President.

Thereafter, when the president transmits to the President pro tempore of the Senate and the Speaker of the House of Representatives his written declaration that no inability exists, he shall resume the powers and duties of his office unless the Vice President and a majority of either the principal officers of the executive departments or of such other body as Congress may by law provide, transmit within four days to the President pro tempore of the Senate

and the Speaker of the House of Representatives their written declaration that the President is unable to discharge the powers and duties of his office. Thereupon Congress shall decide the issue, assembling within forty-eight hours for that purpose if not in session. If the Congress, within twenty-one days after receipt of the latter written declaration, or, if Congress is not in session, within twenty-one days after Congress is required to assemble, determines by two-thirds vote of both Houses that the President is unable to discharge the powers and duties of his office, the Vice President shall continue to discharge the same as Acting President; otherwise, the President shall resume the powers and duties of his office.

Amendment XXVI (1971)

Section 1. The right of citizens of the United States, who are 18 years of age or older, to vote shall not be denied or abridged by the United States or any state on account of age.

Section 2. The Congress shall have power to enforce this article by appropriate legislation.

Amendment XXVII (1992)

No law, varying the compensation for the services of Senators and Representatives, shall take effect, until an election of Representatives shall have intervened.

INDEX

ABA, *see* American Bar Association
ACLU, *see* American Civil Liberties
    Union
Adams, Brock, 31
Adams, John, 39, 44
Adams, Sherman, 46
AFDC, *see* Aid to Families with
    Dependent Children
Atomic Energy Commission, *see*
    Nuclear Regulatory
    Commission
Afganistan, 20
Afroyin v. *Rusk,* 124
Agriculture, Department of, 49, 153
Aid to Families with Dependent
    Children, 6
Allen, Richard, 52
AMA, *see* American Medical
    Association
American Bar Association, 133
American Civil Liberties Union, 144
American Communist Party, 74
American Legion, 182
American Medical Association, 182
Amicus Curiae briefs, 144
Argersinger v. *Hamlin,* 126
Arizona v. *Fulimante,* 127
Army of the Potomac, 18
Arthur, Chester, 170
Articles of Confederation, 2, 4
Aspin, Les, 88

Baker, Howard, 84, 110, 112
Baker, James, 53, 62, 157
Baker v. *Carr,* 76, 132
Barbary Wars, 19

Barmet Aluminum Co. v. *EPA,* 149
Barron v. *Baltimore,* 126
Baum, Lawrence, 145
Bentsen, Lloyd, 13, 44, 89
Biden, Joe, 89
Bill of Rights, 3–4, 125–126, 131,
    142
Blackmun, Harry, 134, 137, 138
Block grant, 6
Blumenthal, W. Michael, 31
Bonier, David, 81, 83
Bork, Robert, 138
Bowen v. *Kendrick,* 134
Bowsher, Charles, 73
Breaux, John, 32
Brooks, Jack, 88
Brown, George, 88
Brown v. *The Board of Education,*
    125, 129
Bryner, Gary, 185
Brzezinski, Zbigniew, 52
Buchanan, James, 38
Buckley v. *Valeo,* 124
Budget and Accounting Act of 1921,
    28
Budget and Impoundment Control
    Act of 1974, 30, 103
Budgetary process, 103–107
Bundy, McGeorge, 52
Burch, Dean, 163
Bureau of the Budget, *see* Office
    of Management and the
    Budget
Bureaucracy:
    appointive policy making posi-
        tions, 171

Bureaucracy (*continued*)
    autonomy of units within depart-
        ments, 158–159
    characteristics of, 151–152
    civil service, 169–171
    extragovernmental influences on,
        181–182
    general schedule pay system, 172
    government influences on,
        178–181
    institutional loyalty, 183
    internal influences on, 182–183
    leadership, 174–178
    limitations, 178–183
    organization, 152–169
    personnel, 171–174
    relations with Congress, 179–181
    relations with the judiciary, 181
    relations with the president,
        178–179
    size, 17
    specialization, 175
    spoils system, 169–170
    successes, 183–184
Burford, Anne, *see* Anne Gorsuch-
    Burford
Burger, Warren, 134
Burger Court, 124, 127, 134
Burr, Aaron, 39
Bush, George:
    administration, 58
    cabinet members, appointment of,
        157–158
    cabinet, use of, 50
    dealing with Democratic Con-
        gress, 7–8

215

George Bush (*continued*)
  decision regarding Superfund reauthorization in 1991, 63, 188
  delegation to staff, 52
  deregulation, attitude toward, 164
  electoral college, 1988 vote, 34, 42
  election, 1988 results, 34
  election, 1992 results, 34, 58
  judicial nominations, 135–137, 139
  nominations by, 30
  OMB director, 54
  Persian Gulf War, and 7, 19
  popularity of, 7, 58
  vice president, selection of, 45
  veto record, 67
  White House Office, management, 52–53
Butterfield, Alexander, 47
Byrd, Robert, 84, 89, 110, 112

CAB, *see* Civil Aeronautics Bureau,
Cabinet:
  as advisory body, 50
  autonomy of units within departments, 158–159
  characteristics of members, 157–158
  growth in size, 153, 156–157
  origins, 49
Calendar Wednesday, 100
Califano, Joseph, 31
Campbell, Colin, 59
Cannon, Joe, 81
Carp, Robert, 145
Carter, Jimmy:
  amnesty program, 179–180
  appointment of ambassadors, 24
  cabinet members, firing of, 31–32
  as commander-in-chief, 18
  dealing with congress, 7
  deregulation and, 162
  election of 41, 42
  and hostages in Iran, 7
  judicial appointments, 136
  leadership, 57
  merit appointment, 24
  national security advisor, use of, 52
  National Security Council, 54
  Office of Drug Abuse Policy, and, 55
  organizational style, 48

Jimmy Carter (*continued*)
  outsider status, 40
  pocket vetoes, 68
  power to pardon, use of, 30
  Superfund law, 59–61, 108–109, 145–146, 185
  as treaty negotiator, 21
  vetoes by, 68
  vice-presidential role, expansion of, 45
  White House staff, use of, 52
Categorical grant-in-aid, 5
Cavazos, Laura, 157
CBO, *see* Congressional Budget Office
Central Intelligence Agency:
  duties, 55
  role in the Watergate affair, 47
  selection of director, 55
CEQ, *see* Council on Environmental Quality
CERCLA, *see* Superfund law
Chamber of Commerce, 182
Chase, Samuel, 120
Checks and balances, 7
Chemical Manufacturers Association, 110, 186
China, 24, 57
Chisholm, Shirley, 94
CIA, *see* Central Intelligence Agency
City of New York v. *Exxon,* 149
City of Richmond v. *J. A. Croson,* 134
Citizens for Kennedy, 137
Civil Aeronautics Board, 165
Civil Rights Act of 1964, 102
Civil Rights Act of 1968, 102
Civil service, 169–174
  creation, 169–171
  distribution of personnel, 172–173
  salaries, 172
  spoils system, 169–170
Civil Service Reform Act of 1883, 170
Clay, William, 88
Clayton Anti-Trust Act of 1914, 194
Cleveland, Grover, 38
Clinton, Bill:
  challenges facing, 58
  election of, 34, 58
  and Maine's electoral vote, 42
  selection of running mate, 44, 45

Bill Clinton (*continued*)
  victory margin and numerical majority, 34
  vote in 1992, 34, 58
Cloture, 101–102
CMA, *see* Chemical Manufacturers Association
Colegrove v. *Green,* 76
Commerce, Department of, 49, 153, 183
  Subcommittee on Transportation, 109
Commerce Clause, 66
Commission on Drug Abuse, 56
Commission on Obscenity and Pornography, 56
Commissions within EOP, 56
Committee for the Reelection of the President, 46–47
Committee of the Whole House, 101
Community Action Program, 196
Comprehensive Environmental Response, Compensation, and Liability Act, *see* Superfund law
Congress, *see also* House of Representatives; Senate
  activities of members, 78–80
  adjournment, 27
  appelate jurisdiction, right to limit, 120–121
  apportionment, 75–76
  appropriations, 103, 179
  authority to police itself, 69–71
  authorizing legislation, 103, 180
  bill, introduction of, 96
  bill becomes law, 96–102
  budgetary process, 103–107
  bureaucracy, relations with, 179–181
  cabinet departments, right to establish and abolish, 153
  calendars, 100
  campaign contributions, power to regulate, 71
  characteristics of members, 77–78
  committee action on bills, 98–100
  committee chairpersons, 87–90
  committees, 90–96
  conference committees, 102
  constituent service, 79–80
  constitutional prerogatives, 65–71
  court system, power to organize, 118–119

Congress (*continued*)
  dependence on the president for implementation, 24–25
  electoral procedures, 75–77
  executive agreements, concern with, 22–23
  government policy, legitimation of, 74–75
  hearings, 72–73
  House and Senate compared, 75, 76
  impeach and try, authority to, 69
  independent executive agencies, right to establish, 165–166
  independent regulatory commissions, creation of, 159
  issue creation and clarification, 72–73
  joint committees, 95
  judiciary, control over size of, 121–122
  lawmaking, 74
  leaders, 80–90
  Legal Services Corporation preserved, 178
  lobby registrations, requirements of, 70
  military affairs, 19–20
  oversight of the executive branch, 73–74
  party caucuses, 85
  presidential power, role in expansion of, 28
  presidential vetoes, right to override, 67–68
  reforms of the 1970s, 85
  rejection of initial Superfund proposal, 60–62, 108–109
  reorganization of the EOP, right to reject, 55
  representation, 71–72
  salaries, 69–70
  seniority system, 86–87, 94
  session length, 17
  size, 75–76
  special or select committees, 95
  staff, 80
  subcommittee action on bills, 98–99
  subpoena power, 96
  Superfund passage, 108–113
  veto overrides, 67–68, 102

Congressional Budget Office, 73, 103, 104–105
Congressional–executive agreements, 21–22
Congressional Quarterly, 108, 145
Consent Calendar, 99–100
Conservatives, 9–11, 12, 15
  and individual rights, 10
  and the free market, 10
  and the welfare state, 10
  and the international arena, 10
Conservation Law Foundation of New England v. *EPA,* 150
Conservatism, 9–11, 15
Constitution, *see also* Amendments (listed by number):
  authorization of the judicial system, 118–120
  commerce clause, 66–73,
  elastic clause, 66–67, 130
  framework of change, 17
  granting of specific powers, 72
  prerogatives and limitations, 2–8
  prerogatives of Congress, 65–71
  prerogatives of the Judiciary, 117–120
  prerogatives of the President, 17–31
  supremacy clause, 125
Constitutional amendments, 5, 121
Constitutional Convention, 2–3, 17, 123
Consumer Product Safety Commission, 194
Continental Congress, 38
Conventions, 439–40
Conyers, John, 88
Coolidge, Calvin, 33
Cooper, Phillip J., 145
Cooperative federalism, 6–7
Corporations, development of, 193–194
Costle, Douglas, 60
Council of Economic Advisors, 54, 55
Council on Environmental Quality, 61
Council on Wage and Price Stability, 55
Courts:
  administrative courts, 120, 142
  Court of Claims, 142
  Court of International Trade, 141

Courts (*continued*)
  Court of Military Appeals, 142–143
  Courts of Appeals, 118–119, 132–133, 135–136, 140–141
  district courts, 118–119, 132–133, 135–136, 141
  special judicial courts, 141
  Tax Court, 142
  territorial courts, 142
COWPS, *see* Council on Wage and Price Stability
Cranston, Alan, 81
CREEP, *see* Committee for the Reelection of the President
Crime Control Act of 1976, 158
Cuba, 24, 74
Cuban Missile Crisis, 54
Culver, John, 110, 111

Darby, Fred, 66
Darman, Richard, 54
Darwin, Charles, 192
Davidson, Roger, 108
Davis, Swep, 110
Defense, Department of, 172, 174, 176, 180
Dellums, Ron, 88
Democratic National Committee, 47
Democratic Republicans, 170
Democratic Steering and Policy Committee, 82, 93–94
Dingell, John, 88, 115
Discharge Calendar, 100
Doe v. *Bolton,* 127
Dole, Elizabeth, 157
Dole, Robert, 81, 84, 113
Douglas, William O., 138
Dred Scott case, 124
Dual federalism, 5
Dukakis, Michael, 13, 34, 44

Eckhardt, Bob, 112
Economic Opportunity Act of 1964, 196
EDF, *see* Environmental Defense Fund
Education, Department of, 156, 157
Ehrlichman, John, 54
1887 Act to Regulate Commerce, 161
Eisenhower, Dwight D.:
  cabinet, use of, 50

Eisenhower, Dwight D. (*continued*)
as commander in chief, 19
disability, 45–46
National Security Council, use of,
54
Supreme Court appointments,
134
White House staff, use of, 48,
52
Elastic clause, 66–67, 130
Electoral College, 40–42
Eleventh Amendment, 121
Employment Act of 1946, 28, 54
Energy, Department of, 156
Energy Research and Development
Administration, 156
Engel v. *Vitale,* 129
Environmental Appeals Board, 150
Environmental Defense Fund, 147,
186
Environmental Protection Agency:
environmental groups, relations
with, 185
investigation of Love Canal site,
59
National Contingency Plan,
Responsible for, 185–186
organization, 168
origin of, 194
pressure on, 180
regional headquarters, 167
response to Lesniak case, 160
scandals during Reagan ad-
ministration, 68, 167
size, 166
sued to force promulgation of
regulations, 181, 186
Superfund law, implementation of,
60–61, 186, 185–189
tasks, 166
EOP, *see* Executive Office of the
President
EPA, *see* Environmental Protection
Agency
ERDA, *see* Energy Research and
Development Administration
Executive Agreements, 22–23
Executive Calendar, 100
Executive Office of the President,
50–56
Export–Import Bank, 195
Ex post facto laws, 3, 4
Exxon Corp. v. *Hunt,* 146

Fair Labor Standards Act of 1938,
66
Farm Credit Administration, 167
FBI, *see* Federal Bureau of Investigation
FCC, *see* Federal Communications
Commission
FDIC, *see* Federal Deposit In-
surance Corporation
FEA, *see* Federal Energy, Ad-
ministration
Federal Bureau of Investigation:
agents pardoned by Reagan, 30
background checks on judicial
nominees, 133
impeded by Nixon, 47
independence in Justice Depart-
ment, 158
Federal Communications Commis-
sion, 163–164
Federal Deposit Insurance Corpora-
tion, 167–169
Federal Election Campaign Act, 124
Federal Energy Administration, 156
Federal Highway Act of 1916, 5
Federal Power Commission, 156
Federal Register, 149, 186
Federal Reserve Board, 163, 165,
198
discount rate, use of, 198
Federal Reserve System, 165, 198
Federal Trade Commission, 163, 183
Federalism, 4–6
cooperative, 5–6
dual, 5
Federalists, 123, 170
Ferraro, Geraldine, 38, 44
Fifth Amendment, 3, 96, 126
Filibuster, 101–102
Fillmore, Millard, 38
First Amendment, 3, 70, 131
Fiscal policy, 197
Fishbourne, Benjamin, 90
Florio, James, 109, 110
Foley, Thomas, 81, 82
Ford, Gerald:
dealing with Democratic Con-
gress, 7
efforts at trucking deregulation,
162
election defeat, 41, 42
judicial appointments, 133, 136,
137, 138

Ford, Gerald (*continued*)
pardoning Nixon, 30
as party leader, 36
succession to the presidency, 44
Supreme court appointments, 8
as treaty negotiator, 21
vetoes, 67
White House Staff, use of, 52
Ford, Wendell, 89
Ford, William, 88
Fortas, Abe, 135
Fourth Amendment, 3
Fourteenth Amendment, 3, 121,
125–126, 131
FPC, *see* Federal Power
Commission
Frankfurter, Felix, 139
Franklin, Barbara, 157
Friedman, Milton, 198
Friends of Animals, 144
FTC, *see* Federal Trade Commission

Gallatin, Albert, 170
GAO, *see* General Accounting Office
Garfield, James A., 29, 38, 42,
170
Garner, John Nance, 44
Gates, Robert, 30
Gay Activist Alliance, 74
General Accounting Office, 73, 180
General Schedule Pay System, 172
General Services Administration,
166, 167
Gephardt, Richard, 81
Gibbons v. *Ogden,* 5
Gideon v. *Wainwright,* 126
Gingrich, Newt, 89
Ginsberg, Douglas, 135
Gitlow, v. *New York,* 126
Glenn, John, 89
Gonzalez, Henry, 88
Goldwater, Barry, 11, 138
Gore, Al:
association with environmental
issues, 45
campaign for vice president, 58
selection as vice-presidential can-
didate, 44, 45, 58
Gorsuch-Burford, Anne, 61–62, 146,
185–187
Government Corporation Control
Act of 1945, 169
Government corporations, 167–169

Government Printing Office, 95
Government Regulation, 193–195
Grant, Ulysses S., 38, 170
Gray, William, 83
GSA, *see* General Services Administration
GS rating, *see* General Schedule Pay System
Great Britain, 8
Great Depression, 5, 196
Great Society, 5
Grocery Manufacturers Association, 115
Grove City College v. *Bell,* 121
Guiteau, Charles, 170

Habeas Corpus, 3
Haig, Alexander, 29, 52–53
Halderman, H. R., 47, 54
Hamilton, Alexander, 2, 39, 50, 169, 193
Hammer v. *Dagenhart,* 128
Harding, Warren G., 42
Harris, Patricia, 157
Harris v. *New York,* 127
Harrison, William Henry, 38
Hatch Act of 1940, 70
Hawaii, annexation of, 21
Hayden, Carl, 43
Hazelwood School District v. *Kuhlmeier,* 134
Health, Education, and Welfare, Department of, 153
Health and Human Services, Department of, 156, 157
Hedeman, William, 186
Hepburn Act of 1906, 161
Hernandez, John, 186
Hickel, Walter, 11, 50
Hills, Carla, 157
Hollins, Ernest, 89
Holmes, Oliver Wendell, Jr., 131
Hooker Chemical Company, 60
Hoover, J. Edgar, 158
House Committees:
 Agriculture, 87, 88, 94, 103
 Appropriations, 88, 91–92, 93, 94, 100, 103, 105–106
 Armed Services, 87, 88
 Banking, Finance and Urban Affairs, 87, 88
 Budget, 88, 92, 103, 104–105

House Committees (*continued*)
 Committee of the Whole, 101
 Committee on Committees, 94
 District of Columbia, 88
 Education and Labor, 88
 Energy and Commerce, 88, 113, 115
 Foreign Affairs, 88
 Government Operations, 73, 88, 186
 House Administration, 88
 Interior and Insular Affairs, 88
 Judiciary, 35, 88, 92
 Merchant Marine and Fisheries, 88, 108
 Post Office and Civil Service, 88
 Public Works and Transportation, 87, 88, 108, 113
 Rules, 82, 88, 90–91, 92, 93, 94, 97, 99–100, 109, 118
 Science and Technology, 88
 Select Committee on Narcotics Abuse and Control, 95
 Small Business, 88
 Standards of Official Conduct, 88, 92
 Steering and Policy, 82, 93
 Ways and Means, 82, 88, 91, 92, 93, 94, 119, 124
 Veterans Affairs, 88, 94
House of Representatives:
 appointment to committees, 93–95
 apportionment, 75–76
 calendars, 99–100
 committees, 90–96
 Committee of the Whole, 101
 discharge petition, 99, 100
 floor procedures, 101–102
 majority leader, 81, 82
 majority whip, 81, 82–83
 minority leader, 81, 83
 minority whip, 81, 83
 reforms of the 1970s, 82, 85
 right to impeach, 69
 role in choosing a president, 40–41
 subcommittees, 92
 tenure of members, 77
 voting procedures, 101–102
House Speaker:
 coordinator of budget process, 82
 line of presidential selection, 43
 selection, 81–82

House Speaker (*continued*)
 strengthened by Democrats, 82
 succession to, by majority leader, 82
Housing and Urban Development, Department of, 49, 156, 157
Hughes Court, 124
Humphrey, Hubert, 34
Hunt, E. Howard, 159

ICC, *see* Interstate Commerce Commission
Impeachment, 46–47, 69
Impoundment, 25, 103
Incrementalism, 15, 37
Independent Executive Agencies, 165–167
Independent Regulatory Commissions, 159–165, 194–195
Indochine War, 7, 19, 20, 30, 50, 57, 73, 80, 144
Industrial Revolution, 193
In re Torwico Electronics, 149
Interest Groups, 13–14, 177–178, 181–182
Intergovernmental relations, 5–6
Interior, Department of, 50, 153, 157
Internal Revenue Service, 142, 184
International Agreements other than treaties:
 congressional executive, 21–22
 number of, 23
 presidential negotiations of, 21–22
 pure executive, 22–23
Interstate Commerce Commission:
 development of, 159–161, 162, 194–195
 organization of, 159
 regulation as protection from competition, 161–162
 regulatory commissions as decision makers, 162–163
IRS, *see* Internal Revenue Service
Iran-Contra scandal, 30
Item veto, 28, 68–69

Jackson, Andrew, 32–33, 39
Japanese-Americans, internment of, 26
Jay Treaty, 22
Jefferson, Thomas, 25, 27, 50, 169–170
Johnson, Andrew, 38, 46, 56, 67

Johnson, Lyndon:
    cabinet, 153
    failures in presidential leadership,
        56–57
    Fortas nomination, 135
    and the great society, 5, 196,
        198
    and J. Edgar Hoover, 158
    judicial appointments, 136
    as majority leader, 94
    reaction to Kerner Commission
        report, 56
    Supreme Court appointments, by,
        136
    vetoes, 68
    and the Vietnam War, 7
    White House staff, use of, 52
Johnston, J. Bennett, 89
Joint committees:
    economic, 95
    library, 95
    printing, 95
    taxation, 95
Joint resolution, 98
Jones, Walter
Judicial courts, see Judiciary
Judicial philosophies:
    activism, 130–132
    loose constructionism, 130–131
    myth of the law, 139–140
    restraint, 130
    strict constructionism, 130–131
Judicial review, see Judiciary
Judiciary:
    abortion cases, 121
    administrative courts, 120, 141,
        142–143
    and bureaucracy, 181
    busing cases, 121
    civil cases, 122
    criminal cases, 122
    interdependent with other
        branches, 117
    judges, 120, 135–139
    judicial courts, 118–119
    jurisdiction, 122
    leadership, 123–130
    operation, 140–144
    route of appeal, 119
    school prayer cases, 121 size,
        121–122
    special judicial courts, 141
Judiciary Act of 1789, 123

Justice, Department of, 137, 148,
    153, 158

Keagle, James, 185
Kennedy, Arthur, 138–139
Kennedy, Edward, 11, 89
Kennedy, John, 32, 38
    assassination of, 42, 43
    cabinet, 50
    and civil rights concerns, 172
    and FBI, 158
    National Security Council, use of,
        54
    nuclear threat, use of, 18
    Supreme Court appointment,
        137–138
    vetoes by, 68
    White House Staff, use of, 47, 48
Keynes, John Maynard, 197
Keynesian economics, 197–198
Kissinger, Henry, 52, 54
Korean War, 19, 26, 124
Kornacki, John, 108
Kozak, David, 185
Kreps, Juanita, 157
Ku Klux Klan, 74

Labor, Department of, 49, 177
LaFalce, John, 88, 112
Laissez-faire, 191–193
Lautenburg, Frank, 115
Lavelle, Rita, 167, 187
League of Nations, 20–21, 33
Leahy, Patrick, 89
Legal Services Corporation, 68, 176,
    178
Lesniak et al v. United States et al,
    145–146
Liberalism, 8–11
Liberals, 9, 10, 15
    and individual rights, 9–10
    and the free market, 10
    and the welfare state, 10
    and the international arena, 10
Liberty Lobby, 144
Libya, 74
Liddy, G. Gordon, 96
Lincoln, Abraham, 18, 25–26, 42
Lobbying Disclosure Act of 1946, 70
Logrolling, 6
Long, Russell, 111
Lott Trent, 94
Louis Harris poll, 109

Love Canal, 60
LSC, see Legal Services
    Corporation
Lujan, Manuel, 157
Luther v. Borden, 132

Macromanagement of the economy,
    197–198
Madigan, Edward, 112
Madison, James, 6–7, 123–124
Maher v. Roe, 127
Maine, as electoral college excep-
    tion, 40, 41–42
Marbury, William, 123–124
Marbury v. Madison, 123–124
Marcy, William Learned, 169
Marshall, John, 67, 123–124,
    125
Marshall, Thomas, 46
Marshall, Thurgood, 137, 139
Martin, Lynn, 157
Martin v. Hunter's Lessee, 5
McCormick, John, 43
McCulloch v. Maryland, 5, 67
McGeorge School of Law, 138
McKinley, William, 42, 158
Medicaid, 196
Medicare, 184, 196, 200
Mexican-American War, 19
Michel, Robert, 81, 83
Miller, George, 88
Miller, James, 62
Miranda v. Arizona, 127
Missouri v. Independent
    Petrochemical Corp., 148
Mitchell, George, 81, 84
Moakley, John, 88
Moffett, Toby, 186
Mondale, Walter, 38, 44, 45
Monetarists, 198
Monetary policy, 198
Monroe, James, 29
Monsanto Co., 110
Montgomery, G. V. (Sonny), 88
Moore, Curtis, 110
Morehouse School of Medicine,
    157
Mossbacher, Robert, 157, 158
Motor Carrier Act of 1980, 162
Mueller, John, 35
Murphy, Paul, 161
Muskie, Edmund, 110, 111
Myers v. United States, 56

Nader, Ralph, 194
National Abortion Rights League, 144
National Aeronautics and Space Administration, 166, 167, 184
National Association of Counties, 6
National Association of State Legislators, 6
National Contingency Plan, 146–147, 185–186
National Endowment for the Arts, 166
National Football League, 138
National Highway Traffic Safety Administration, 194
National Labor Relations Board, 163, 183, 194
National League of Cities, 6
National Priorities List, 148–149, 188
National Response Team, 147
National Right to Life Committee, 144
National Science Foundation, 166, 167
National Security Act of 1947, 54
National Security Council, 54–55
Navy, Department of, 153
NCP, *see* National Contingency Plan, *Near* v. *Minnesota,* 126
Nebraska, as electoral college exception, 40
"Necessary and Proper" Clause, 66, 131
Neustadt, Richard, 31, 59, 65
New Deal, 5, 12, 122, 124, 131, 196
New York Health Commissioner, 59
New York State Department of Environmental Conservation, 59
Ninth Amendment, 131
Nixon, Richard:
    cabinet, use of, 50
    failed presidency, 7
    judicial appointments, 136, 137, 138
    National Security Council, use of, 54
    organizational style, 48
    pardoned by Ford, 30
    partial recognition of China, 24
    regulation as harassment, use of, 163–164
    relations with the bureaucracy, 176

Richard Nixon (*continued*)
    reorganization of OMB, 53
    resignation, 47, 69
    secret service, misuse of, 158–159
    Supreme Court, appointments, 137, 138
    as treaty negotiator, 21
    and Watergate, 7, 35, 96, 141, 158–159
    White House staff, use of, 52
Nixon v. *Sirica,* 141
N L Industries v. *Kaplan,* 149
NLRB, *see* National Labor Relations Board
Norton, Eleanor Holmes, 78
Northern Pipeline Construction Co. v. *Marathon Pipe Line Co.,* 124
NPL, *see* National Priorities List
NRC, *see* Nuclear Regulatory Commission
NRT, *see* National Response Team
NSC, *see* National Security Council
Nuclear Regulatory Commission, 163, 194
Nunn, Sam, 89

O'Callahan v. *Parker,* 143
Occupational Health and Safety Administration, 194
O'Connor, Sandra Day, 137, 138
OERR, *see* Office of Emergency and Remedial Response
Oestereich v. *Selective Service Board,* 128
Office of Administration, 51
Office of the Comptroller General, 180
Office of Drug Abuse Policy, 55
Office of Emergency and Remedial Response
    implementation of Superfund law, 186–187
Office of Hazardous Emergency Response, *see* Office of Emergency and Remedial Response
Office of Management and the Budget, 53–54, 55, 103, 104, 105, 179
    role in Superfund implementation, 62
Office of Policy Development, 51

Office of Science and Technology, 51
Office of U.S. Trade Representative, 51
OHER, *see* Office of Hazardous Emergency Response
Olney, Richard, 161
OMB, *see* Office of Management and the Budget

PACs, *see* Political Action Committees
Panal Canal Treaty, 21, 57
Panetta, Leon, 88
parliamentary system, 8
Pell Claiborne, 89
Pendleton Act, *see* Civil Service Reform Act of 1883
Perot, H. Ross, 12, 34, 58
Peterson, Mark, 108
Planned Parenthood v. *Casey,* 127
Pocket veto, 28, 68
Political Action Committees, 13–14, 71
Political parties:
    decentralization of, 13–14, 36
    lack of patronage jobs, 14, 36
    minor parties, 11–12
    nomination of presidential candidates, 39–40
    origin, 39
    two-party system, 11–14
Polk, James, 21, 23
Pollock v. *Farmers Loan and Trust Co.,* 121
Pork Barrel, 72
Powell, Lewis, 134
Powell v. *Alabama,* 126
Pratt, John, 148
President:
    appointive policy-making positions, 171
    appointments of agency heads, 153–158, 159, 165–166, 169
    appointments on Senate Executive calendar, 100
    as chief administrator, 29–30
    as chief diplomat, 20–24
    as chief executor, 24–27
    as chief policy initiator, 27–29
    combined constitutional prerogatives, use of, 25–27
    as commander in chief, 17–20

President (*continued*)
  and Congress, 32–35
  current services budget, submission of, 103, 105
  eligibility for office, 38
  as head of state, 30–31
  impeachment, 46–47, 69
  impoundment, use of, 25, 103
  institutionalization, 47–56
  item vetoes, 28, 68–69
  media, use of, 32–34
  as "moral leader," 35
  as party leader, 36
  persuasion, use of, 31–35
  pocket vetoes, 68
  political context of power, 36–38
  popularity, 35–37
  power to address Congress, 27
  power to appoint ambassadors, 23–24
  power to appoint bureaucrats, 24
  power to convene and adjourn Congress, 27
  power to execute laws, 24–25
  power to grant pardons, 30–31
  power to make the state of the union address, 27
  power to negotiate international agreements, 20–23
  power to nominate judges, 28–29
  power to receive ambassadors, 24
  power to recommend legislation, 27–28
  power to run the bureaucracy, 29
  power to veto bills, 28
  press conferences, 33
  prestige of office, 35
  reelection chances and leadership, 56–57
  relations with the bureaucracy, 178–179
  role in the budgetary process, 103–105
  selection, 39–42
  succession, 44–44
  terms of office, 42
Private Calendar, 100
Pryor, David, 115
Proportional representation, 11

Quayle, J. Danforth, 45, 81, 164, 195
Randolph, Jennings, 111

Rayburn, Sam, 85
Reagan, Ronald:
  ambassadorial appointments policy, 24
  appeal of, 184
  cabinet, 50, 157
  campaign, basis of, 193
  CIA, weakening controls on, 55
  commission on regulatory reform, 55–56
  dealing with a Democratic congress, 7
  elections, 44, 111
  environmental policies, 61–63, 185–188
  EOP, organization of, 55
  implementation of Superfund law, 61–63, 185–188
  item veto, support for, 28
  judicial appointments, 136, 137, 138
  legislative successes, 7, 37–38
  military spending, support of, 20
  National Security Advisor, use of, 54–55
  organizational style, 48
  pardoning of FBI burglars, 30
  pocket vetoes, 68
  reductions in force, 174
  strengthening of OMB, 53–54
  Supreme Court appointments by, 137, 138
  trucking regulations, political issue, 162
  vetoes, 67
  vetoes overridden, 67
  veto threat, use of, 68
  White House staff, use of, 52–53
Reciprocal Trade Agreement Act, 21
Reconciliation, 105
Reed, Thomas, 81
Reedy, George, 49
Regulatory Commissions, 159–165
Rehnquist, William, 122, 133, 137, 138, 139
The Rehnquist Court, 127, 128, 134–135
Reilly, William, 115, 188
Reorganization Act of 1953, 54
Reynolds v. *Sims,* 126, 132
Rhodes, John, 83
Riegel, Donald, 89
Riley, Dennis, 185

Roberts, Owen, 8, 122
Rockefeller, Nelson, 44
Roe v. *Wade,* 131, 135
Romney, George, 38
Roosevelt, Franklin:
  breaking two-term tradition, 42
  Bureau of the Budget, control over, 53
  court-packing effort, 8, 36, 121–122
  Democratic Party, rejuvenation of, 36
  fireside chats, 33
  Japanese-Americans, internment of, 26
  Naval expenditures, and, 49
  organizational style, 48
  pocket vetoes, 68
  vetoes, 68
Roosevelt, Theodore, 27–28, 33
Rostenkowski, Dan, 88
Rostow, Walter, 52
Rourke, Francis, 185
Ruckelshaus, William, 167, 187
"rules of the political game," 1
Rust v. *Sullivan,* 125

Saint Lawrence Seaway Development Corporation, 169
Sanders, Bernie, 11
Sasser, Jim, 89
Savings and loan bailout, 73, 195
SCA Services of Indiana, Inc. v. *Thomas,* 148
Scalia, Antonin, 137, 138
Schattschneider, E., 182
Scott, William, 90
SEC, *see* Securities and Exchange Commission
Secret Service, 158–159
Securites and Exchange Commission, 163, 194
Seidman, Harold, 183
Selective Service Act, 30, 128
Senate:
  apportionment, 75
  calendars, 100
  cloture votes, 101–102
  committees, 92–93, 94–95
  confirmation of appointments, 30, 132–135
  discharge motions, 99
  filibusters, 101–102

Senate (*continued*)
  floor proceedings, 101–102
  as jury in impeachment trials, 69
  president, 44, 81
  president pro tempore, 81
  reception of electoral votes, 39
  reforms of the 1970s, 85
  senatorial courtesy, 90, 133
  subcommittees, 93–93
  tenure of members, 77
  treaty approval, 20–21
  Vice President, role in choosing,
    41
  voting procedures, 101–102
  Watergate committee, establish-
    ment of, 47
Senate committees:
  Agriculture, Nutrition, and Phar-
    macy, 89
  Appropriations, 89, 93, 105
  Armed Services, 89
  Banking, Housing, and Urban
    Affairs, 89
  Budget, 89, 103, 104–105
  Commerce, Science, and
    Transportation, 89
  Democratic Steering, 94
  Energy and Natural Resources,
    89
  Environment and Public Works,
    89
    consideration of Superfund bill,
      108, 110
  Finance, 89, 93
    consideration of Superfund bill,
      111, 114
  Foreign Relations, 21, 89, 95
  Governmental Affairs, 89
  Judiciary, 89, 134
  Labor and Human Resources, 89
  Republican Committee on Com-
    mittees, 94
  Rules and Administration, 89, 93
  Select Committee on Intelligence,
    95
  Select Committee on Presidential
    Campaign Activities, 95
  Select Committee on Small
    Business, 95
Senate majority leader, 81, 84
Senate minority leader, 81, 84
Senate whips, 81, 84
Senior Executive Service, 179

Separation of institutions sharing
    power, 6–8
SES, *see* Senior Executive Service
Sessions, William, 158
Shell Oil Co., 110
Sherman Anti-Trust Act of 1890,
    194
Simple resolution, 98
Simpson, Alan, 81, 84
Sirica, John, 47, 141
Sixteenth Amendment, 121
Skinner, Samuel, 158
Small Business Administration, 166
Smith, Adam, 192
Smith, James, 161
Smithsonian Institute, 166
*Snediker Developers Ltd. Partner-
    ship* v. *Evans,* 150
Social Security, 9, 200
Social Security Act, 196
Social Security Administration, 184
Sorenson, Theodore, 47
Souter, David, 137, 139
Spanish-American War, 19
Special Assistant for National
    Security Affairs, 52–53
Spoils system, *see* bureaucracy
Stafford, Robert, 62, 111, 112
Stagflation, 198
Stalwart, 170
Stanford Law School, 138
Stanton, Edwin, 46
State, Department of, 21, 43, 49,
    151, 152, 153
State of the Union address, *see*
    President
Stevens, John Paul, 137, 138
Stevens, Ted, 84
Stidham, Ronald, 145
Stokes, Louis, 88
Strauss, Lewis, 30
Strict constructionism, *see* judicial
    philosophies
Stumpf, Harry, 145
Succession Act of 1947, 43
Succession Act of 1792, 53
Sullivan, Louis, 157
Sununu, John, 158
Superfund law:
  alternative remedial contract
    strategy, 188
  ARCS, *see* alternative remedial
    contract strategy

Superfund law (*continued*)
  congressional efforts at influencing
    implementation
    through publicity, 180
  development at EPA, 185–189
  disputes over committee jurisdic-
    tion, 109–111, 113–114
  House floor action, 112–113
  initial Carter proposals, 59–60
  legal challenges, 145–150
  liability provisions, 111, 148
  lobbying, 109–111, 188–189
  Reagan influence on, 61–62, 114,
    147, 186
  SARA, *see* Superfund Amend-
    ments and Reauthorization Act
  Senate floor action, 112
  Superfund Amendments and
    Reauthorization Act, 62–63,
    113–116, 148–150, 187–189
Supply-side economics, 198
Supremacy clause, *see* Constitution
Supreme Court:
  abortion issue, 127, 131, 135
  amicus curiae briefs, 144
  appelate jurisdiction, 120–121
  appointment of judges, 134–135
  apportionment decisions, 76, 126,
    132
  authorized in Constitution, 118–120
  caseload, 143–144
  disallowal of steel seizure, 26
  Friday conference, 144
  impeachment threat, 120
  income tax case, 121
  interpretation of federal statutes,
    128
  issue creation and clarification,
    129
  judicial activism, 130
  judicial constraint, 130
  leadership functions, 128–129
  legitimation role, 129
  limitations on, 120–122
  loose constructionism, 130–131
  "myth" of the law, 139–140
  noncompliance with decisions,
    129
  order to Nixon to surrender tapes,
    141
  original jurisdiction, 120–121
  oversight function, 129
  as policy maker, 129

Supreme Court (*continued*)
political nature of decisions, 139–140
political question doctrine, 132, 144
procedures, 143–144
representation function, 128–129
review of acts of Congress, 124
review of presidential actions, 124–125
review of state and local actions, 125
role of chief justice, 144
selection of cases, 143–144
size, 121–122
strict constructionism, 130–131
tenure of justices, 120
voting order, 144
writ of certiorari, 143–144

Taft Court, 132
Taney, Roger, 132
Teamsters Union, 162
Tennessee Valley Authority, 169
Tenth Amendment, 22, 130
Tenure of Office Act of 1867, 56
Thomas, Clarence, 137, 139
Thomas, Lee, 69, 187–188
Thurber, James, 108
Tower, John, 30
Train v. *City of New York*, 125
Transportation, Department of, 31, 156, 158
Transportation Leasing Co. v. *CA,* 149
Treasury, Department of the, 31, 153, 157, 158
Treaties, 18, 20–22, 23
on Senate Executive calendar, 100
Treaty of Versailles, 20–21
Truman, Harry:
impoundment of funds, 25
seizure of steel mills, 26, 124–125
succession to office, 45
Turner, David, 170

TVA, *see* Tennessee Valley Authority
Twelfth Amendment, 39
Twentieth Amendment, 27
Twenty-fifth Amendment, 42, 43–44
Twenty-second Amendment, 42
Twenty-sixth Amendment, 121
Tyler, John, 21, 38, 42

Union Calendar, 100
United Negro College Fund, 83
United Parcel Service, 169
United States Air Force, 153
United States Attorney, 141
United States Government Manual, 152
United States Postal Service, 169
United States Treasury, 180
United States v. *Darby,* 66
United States v. *Maryland Bank and Trust,* 149–150
United States v. *Mitchell et al,* 141
United States v. *Northeastern Pharmaceuticals and Chemical Co.,* 148
United States v. *Tempia,* 142
University of Chicago, 138

VA, *see* Veterans Administration
Vance, Cyrus, 52
Department of Veterans' Affairs, 79–80, 156–157, 172, 177, 182
Vice President:
authority, 44–46
office in the EOP, 51
role, 45–46
Selection by presidential candidate, 44–45
succession to office, 45–46
Vietnam War, 7, 19, 20, 30, 50, 57, 73, 80, 144
Volcker, Paul, 199
Voting Rights Act of 1965, 79, 102

Wabash, St. Louis and Pacific Railroad v. *Illinois,* 161
Wallace, George, 184
War, Department of, 153
War on poverty, *see* Economic Opportunity Act War Powers Act, 20
Warren, Earl, 8, 123, 126, 134
Warren Court, 8, 123, 126 129, 132
Washington, George, 18, 20, 49
cabinet appointments, 153
vetoes, 67
Watergate, 7, 35, 46–47, 134, 158–159
FBI improprieties, 158
role in Nixon's resignation, 47
tapes, 134, 141
The Wealth of Nations, 192
Weber, Max, 151–152
Weberian model, 152
Webster, Daniel, 65
Webster, William, 158
Webster v. *Reproductive Health Services,* 127
Weicker, Lowell, 11
Welfare State, 195–197
Welsh v. *United States,* 128
Wentworth, Marchant (Lucky), 110
Wesbury v. *Sanders,* 76
Whiskey rebellion, 18
White, Byron, 137–138
Whitehead, Clay, 163
White House Office, 50–53
White House Office of Telecommunications Policy, 163–164
Whitten, Jamie, 88
Wilson, Woodrow, 20–21, 26, 27, 38, 45
World War I, 19, 26
World War II, 19, 26, 138, 199
Wright, Jim, 82

Yeutter, Clayton, 157
Youngstown Sheet and Tube Company v. *Sawyer,* 124–125

TO THE OWNER OF THIS BOOK:

We hope that you have found *Politics and Structure, Sixth Edition,* useful. So that this book can be improved in a future edition, would you take the time to complete this sheet and return it? Thank you.

Instructor's name: _____

Department: _____

School and address: _____

_____

1. The name of the course in which I used this book is: _____

_____

2. My general reaction to this book is: _____

_____

_____

3. What I like most about this book is: _____

_____

_____

4. What I like least about this book is: _____

_____

_____

5. Were all of the chapters of the book assigned for you to read?   Yes   No

    If not, which ones weren't? _____

6. Do you plan to keep this book after you finish the course?   Yes   No

    Why or why not? _____

_____

7. On a separate sheet of paper, please write specific suggestions for improving this book and anything else you'd care to share about your experience in using the book.

Optional:

Your name: _____   Date: _____

May Wadsworth quote you, either in promotion for *Politics and Structure, Sixth Edition,* or in future publishing ventures?

Yes: _____   No: _____

Sincerely,
Thomas G. Ingersoll
Robert E. O'Connor
Robert F. Pecorella

FOLD HERE

BUSINESS REPLY MAIL
FIRST CLASS   PERMIT NO. 34   BELMONT, CA

POSTAGE WILL BE PAID BY ADDRESSEE

Thomas G. Ingersoll/Robert E. O'Connor/Robert F. Pecorella
Wadsworth Publishing Company
10 Davis Drive
Belmont, CA 94002